NEHRU

a voice for mankind

the john day company · *new york*

bani shorter

NEHRU

a voice for mankind

TO INDIA NOW

"We are small people,"
Panditji said,
"but when we attempt big things,
we too become somewhat big."

The John Day Company, Inc., 257 Park Avenue South, New York, N.Y. 10010
an Intext *publisher*

Library of Congress Catalogue Card Number: 71-89037
Printed in the United States of America
Designed by The Etheredges

921
'31Sh

contents

ILLUSTRATIONS FOLLOW PAGE 152

acknowledgments

I am indebted to members of the Nehru family: to Jawaharlal Nehru, then Prime Minister of India, to his sister, Madame Vijaya Lakshmi Pandit, and to his daughter, Indira Gandhi, Prime Minister of India at present, for their willingness to see me and to talk with me at length about the writing of this book. Our visits were not interviews in the usual sense. They were conversations during which we reflected on incidents together and directions for the writing of the book were defined. Through the gracious auspices of the Nehru family, I also became acquainted with dear friends and associates of the Prime Minister.

Among the friends and associates of Jawaharlal Nehru who were particularly helpful to me were H. V. R. Iyengar, Diwan Chaman Lall, M. O. Mathai, Dr. Syed Mahmud, B. F. Tyabji, and the Indian biographer of the Nehru family, B. R. Nanda. Each one of these people contributed information and friendly concern to the project. A special word of gratitude must also be expressed to wise and kindly Tarlok Singh, once Principal Private Secretary to the Prime Minister. His good counsel and generous intervention opened many doors and his affectionate friendship was sustaining.

Other persons in India and elsewhere have helped substantially with this undertaking. Characteristically, each contributed according to his individual talent and at a particular time. Such people include the late Annemis Helland-Hansen of Norway, Tara Bhattacharjee, Helen and Albert Baily, and Charlotte Bauer.

My son, Rangit, who was Indian by birth, has always had a special enthusiasm for this book. We traveled to New Delhi together and while I worked upon it, he proved to be a fine companion.

Still others, behind the scenes, both in India and America, have given much. Some of them have been beside me all the way and their comradeship has helped to make the journey worth the making. I thank them, every one.

BANI SHORTER

part 1 *1889–1920*

On the last day of the sixteenth century, December 31, 1599, Queen Elizabeth the First of England placed her signature upon a document of far-reaching and momentous consequence. She was a shrewd woman and thought twice before she risked having her sailors come into contact with vessels that belonged to other monarchs. She could hardly afford to have them embroil her country in a new and costly war. However, she was also a proud woman and she had no intention of losing England's advantage in trade, commerce, or dominion. Her title read, ELIZABETH BY THE GRACE OF GOD QUEEN OF England France and Ireland. She was not averse to adding to the list of subject nations Spain, or any other state that could be won without paying too great a price. Not averse to adding Spain or even the newer lands her merchants had visited farther to the east and where this document gave them permission to travel and trade on her behalf.

England was the last of the European countries in the race for trade and holdings in the Far East. The Portuguese had landed in India a hundred years before the time of Elizabeth and the Dutch had already established themselves in the Spice Islands. Men who came late to the game and who wanted to stake out rights to goods and wealth had to have backing and prestige, as well as money at their disposal. Moreover, they had to be cunning and sometimes ruthless, to make decisions without reference to a government that was seven thousand miles away. With certain foresight, the Queen's cousin, George, Earl of Cumberland, and a group of chosen associates had petitioned Her Majesty for permission to set sail for the East Indies *"for the honour of this our realm of England,* as for the increase of our navigation, and advancement of trade of merchandise." Elizabeth, after having waited for what she deemed to be a suitable period and until affairs were going well in current battles against Spain, granted these men a charter to which she affixed her name and seal.

"Know ye therefore . . . that they . . . shall be a body Corporate and Politic in deed and in name by the name of the Governor and Company of merchants of London trading into the East Indies" the charter read. In 1607 the "East India Company" fitted out a crew and sailed with three vessels. Sixteen months later one of the ships reached the west coast of India at a place not far from modern Bombay. After minor skirmishes with the Portuguese, William Hawkins, who served as lieutenant of the company, arrived at the court of Akbar the Great in Agra to present his credentials and to ask for permission to trade and build a warehouse on the coast.

Akbar the emperor, "The Great Mogul," had died in 1605 while the ships of the East India Company were still being outfitted; but the Mogul Empire, which spread across the plains of northern India, including the territory of what is now modern Pakistan, an empire that extended as far east as Burma and south to Hyderabad, survived in the hands of his son. This was an area nearly equivalent in size to all of Europe, and Akbar had ruled it with wisdom and with splendor.

If anyone could ever have been a match for the fiery Elizabeth, it would have been Akbar, with his lands and influence, his tremendous vigor, and his lively temper. As a man, he was utterly fearless: he had disarmed and struck down with his bare fists a rebel who had tried to assassinate him; he had leapt daringly from the neck of one fighting elephant to another in an effort to separate them; he was an emperor who tooled and molded his own weapons, including cannon, with craftsmanship and skill. Like Elizabeth, he encouraged the arts. He, too, established a strong government, carefully knit and held together largely by the force of his own personality.

In wealth, Akbar the Great far outshone Elizabeth of England. His court was a glittering display of silks and jewels, costumed servants and graceful dancers, horses and elephants bedecked with gold, magnificent palaces, gracious gardens, and flowered carpets. The Englishmen who first beheld the cities of Agra and Delhi saw the glories of London magnified a hundredfold. Without moving any farther across the plains of India, without realizing or caring at the time that such lavish display was possible only because of the backbreaking labor of millions of peasants, members of the East India Company returned to England with tales of unmatched riches. "The wealth of fabulous India" summoned men from all walks of English life and lured them east for adventure, gain, and power.

Akbar had been a jealous emperor, a Muslim, one of the line of conquerors who had swept across India from the west in the twelfth century, a cruel man, but also generous and intelligent. He had tried to establish a splendid and enduring empire, taking as his model the plan of Asoka, the greatest and wisest of India's ancient rulers. Akbar never succeeded in conquering quite as much territory as Asoka, and he chose to rule by the sword, whereas Asoka had abandoned force and rested his authority upon the goodwill of the people. Like his predecessor, however, Akbar did succeed to an amazing degree in uniting the people under his control.

While Asoka had tried to get all the people of the Hindu faith to live together in harmony, it became a tenet of Akbar's reign that Muslims, as converts to the religion of Islam were called, should live at peace with Hindus. Akbar chose officers who were indifferent to religious conflict, both Muslims and Hindus, men who by the example of their behavior would attract and hold the loyalty of their subjects. Also, Akbar saw that if his empire were to last beyond his lifetime, he could not afford to exploit any of his laborers unduly. He exacted a fair rent from his peasants and discouraged excessive spending.

Excess there was, of course—luxury at court and sometimes selfish, high-handed behavior on the part of local officials who were far from Agra or Delhi and out of sight and hearing of the emperor. Akbar strengthened his position by making agreements with petty princes who were neither enlightened nor sensitive in their treatment of subjects. These arrangements brought great rewards to the princes but offered them nothing in the way of permanent security.

A man might wear jeweled robes one day and be invited to sit "inside the red rails" with the emperor while he held audience; yet, the same man might find himself out of favor and bereft of his wealth on the following day. Ideas about limiting the power of a sovereign were only beginning to take root, even in Europe, and no one had yet begun to say very much about the rights of the common man. The American and the French revolutions, which would bring the idea of equality to the fore and help establish democracy in the West, were still over one hundred and fifty years in the future.

This, then, was the empire with which the British came in contact through the East India Company, the land that they gradually usurped and ruled for over three hundred and fifty years, adding to it the southern and western parts of the Indian peninsula as well. It was a magnificent land of towering mountains and scorching deserts, wide rivers, fertile plains, and sun-washed seacoasts. It offered abundant resources for the man who was willing to withstand the torturous extremes of the climate, who knew how to tame or coax the native people into making agreements for trade or barter. There was grain as well as gold, jute as well as silk, indigo in addition to spice, cotton, and jewels. The list of what India could produce for European markets was endless, lying in wait, as it were, for exploitation and trade in the seventeenth century, ripe for the advent of the industrial revolution in the eighteenth and nineteenth centuries.

To this hot, rich land came a handful of Englishmen to trade and not to govern. But they were forced to govern, to some extent, in order to trade. They, too, had to concern themselves, as Akbar had done, with the vast, illiterate peasantry who undergirded their wealth and whose own rewards had to be sufficient to maintain production. From their predecessors the British inherited as well the unresolved conflict between Hindus and Muslims, which differed from the tensions between men of other faiths because it also reflected the resentment of Indian subjects toward their Mogul conquerors.

Beset by such problems in a strange, far-off country, the men of the East India Company groped for ways of doing things which were familiar and reliable. They were glad to have found in India an empire which was held together by the powerful personality of one leader who ruled by making arrangements with petty princes, as well as by choosing loyal, able administrators of his own. Englishmen could make use of such a set-up by negotiating their own arrangements with the emperor, his princes, and, when necessary, with his civil servants.

Having found a system for control already in existence in India, the British began to use it to serve ends which by the nature of things were their own and not Indian. These men were not missionaries. They had not come to India to help to develop the country in the modern sense of the term. Neither did the servants of the East India Company care very much about how the majority of the people fared, so long as their own business was not interfered with. Therefore, they quickly formed alliances with the Moguls in the name of the English Crown, raised an army of Indians and paid them for their service, routed other European contenders for trade, and used whatever means they deemed necessary to insure that their ships would be plentifully filled with cargo that would bring a quick and profitable return in Europe. Men in other times might think ill of them for their attitude, but their own age saw no harm in such enterprise.

What the British adventurers did not consider either

was that the Mogul empire, which seemed so secure, was a very recent event, historically, on the subcontinent of India. It lay, as the delicate domes and lacey arcades of its palaces suggested, like decorative icing over the substance of Indian life. Later, Englishmen would discover tangible evidence of a civilization in India that had rivaled those of Mesopotamia and Egypt in ancient times, a civilization whose boats had reached the coast of North Africa in the third millennium before Christ, whose government had controlled a far-flung network of principalities long before the rise of Greece or Rome. To the east and south of Agra stood wondrous temples whose magnificence was astounding, considering the intricacy of their design and the methods by which they must have been erected.

Out of the rich soil of India had risen not one but two of the world's major religions: Hinduism, which had moved south and east to the islands and jungles of the Pacific; and Buddhism, which had spread north to China and east to Japan. The fact that the Indian peasantry could not read or write at the time of the arrival of the Europeans did not mean that they had no learning. They knew, and many of them could recite, tales of epic proportions, dramas and poetry, as well as folk stories. In all walks of Indian life, the sense of a great and glorious past was alive, even among humble people, while among the nobility, learning and culture asserted themselves proudly.

So, even during the most extravagant days of Mogul rule, when the empire was at its height, the core of the subcontinent had remained Indian, not Mogul, in its loyalties; and, moreover, there were Hindu families who had been recognized at court and enjoyed the favor of the emperor. In later years, one of these favored families was named Kaul. This was a family noted for its handsome men and gracious women. They were scholars and people of refinement, Brahmins by caste, aristocrats among Hindus. They had come originally from the beautiful, lush valley of Kashmir, deep in the heart of the Himalaya mountains.

In the year 1716, when the fortunes of the East India Company were well advanced in India, but while Mogul rule was still in force over a large part of the country, one of the Mogul kings took a pleasure trip to the valley of Kashmir and there he met and was very much impressed by Raj Kaul, a scholar who could read both Persian and Sanskrit, the language of the Hindu scriptures. The king invited Raj Kaul to bring his family to Delhi, where he promised to grant him land and distinction.

Raj Kaul moved down from Kashmir with his family and continued his life as a scholar in what had become the imperial capital. The land that the king gave to Raj Kaul was situated along a canal, called a *nahar* in the language spoken at court. At first the aristocratic family was referred to by the local inhabitants of Delhi as the Nahars, the people who lived by the canal; but, as time went on, they became known as the Nehru family.

The fortunes of the Nehrus increased in Delhi, for they were a family who combined learning and culture with the ability to negotiate, administer, and control. Under the increasing influence of the British in India, the men of the family were attracted to the practice of law. One of them acted as the first legal adviser for the East India Company at the court of the Moguls. In 1857, another of the Nehru family was serving as police chief of Delhi.

The year 1857 was a dividing line in the history of India because it marked a turning point in relations between the East India Company and its government and between England and India. Another queen, Victoria, then sat

upon the throne of England. Her reign, though not as colorful and flamboyant as that of Elizabeth, was equally noted
for its commerce and especially for its spread of power and
influence. Under Victoria's rule, the British Empire reached
its widest dimensions.

In the years between 1607 and 1857 the fortunes of the
East India Company and, to some extent, the fortunes of the
British government in India had flourished, while those of
the Mogul Empire had steadily declined. Having arrived at
the court of Akbar as petitioners for the right to build a
warehouse, the men of the East India Company had found
that in order to be secure, they had had to have soldiers
to protect their warehouse and force with which to make
and keep agreements, whether with the emperor or with
his princes. This had led to the gradual expansion of
English territory and the tightening of English control in
India.

Although the East India Company continued to rule by
virtue of its name and charter, over the centuries the company became established as an instrument of the British
throne. By each of three "Government of India Acts," passed
by the British Parliament in 1813, 1833, and 1853, the
Crown assumed wide responsibilities for governing English
territory in India and in 1858 the sovereignty of Great Britain became complete. Long before this, the original situation had been reversed, and emperors of the Mogul court
had had to come as petitioners to the powerful sahibs of the
East India Company; but, after 1858, Mogul power was forever destroyed in India. In the eighteen seventies, it was
Queen Victoria, Elizabeth's proud, illustrious descendant,
who took the title "Empress of India."

The situation that provoked the transfer of power from
the East India Company to the Queen was sparked by the

Indian Mutiny of 1857. Historians have explained the Indian Mutiny in various ways. Some have called it the last bid of the Moguls for power and an attempt on their part to reestablish their weakened empire. Others have interpreted it as an upsurge of democratic feeling, the first expression of the will of the Indian people to be free, a revolution of the peasants. Still others have seen in the mutiny an inevitable clash between peoples of very different backgrounds, customs, and institutions, a clash that occurred at a time when no one was concerned with more than his own immediate advantage.

Whatever may be the long-range interpretation of the Indian Mutiny of 1857, certainly it was the lack of understanding and respect for peoples of different backgrounds that touched off the conflict. It all began in England, in an office of the Ordinance Department for the army, with men who had never been to India and who did not know the depth of feeling which Indians have for their own religions and what that means to them in terms of daily practice.

English ordinance officers packed and sent out to India heavily greased cartridges for use in new rifles. The cartridges had to be torn open at the ends in order to release their powder. The easiest way to tear open a cartridge was to bite it. After a rifle had been loaded, its muzzle was to be smeared with the grease that had coated the cartridge. The grease was a mixture of suet and lard. Orthodox Hindus, of which there are many in the Indian army, would be profaned by touching suet and Muslims would be equally profaned by touching lard.

The greased cartridges were distributed to army depots in India, ready for issue to the troops. By the time that officers in the field realized the mistake that had been made and were ready to make amends, it was too late. Eighty-five Indian soldiers stationed at Meerut refused to use the cartridges. As a consequence, these men were stripped of their uniforms and shackled. Reports of this spread rapidly among the troops and they revolted. Delhi was seized by mutineers. There was panic in Calcutta. It looked as if England were going to lose control of its hardwon territory.

In 1857 Englishmen and Indians were in the proportion of one to four thousand in India. The East India Company had kept control of its holdings by using an army of mercenaries. There had been mutinies before, but they had been localized. Faced with widespread revolt in 1857, the English were hard put to defend their stations. The course they took was determined by a need to make a strong show of force in the beginning or, in all probability, to be wiped out.

Englishmen in the field displayed quick judgment, but ferocious cruelty and almost indiscriminate violence. Treachery, torture, and pride were the order of the day. Savagery ran rampant on both sides. In the end, the capital at Delhi was won back for England, order was reestablished, and Queen Victoria was crowned Empress of India, but at a terrible price in bloodshed and ill feeling. The record of the Indian Mutiny is regarded today with embarrassment and shame.

In the midst of the uprising, when Delhi had become an inferno, the Nehru family fled, joining the throng of refugees that poured out of the capital and into the countryside. On their way to Agra, which they had set as their immediate destination, the Nehrus carried a little girl, the younger sister of two strikingly good-looking and intelligent brothers. The child was fair-skinned, as Kashmiri children often are, and very lovely. On their way to Agra, the family encountered a couple of English officers who caught sight of the little girl and assumed that she had been kidnaped from a British home and was being smuggled out of Delhi.

It was a time when tempers were short. The officers proposed to avenge a supposed crime then and there. They seized the two Nehru brothers and might have hung them from the nearest tree if one of them had not been able to speak English and explain the situation. So the family was saved from a certain and violent end. They proceeded to Agra. There they established themselves, prospered over the years, and were able to educate three sons, the two who had come from Delhi, and another who was born later, named Motilal.

Motilal Nehru grew up in the care of one of his elder brothers who became a lawyer in Agra. From his mother he inherited a will to get what he wanted and a terrible impatience with anything that stood in his way. He was impetuous and mischievous; but, at the same time, bright, jovial, and alert. He learned Persian and Arabic, as well as Hindustani and English. Because he was anxious to get on in the world, and that meant serving his British governors in some capacity, he had an ambition to acquire Western knowledge and to deport himself according to Western fashion. He trained for the law. He served a three-year apprenticeship in Cawnpore and then went to work at the High Court in the city of Allahabad.

Affairs looked rather promising for Motilal Nehru. He was endowed with vigor and learning. Clients trusted him. He acquired friends easily. He did not hesitate to display his talents in such a way as to impress his English superiors, although he carefully maintained contacts with members of his own Indian community, both Muslim and Hindu. He rapidly made a name for himself in his profession.

Though his wife was a devout Hindu, this promising young lawyer refused to profess belief in any *one* religion. Actually, he showed more interest in material possessions than in questions of dogma at the time. Likewise, he evidenced distress but not necessarily dismay when confronted with the social conditions around him: the poverty of most of his countrymen, their lack of learning, and subservience to foreign rule. His style, his entertaining, and his ways of looking at things became more and more like those of an English gentleman. He enjoyed the opportunities and, above all, the status his position offered.

After the Indian Mutiny of 1857, England was at the height of its power in India. The Suez Canal opened in 1869, cutting the distance from Bombay to Liverpool by four thousand miles. Steamships replaced unpredictable sailing vessels. Gone were the days when a few men would tenaciously protect lonely warehouses and trading posts. English companies were ready to invest heavily in India and that meant bringing out hundreds and thousands of young company managers and supervisors.

Wives and sweethearts of English officers were tempted to brave the trip from home to the tropics. English families began to move onto the tea plantations in the foothills of India. They lived in bungalows alongside newly built factories; they erected churches and opened schools and clinics for their children. They began, too, to show a concern for more than their own welfare. Englishmen evidenced interest in Indian matters as well, in the uplift of "the natives," as they called them, and especially in the encouragement of young Indians who could be a help in the work of the empire.

Motilal Nehru was one such person of promise, and Western ways obviously appealed to him. In the late 1800's he stood very close to the pinnacle of success. He was enjoying the best of both cultures, English and Indian. Associations with England brought him money, advantage, and prestige, a sense of "being in tune with the times," while his traditional ties to India gave him a feeling of belonging to something long established and familiar, of being part of the community into which he had been born. He had suffered minor setbacks and disapproval on his upward climb to prominence but he had been able to win over most of his opponents by generosity and good humor. Only one thing was now lacking in his life, as he saw it, and that was a son, a son to inherit his name, a son upon whom he could lavish his affections, and who would equal or even surpass, his own accomplishments.

There was great rejoicing in the home of Motilal and Swarup Rani Nehru when a son was born. Unfortunately, that first child did not live. The anxious parents had to wait a few years before a second son was born to them. The passage of time merely intensified their longing. Therefore, it was with heightened pleasure and anticipation that they greeted the birth of their second child on November 14, 1889.

He was named Jawaharlal, "bright and shining jewel." To his father, the handsome little boy was the most precious gem which adorned his crown of success. As a baby and as a growing child the Nehru boy was very shy, but, even so, there was playfulness and good humor about him which shed luster upon anyone who came in contact with him. The name Jawaharlal, chosen by his father, was a good one.

Jawaharlal enjoyed being the son of Motilal Nehru and the only child in the family. His sister Sarup Kumari was not born until he was ten. He was forbidden ever to go out alone, but Anand Bhawan, the house his father built just before Sarup Kumari was born, was like a small palace. Its halls were spacious and cool, with plenty of room for games and entertaining older cousins and friends. Surrounding the house were tennis courts, an enormous garden, and two swimming pools. There was a stable of well-groomed horses;

and when he was eight, Jawaharlal was given a pony of his own. He did not attend public schools, but was instructed by tutors. He first learned Persian, as he might have done had he lived at the Mogul court; and then he gradually began to study history and other subjects. When he was twelve, an English tutor named Brooks was invited to live at Anand Bhawan to teach him mathematics, science, and the so-called "Western" subjects.

From the beginning, Jawaharlal Nehru was introduced to both the Indian and the English ways of doing things. Among the earliest photographs of the child is one that shows him in a flowered court dress reminiscent of his Delhi ancestors. Another photograph, taken when he was a year or two older, shows him wearing a sailor suit and mounted upon an English tricycle. Anand Bhawan had three kitchens, two which cooked the pungent, spicy foods that were such favorites with Indians, and one in which European foods were prepared. The Nehru family sat at a table and ate with knives and forks, in the English manner, rather than with their fingers, as well-brought-up Indians did at that time. And, one day, Jawaharlal's father proclaimed that henceforth only English was to be spoken in his house. Although everyone became very good at it eventually, the first response to that edict was silence, because no one could speak any English except Motilal himself.

This was an exciting time to be growing up, especially when one was a member of such a family as Jawaharlal's, a family with access to inventions, education, and wealth. Electricity was soon installed at Anand Bhawan. Brooks, Jawaharlal's tutor, helped his young pupil to fit out a science laboratory where he could perform experiments. There was much talk of travel, too. Together, Brooks and Jawaharlal read books about adventurers and explorers of their own times. In 1899, Motilal Nehru went to Europe for a visit. The family spent its summers in the mountains. The head of the household earned enough from just a few days of his work to support his children for a year. In fact, there was nothing which a son could have asked for which would not have been sought for Jawaharlal.

At the same time, India itself was waking and stretching through its contact with ideas current in Europe and America, ideas about government as well as science and technology. In 1885, four years before Jawaharlal Nehru had been born, a group of seventy-two Indian gentlemen had gathered in Bombay at the invitation of an enthusiastic Englishman named Hume to discuss reforms in British rule which benefit the Indian people as a whole. This group had called itself the "Indian National Congress," and had decided to meet annually thereafter.

Despite the fact that the Congress was founded by an Englishman, most English officials did not take it very seriously. But in 1888, the Indian National Congress convened in Allahabad and received quite a bit of local notice. Motilal Nehru found himself interested in its meetings. Three years later, when the Congress again met at Allahabad, he offered to serve as chairman of the reception committee. According to reports of the session, his arrangements "surpassed in elegance and finish" the best efforts previously made.

The innovations in everyday life, in communications, and in politics that came to the world during the last days of the nineteenth century were spectacular; but, they were nothing compared to what would appear in the next fifty years. The motorcar, the airplane, movies, the radio, atomic energy, and the United Nations—all these were yet to be.

Jawaharlal Nehru was born at a time when gigantic forces were fusing to create universal changes, and he was destined for leadership. Of course he did not realize this, any more than Queen Elizabeth I had realized on the last day of the sixteenth century that Englishmen would be ruling the subcontinent of India three hundred years later. The little boy thought of himself first of all as a Nehru and as an Indian. He knew he lived in luxurious surroundings in the city of Allahabad and he hardly ever went out. When he grew up, he hoped to have a look at the rest of his world; but meanwhile, like most other children, he made a game of life and played at being big. He had no idea that mixed in his games were elements of future greatness.

The problem with becoming great is just that. Along the way, no one ever knows for certain that a little boy, even a child of such an illustrious father as Motilal Nehru, will become great. So the things that Jawaharlal did, the clothes he wore, and the impressions he received were not recorded at the time. Or, even if such things were noted down, as some of them were, information was not given in sufficient detail so that the picture of a lively human child emerges from the somewhat musty letters and photographs. The person who wishes to recreate the early years of this great man's life has to use his imagination. A biographer must improvise upon the facts in the same way that a musician improvises upon a scale to make his melody.

"In the midst of that great family," Jawaharlal wrote later, "I felt rather lonely and was left a great deal to my own fancies. But more than all other festivals I was interested in one annual event in which I played a central part— the celebration of the anniversary of my birth. This was a day of great excitement for me. Early in the morning I was weighed in a huge balance against some bagfuls of grain and other articles which were then distributed to the poor, and later in the day there was a party. I felt the hero of the occasion. My chief grievance was that my birthday came so rarely. I tried to start an agitation for more frequent birthdays."*

"Oh, yes," his sister said, when she talked with the author about this book. My brother's birthdays were always like that—so many seers of growth, so many more seers of rice for the poor. The poor surrounded us. We never had much contact with them, of course, but they were always there, and on birthdays we were reminded of them."

An Indian child, a delicate boy, a handsome and a lonely boy, the pride of his father's heart had a birthday. He found himself the center of attention for one brief moment; but on that occasion, he came face to face with the ugliness of poverty. His family and the servants were at hand. His tutor, Brooks, was with him. It all occurred at gorgeous Anand Bhawan. When we know that, and when we think what happened afterward, we improvise and can suppose that Jawaharlal behaved somewhat in the following way.

* To provide ease of reading of direct quotations, I have in many cases dispensed with scholarly apparatus to mark minor deletions and additions. The reader is assured, however, that neither the import nor the tone of the quotations has been altered.—*Bani Shorter.*

at anand bhawan, the home of joy *

The boy Jawaharlal stood before a long mirror and inspected himself. Self-consciously, he made sure that he looked exactly as he wanted to look. He retied the laces of his shoes and for the third time that morning he smoothed down the collar of his handsome new suit. Outside, servants called to him impatiently. The majestic voice of his father resounded from the courtyard, demanding, "Jawahar, come down here! We are waiting for you."

Jawaharlal smiled. On other days a call from the courtyard would have sent him running to his father's side, but right now he did not budge. He knew that his father would wait. Before long someone was going to be sent upstairs to fetch him. Amid laughter and with a pretense of scolding he

* The plan of this book was discussed with Jawaharlal Nehru himself. The interior and exterior dialogue in this chapter is reconstructed to approximate the reality as closely as possible.

would be hustled out; but no one would think of punishing him. After all, it was his birthday! He had looked forward to this day for so long that he could hardly bear to have it begin. He hated the thought that some of its precious minutes would slip away and be gone.

What occurred next was precisely what Jawaharlal had hoped. He tingled from head to toe with excitement when the servant hurried him out into the hall at last. Through the wide corridors of the splendid house, across the balcony, and down the stairs they went. Other servants beamed with approval the minute that they laid eyes upon the birthday boy; and all along the way, he saw evidence of wonderful, tantalizing preparations.

As it nearly always happened on festive days, Munshi, an old friend and teacher of the Nehru family, had come to present a bouquet of flowers. He was waiting outside the door of the study. When the boy approached him, Munshi lowered his eyes, touched his forehead respectfully, and murmured, *"Salaam."* Flattered by this gesture, Jawaharlal extended his hand to the man and accepted the flowers grandly. Munshi patted the child's shoulder and they hurried toward the courtyard together.

In the kitchen compound, however, it was not as easy for Jawaharlal to maintain his air of self-control. There he was face to face with his father and he felt altogether small before the masterful figure of Motilal. "Are you ready at last?" the jovial man asked, with just a hint of irritation in his voice. "Yes, sir," Jawaharlal replied, trying desperately to maintain his confidence.

This was November 14, 1902, the thirteenth birthday of Jawaharlal, only son of the wealthy lawyer and acknowledged head of the High Court, Motilal Nehru of Allahabad. For father and son it was the day of days. If an observer had seen them together, the strong, dominating man and the timid, delicate boy, could he have foreseen that eventually this child would lead them both, along with millions of others in their country of India, on unknown paths to a world as yet undreamed of? Yes, in later years, when the story of the Nehrus had become part of history's record, one might look back and say, "It all had its beginnings in the city of Allahabad, at Anand Bhawan, 'The Home of Great Joy.' " But that morning neither father nor son thought beyond the very moment.

The courtyard was abuzz with activity. Anand Bhawan served as home to the extended family of the Nehrus, and the sons of Motilal's brother as well as his more immediate relatives lived there. The place was like a vast estate and just at that moment, everyone on the premises excepting baby "Nanni" and her nurse was trying to squeeze into the kitchen compound.

Jawaharlal's pretty mother was on hand, bustling around and giving orders. Her sister was setting up tables, with the help of Jawaharlal's older cousins. One or two of Motilal's lawyer friends had dropped by, and Brooks was expected to put in an appearance momentarily. A host of servants was attending this crowd, and their wives and children were around as well. Everyone was talking at once and an air of happy anticipation pervaded the crowd.

It is strange that in the midst of such a familiar group Jawaharlal could ever have felt shy; and yet, he had to admit that he did. It is also hard to imagine that in such surroundings he was ever lonely; though he was at times. He liked being the only son of the head of the family and he enjoyed being the focus of attention, but he was always just a little bit afraid of the illustrious man who was his father; and, so, he usually tended to hang back and avoided getting into the midst of things. His mother was tender and sympathetic but her interests seemed rather separated from the world that appealed to him most. Unfortunately, there was no one else at Anand Bhawan who happened to be his own age. He could honestly say that sometimes he thought of himself as a prisoner within the flowered walls of his father's mansion, and that was partly what made days such as this one so very special.

Out of the house came a line of kitchen servants bearing heavy trays and baskets. With Oh's and Ah's of delight, people jostled to one side in order to make room for the procession. The baskets were piled high with shirts, blankets, and bright saris. The trays were laden with sweetmeats, fresh and temptingly arranged on rows of green leaves. There were tins and tins of candies too, hard candies wrapped in papers marked MADE IN ENGLAND, candies of a kind most children in India could not afford to buy.

The trays and baskets were placed on the tables which stood either at the ends or behind a set of huge balance scales. In a few minutes Jawaharlal was going to stand on one of the platforms of those scales; and his exact weight in rice was going to be poured onto the boards at the other end. This was how he was weighed once a year; and after the weighing was over the rice and all the blankets and candies were distributed to the poor people of the neighborhood. The weighing ceremony was a tradition in the Nehru family. Such an event always marked the birthday celebrations of Motilal's son. It was one way the family shared its good fortune.

As the boy watched the goings-on, his heart raced. He was eager to find out just how much he had grown since he had been weighed the year before; but he also knew that when he was weighed, the door to the street was going to be open and everyone from round about would be looking at him. The thought of such eminence frightened him a little; but all the same it was nice to show himself off once in a while and have everybody tell him how pleased they all were with him.

The bustle of the courtyard was suddenly interrupted. The door that led from the compound to the street received such a pounding that its hinges rattled. "Hi, hi," someone shouted raucously. Hastily, the gatekeeper jumped from his stool and fumbled for one of the many keys that hung from his belt. He fitted a gigantic iron key to the padlock and the door sprang open immediately. Two coolies appeared, carrying tremendous bags of rice.

Motilal Nehru looked with satisfaction from the bags of grain to his son. Jawaharlal smiled gleefully. By now Brooks had joined the party and when he observed the coolies dump the rice onto the ground, he commented to Motilal in jest, "I doubt that your son will be heavy enough to tip the scales with that much of a load, sir."

Motilal turned to the young Englishman with a look of defiance, which was his instinctive response when challenged; but there was mischief in his voice as he boasted, "Well, if he's not big enough, then we'll have to weigh him twice." The two men laughed, but Jawaharlal's face clouded momentarily. He drew himself up to his full height and tried to look as big as he possibly could.

Excitement gave urgency to the preparations. The head servant held back outsiders who were waiting in the alley. He urged members of the Nehru family and their friends to move closer to the house. Then he spoke to those who had assembled in the lane and invited them to come in and squat on the floor of the compound. He approached the group standing on the veranda and, taking Jawaharlal by the hand, he led him out to the platform that hung suspended at one end of the scales.

On that day, Jawaharlal Nehru was the image of all an Indian mother could ever have hoped one of her sons to be. Those who were present saw a slim, fair-skinned boy dressed in expensive clothes of foreign design. He had the fine countenance of a Kashmiri Brahmin, regarded as one of noble birth. His face was alert, but his look faraway, as if his thoughts were somehow detached from his immediate surroundings. His body showed no sign of illness. Behind him towered a rich man's home. Though he was an Indian and, so, one of the ruled, he associated freely with his English rulers. The young man bore himself like a prince. Expressions of adoration came spontaneously to the lips of those who saw him.

News spread quickly that the door to the Nehru compound had been opened. People flocked through the street and tussled to get places where they could see what was happening. Smiling broadly, Motilal raised his son above his shoulders so that no one would miss having a look at him. "This is the boy, thirteen years old," he said, parading back and forth a few steps.

Exclamations of delight again broke from the audience. Men, women, and children leaned forward in order to look more closely and many touched their foreheads to the dust as a mark of respect and approval. From the line of servants a little girl was pushed forward, clutching a necklace of jasmine for Jawaharlal. Motilal set his son down so that the flowers might be slipped over his head. Then he lifted the boy onto one of the platforms of the scales.

Jawaharlal grinned and stood up boldly. He planted his feet firmly, lest he topple, and grasped the chains at diagonal corners of his platform. At the other end of the scales, a bag of rice was ripped open. Slowly, scoop by scoop, the white and shining grain was ladled onto the upraised boards.

It took quite a while to accumulate a pile of rice that would balance the weight of the child and raise him off the ground. The first bag was emptied and the second one opened. This made Jawaharlal especially proud. So far as anyone could remember, such a thing had never happened on one of his birthdays before. A single bag of grain had yielded more than enough for the other celebrations.

The boy was anxious to see just how big the pile of rice was going to be at the other end of the scales. He twisted himself around, hoping to get a glimpse of the boards, but he thought better of that idea when the platform on which he was standing began to sway. He giggled nervously and stayed as still as he could.

His end of the scales rose, wavered slightly, and became suspended a short distance above the ground. Jawaharlal had no idea of exactly how much rice was balanced against him, but he could tell from his father's hearty cheer that he must have put on enough weight during the last year to satisfy both of them. The rest of the family applauded and shouted congratulations. The onlookers from the street nodded their approval.

As soon as his weight had been balanced, however, the crowd's attention moved directly from the boy to the gifts. Jawaharlal was promptly pulled down to the floor of the compound and his father's firm hands helped him off the scales. Servants released their hold on the empty boards and the platform that held the rice clattered to the ground. Impatiently, the poor people began to shove forward to claim their shares, ignoring the admonitions of the gatekeeper, and even brushing against Jawaharlal's immaculate new suit in their eagerness to get their grain. Within seconds the birthday boy found himself shunted to one side. The family courtyard at Anand Bhawan took on the appearance of a crowded bazaar on market day.

At a safe distance, Jawaharlal stood and watched what was happening. Like shopkeepers, the kitchen servants dealt out rice to each of the families, who were made to form a line. Motilal, Munshi, the cousins, and the lawyer friends presided behind the mountainous piles of shawls and blankets. Swarup Rani gave out saris to the women and Jawaharlal's aunt produced a sweetmeat for every empty-fisted child. These birthday celebrations were well remembered from year to year in Allahabad and hungry people from all over the city thronged the lane. As long as they could do so, the Nehrus would give unstintingly to everyone who came.

Fascinated, Jawaharlal had a good look at these visitors. He had seen poor people before, of course, when he had gone out for drives or ridden his pony to the park; but, somehow, he hadn't paid very much attention to them. Last year when they had come, his mother had taken him away for religious ceremonies, because he had been twelve and that signified that he had come of age as a Hindu. Previous to that, he had been considered too young to be allowed in the courtyard after the weighing and so he had never really observed the gift-giving.

While they sucked their candies and waited for their mothers and fathers to leave, some of the children sauntered over to the place where the Nehru boy was standing. He looked at them curiously. Every bit as interested as he was, they gave him stare for stare. Keeping a respectful distance, they inspected young Jawaharlal from head to toe and gazed at his gorgeous house. Grown-ups came by, clutching bowls of grain, keeping a firm hold on their blankets. Wonderstruck and full of admiration, they too gaped at the boy and his surroundings.

Jawaharlal began to feel embarrassed in front of such an audience. For the most part these were rather skinny people, he thought, ill clothed and poorly fed compared with himself. Their hair was unkempt and the babies they toted around with them were not very lively. The children didn't seem inclined to have anything to say to him, although they certainly didn't look unfriendly. There was no malice in their stares, or ridicule, only resignation and a kind of awe. All the same, their presence made the Nehru child feel strangely uncomfortable and somehow out of place.

Jawaharlal glanced from one to another of his admirers. How old were the old folk, he wondered, the mothers and grandmothers of so many children? Even the young women looked tired to him, and the boys and girls didn't appear to have any spunk or merriment left in them. All in all, it was a sober gathering.

One of the elders in the crowd addressed a question to him in a dialect that Jawaharlal had difficulty understanding. The child had to ask the older man to repeat what he had said, and the fact that he himself couldn't answer right away made the boy more self-conscious than ever. He choked. Shyness threatened to get the better of him. He bit his lip and looked away. As soon as he had stammered out a reply, he turned and fled into the cavernous recesses of the house.

Along the familiar halls, in and out of the lofty rooms, and up the stairs Jawaharlal scampered. He didn't know exactly where he wanted to go; but for the moment it was enough for him to be out of sight of the unfamiliar people, out of reach of their probing eyes. Tears threatened him and suddenly he felt much too hot in his lovely suit.

The rooms at Anand Bhawan were deserted that morning. Hearing the boy pattering about the hall, Nanni's nurse shooed him off on the pretense that his baby sister was asleep. Quite alone, Jawaharlal took his way from room to vacant room until at last he discovered Brooks standing on a balcony above the courtyard.

The child was bothered. What little personal enjoyment he might have derived from his birthday celebrations had been marred by the unexpected encounter with an inquisitive audience. That had made him feel uneasy and out of place. Yet, for the very same reason, he couldn't bear to be alone. He didn't want to be separate from what was going on. It was too lonely! He hid in the curtain behind Brooks for a few minutes and waited until he could catch his breath. Then he leaped out of the shadows and surprised his tutor.

Brooks swung around immediately. He felt inclined to scold Jawaharlal for coming upon him so unexpectedly but, catching sight of the child's troubled face, the tutor reconsidered his impulse. "What ho!" he exclaimed. "That's a sad expression to be wearing on the day of days. Whatever is the matter?"

"Nothing," Jawaharlal replied moodily. He was vexed and troubled, to be sure, but that was nothing he was ready to tell Brooks, at least not yet.

Brooks tried to think of something that would coax the boy out of his quiet. "Have you seen what's happening in the garden?" he asked.

"No," Jawaharlal answered, turning away.

"They are putting up fairy lights, red and green and gold," the tutor explained. "When the lights are turned on, there will be a blaze of color all around the swimming pool. And I hear the birthday cake will serve a hundred people," he added impressively, anxious to get some sort of response from his young charge.

Brooks's description of the party did revive Jawaharlal somewhat. He listened to what his tutor was saying, although he still refused to look at him directly. Brooks went on teasingly, "And today is a holiday," he emphasized. "No lessons. Imagine that. No lessons—and all because of a downcast, silent lad named Jawaharlal."

That was the truth. There were to be no lessons because it was November fourteenth. The reminder of having a day without lessons was enough to change any boy's outlook. A flicker of a smile crept across Jawaharlal's face. He stepped closer to his tutor.

Catching sight of his son with Brooks up on the balcony, Motilal stopped what he was doing for a moment and saluted grandly. Brooks nudged the boy. Jawaharlal peered over the railing. So, without his intending for it to happen, his attention was drawn again, inevitably, to the courtyard and the crowd of visitors.

The boy looked down upon the dwindling stream of people who poured through the door of the compound and the shadow of his pensive mood returned. "Are these all the poor people there are in India, Brooks?" he asked suddenly.

"Good heavens, no," Brooks answered. "I don't suppose anyone rightly knows how many there are, but there are certainly a lot of them. Of that we can be sure."

"Is it the fault of the British that they're poor?" the boy asked his tutor, giving voice to ideas that he didn't understand but had sometimes heard expressed by grown-ups at his father's dinner parties.

"Maybe," Brooks answered warily. "It's probably partly our fault, and partly the fault of the Indians themselves."

Jawaharlal did not know quite how to handle the answer he had been given, but the encounter he had just had, the memory of skinny mothers and so many quiet children, continued to trouble him. "What do the poor people do on days when it is not my birthday?" he asked.

"What do you do?" Brooks asked, looking around with interest.

Jawaharlal grinned. "I dream and I wish," he answered. "I wish it *were* my birthday."

"Maybe that's what they do too," Brooks mused.

Jawaharlal pondered over that reply. "I know of a solution," he volunteered. "I shall have birthdays more often. Don't you think that is a good plan, Brooks? Then I can have the party and the poor people can have my rice."

Sensing the mixed motives behind Jawaharlal's proposal, Brooks laughed out loud. Gaiety reasserted itself. With no one else there to see or comment, Jawaharlal felt more like his usual playful self. "I proclaim," he said, "that every day in all of India shall be Jawaharlal's birthday." With mock dignity he turned to Brooks. "Will you carry out my orders, sir?" he questioned.

His friend Brooks rose to the occasion. The tutor bowed ceremoniously and replied to the child with amusement, "If such a thing could come to pass, I should be the first to comply with your wishes, young Jawaharlal."

The service of the East India Company and of the British Crown in India always attracted capable Englishmen. Many of these men proved to be exceptional leaders and some were outstanding. Two of the greatest were Thomas Munro and Mountstuart Elphinstone. They were ruddy, vigorous officers, fond of sports, both of them Scots of stern countenance. Each served for over thirty years in India in the late 1700's and during the early part of the nineteenth century. Thomas Munro distinguished himself by settling and recording the complex land claims of peasant cultivators in the provinces of Mysore and Madras and he held the post of Governor in Madras. Elphinstone fought a successful war against the hardy Marathas of the Deccan and became Governor of Bombay.

At the time of their service in India, Munro and Elphinstone were acclaimed for their just administration, their skillful planning, and their practical good sense. At the ends of their terms, they were retired to England with honor. Today, however, it is possible to look back upon their careers and see that it was not their military prowess or their administrative skill so much as their prophetic vision of the ends of their rule, their deep respect for the Indian people, an awareness of the innate potential of "the natives" whom they ruled which brought dignity to the work of Munro and Elphinstone and won for it long-lasting recognition.

In the eighteenth century, Munro wrote thoughtfully: "Whenever we [the English] are obliged to resign our sovereignty, we should leave the natives so far improved from their connection with us, as to be capable of maintaining a free, or at least a regular government among themselves." A few years later Elphinstone wrote: "The most desirable death for us [the British] to die should be the improvement of the natives reaching such a pitch as would render it impossible for a foreign nation to retain the government." These were farsighted, courageous words for English administrators to have penned in India before representative government was fully established at home, and while England was still smarting from the loss of her American colonies!

Not all of their countrymen agreed with the views of such men as Munro or Elphinstone, especially in regard to "improvement of the natives," but some of the English did; and, because of them, remarkable forces were set in motion in India during the centuries of British rule. Most notable of these forces, though not the most eye-catching or spectacular in the beginning, was education.

Of course India had had schools long before the traders of the East India Company had arrived upon her shores; and, if those hardy explorers did not immediately concern themselves with the refinements of life in an alien country, it is understandable. At the time of the first Mogul invasions of India, during the eleventh and twelfth centuries, there were already Hindu scholars residing in centers established for religious and scientific study. The influence of the very old and world-famous universities at Nalanda and Pataliputra had waned; nevertheless, the Moguls had immediately come in contact with Hindus of erudition and learning who belonged to scholarly communities. They had found village schools, too, presided over by distinguished elders who gave instruction in Sanskrit. To these the Muslim conquerors had added their own kinds of religious schools; and, through the court, they had given patronage to the arts and sciences. When the empire was at its height, the educational and cultural life of Delhi was described as "the envy of Baghdad, the rival of Cairo, and the equal of Constantinople."

After some years, the British in turn established colleges and universities where they offered instruction in English and administered examinations from English universities. They also provided openings for a few qualified Indians to study in England. In some provinces where they exercised power, they introduced primary education in English; but this was to be given at the discretion of the local governors.

From the point of view of a British governor, there was an immediate and compelling advantage to be gained from

having young Indians qualify for study abroad. The boys
who could afford to go were persons of privilege and influence. Once there, they would experience European ways of
doing things; and when they came back, they would in all
probability extend and interpret the work of empire. They
would make excellent civil servants and company managers.
As a consequence, the burden of British rule would be considerably lightened. This prospect alone was enough to convince doughty English officers to lend their support to education, whether or not they felt it was desirable to educate natives for their own sakes.

But things did not turn out exactly as the British bene-
factors planned. Some of the boys who learned to write and
edit office reports in English, with an eye to applying their
skills in the Civil Service, found themselves attracted instead
to careers in journalism, teaching, and law. Young Indians
who were exposed to the history of Western Europe in the
classrooms of England saw the explosive possibilities of
applying the ideas of modern political philosophers and re-
formers to their own society. Students who mastered the language of trade contracts also read and understood the
Magna Carta. Moreover, at English universities, they became
used to an environment of free inquiry and dissent. They
did not take easily to having their activities curtailed when
they came home. They resented not being listened to ap-
preciatively by men who had encouraged them to train in
England in the first place.

Gradually, the boys who had been educated abroad
began to form a new and powerful elite in India; and
through them a new spirit was released in the country, the
spirit of doubt and questioning. They had acquired not only
European knowledge and skills, but the skepticism and val-
ues of their times. Once home, they began to question

traditional ways of doing things. Their inquiries ranged all the way from matters of religious doctrine to family relationships. In regard to government, they went so far as to ask of their English governors whether colonialism, as it was practiced in India, could be defended by reason; whether it contributed to happiness and was consistent with the dignity of man. These young men had been made restive and, because they were indeed persons of influence, they made others restive too. By 1900 it was fair to say, in the words of Munro, that "the natives were so far improved as to feel new life and vigor."

Coming from the family that he did and having a father who so enjoyed doing things in the British style, it was inevitable that Jawaharlal Nehru would go to a fashionable school when he was ready, and that the school would be in England. At age fifteen he was admitted to Harrow, a famous and exclusive English preparatory school. Upon successful completion of his work there, he was expected to enter Cambridge University. Taking Jawaharlal's sister Nanni with them, Motilal and Swarup Rani made the long sea voyage from India to England in 1905, simply to make sure that Jawaharlal would be well cared for and was comfortably settled.

While Jawaharlal got used to Harrow, the rest of the family went off to Europe for a grand vacation. Whenever he traveled, Motilal Nehru moved in regal fashion. Nanni's astounding beauty and the obvious wealth of the family attracted friends and admirers at every stop and hospitality was pressed upon them. It was a temptation for the family to extend its sojourn, but they returned to England, as they had promised to do, before sailing for home. Motilal had no doubts that his decision to send Jawaharlal to school in Britain was a propitious one. Yet, he found it hard to think of parting with him for so long a time. When he got back to Allahabad, he wrote to his son: "Here we are at last, but somehow or other Anand Bhawan does not appear to be so full of *Anand.*"

Life in an English school had an immediate and noticeable impact upon young Jawaharlal Nehru. For the first time he associated with boys his own age. He learned to play cricket and to row. The school expected him to compete for scholastic honors; and he was delighted when the headmaster praised him in a note to his father at the end of term. He was encouraged to read as much as he wanted to; and he delved into books, not only those assigned, but many others chosen for his own amusement and to satisfy his active curiosity.

During the school terms, days were packed with activities at Harrow; but vacations were set aside for travel and discovery. Jawaharlal went to the continent several times during his first years in England. He made the trip all the way to India twice, alone; and on short holidays, he went mountain climbing with friends.

Mountain climbing was the sport he loved most. He enjoyed the heights, the exhilaration that came from swinging up the path, the beauty of unexpected vistas, new adventures, and the sense of real peace he found at the summit. All his life Jawaharlal was to be attracted to the mountains. Somehow, they symbolized his deep longing for space and freedom.

When the boy was about to move to Cambridge University, he had an awareness of being much more grown-up all of a sudden. He admitted then that he considered preparatory school a little stuffy and he rejoiced in the lack of restrictions his new surroundings promised. His father provided lots of money, and he planned to spend it exactly as he wished. He was gay and stylish and became something of a gadabout for a while.

In after years, when he looked back on school and college, Jawaharlal remembered his dreadful shyness, too, and his lack of confidence; but others remembered him always as a winning and sometimes fiery youth. Long after school days were over, and under very different circumstances, he received a letter from a former teacher which began with the question "Are you the nice Nehru who was in the Headmaster's house at Harrow in 1906?" In fact, the boy made such an impression upon teachers and acquaintances who met him in England that more than a half century later they could recall his youthful looks exactly, his gestures, and his smile.

It is true, however, that he did not succeed in conquering his shyness. At Cambridge he joined a college debating society to which members had to pay fines if they didn't speak during meetings. Many a month Jawaharlal gladly paid his fine rather than risk embarrassment by attempting a speech in front of English colleagues.

With the other Indian boys, he was naturally somewhat less reserved and acquired the reputation of being a genial host, like his father. The Indian fellows palled around together, and Jawaharlal became very fond of some of them, whom he got to know for the first time in England. They became his lifelong friends and included men who acquired fame as patriots—Lala Lajpat Rai, the Ali brothers, Dr. Sherwani, and Dr. Syed Mahmud, a Muslim who figured prominently in his associations later on.

Throughout the seven years he spent at school in England three letters arrived weekly for Jawaharlal. His mother wrote in Hindustani; but the note from Nanni was in English, because she was proud of being able to use the language she was learning from her European governess. In addition, as regular as clockwork, the student received several hand-written pages from his father. These letters from Allahabad formed a strong bond with home.

The head of the Nehru family wrote colorful descriptions of his entertainments at Anand Bhawan. He confided his slight worries about his beautiful little daughter, and he also kept close tabs upon Jawahar, as he called him, his studies, and his health. Soon after he deposited his son at Harrow, Motilal got off a hasty but fatherly note to remind the boy to keep well bundled up until he got used to the English climate. When he replied, Jawahar was expected to account dutifully for the state of his health and his lessons. As time went on, Motilal was roundly shocked at what he considered to be Jawaharlal's mishandling of money and he reprimanded him, demanding that he present a record of his spending. The boy provided not only the record but also vivid descriptions of school, sight-seeing trips, and youthful opinions on the times.

It is through the bits of commentary that he tucked into letters home that those who did not know him have been able to catch vivid glimpses of young Jawaharlal Nehru and to sense what a lively, imaginative boy he was. For example, during the Christmas holidays in 1906, he went off to the automobile show in Paris to have a look at the car Motilal had ordered built for Anand Bhawan. This was to be the first car to be driven in India. Jawaharlal was suitably impressed; but, in his next letter to his father, he warned him that he thought the enjoyments connected with driving autos would be short-lived, because he, Jawaharlal, was certain that the "air age" was at hand. "Everyone seems to be cocksure that aeroplanes will be as common in a few years as motorcars are now," Jawaharlal wrote jubilantly. He proposed to Motilal that, since the air age might not be long delayed, he should plan to fly home for weekends.

Because they shared other ideas, Motilal could not help but report to Jawaharlal some of his views on the political situation at the time. It looked as if trouble was developing in India. The nationalist pot was at the boil, so to speak; and there were very few letters which did not refer in some way to the burgeoning sense of patriotism sweeping the country.

Because of two exceptional spokesmen named Gopal Krishna Gokhale and Lokmanya Tilak, the Indian National Congress had expanded its membership and acquired status during the years since its inception in 1885. Meanwhile, the Muslims, who had felt themselves to be overlooked if not actually out of favor with the British government after the mutiny, had been encouraged to form their own political discussion group. They called it the All-India Muslim League and it met for the first time in Dacca, in what is now Pakistan, in December, 1906. Its founding was timely. Feelings of dissatisfaction with British rule were intensified among Indians of all persuasions because of events that were taking place elsewhere in Asia and that demonstrated the ability of "natives" to get the better of their European overlords. The question of eventual self-government in India was being discussed openly.

For the first time in his life, Motilal Nehru was seriously considering entering politics. He continued to attend the sessions of the Indian National Congress and accepted the presidency of a provincial conference in 1907. Tilak and Gokhale were contending for leadership within the Congress Party and the opinion of professional men was certainly aroused.

One of the most vocal groups in India, however, as well as the one with some of the most active demonstrators, was composed of students. When the famous Gokhale visited Allahabad, Motilal Nehru witnessed enthusiastic university boys unhitch the horses of his carriage and draw it to the auditorium, shouting nationalist slogans at the top of their lungs. As a matter of fact, even in England, the Indian students were electrified by political activities. When they gathered informally, they talked of little else.

Actually, Motilal Nehru was too moderate a person to involve himself in action prematurely, and he certainly did not want Jawaharlal to be mixed up in anything that smacked of danger. He really wanted to wait for a while. He thought it would be better to see what the outcome of political jockeying was going to be before he committed himself; and he expected Jawahar to follow his example.

Occasionally, particularly after he had received one of his father's provocative letters, Jawaharlal Nehru would engage in political speculation with his friends. He became outspoken at such times and sounded dangerously rebellious; but his involvement in such matters was brief. His shyness, his deep affection and respect for Motilal, or his love of fun usually got the better of him in the end.

Political discussions at school or in the university were something of a sideline and a diversion for young men like Jawaharlal. They had exams to study for, games to play, and eventually careers to decide upon. Yet, surprisingly enough, even these occupations were not overly compelling to Jawaharlal while he was at Harrow and Cambridge. Acceptable grades were fairly easy for him to come by and games were no hindrance. He felt he could wait a year or so before he settled upon a career. With plenty of money and friends of his own sort, he preferred to relax and enjoy the lighter side of life.

"I'll never forget him," his dearest friend said afterward. "None of us who knew him then will ever forget him. He was so handsomely turned out, so gracious, so generous; and, yet, so fiery. He certainly gave his father a hard time of it. I remember how he stood behind Tilak, for example. He amazed us all." *

When an open split occurred in the Congress Party, a split between the Extremists and the Moderates, Jawaharlal was on the side of the Extremists. "It is of course a great pity that such a split should have occurred," he wrote to his father. "But it was sure to come and the sooner we have it, the better. You will most probably throw all the blame on Tilak and the Extremists. They may have been to blame for it, but the Moderates certainly had a lot to do with it."

Motilal, the Moderate, was furious. "I am sorry you don't approve of my opinions," Jawaharlal replied, "but really I can't help holding them in the present state of affairs."

* Syed Mahmud, to the author in New Delhi, spring, 1961.

2 on his own *

In a handsomely furnished lounge, the Indian students gathered after dinner. They formed a lively, attractive group, laughing and chiding one another as they came in, shaking the raindrops from their umbrellas and from their turbans. Proud, well-bred, elegantly groomed, and wealthy, these boys represented the most fortunate homes and prominent families of India; and they were further distinguished by having been admitted to Cambridge, one of England's venerable and respected universities.

At the back of the colorful assembly sat a dignified newcomer to these sessions. His name was Jawaharlal Nehru and he was splendidly attired in a suit cut by the King's own tailors. He had come up to Cambridge from preparatory school

---

* The dialogue in this chapter is reconstructed to approximate reality. It is based upon letters exchanged by Jawaharlal Nehru and his father, news reports, and conversations with Dr. Syed Mahmud.

only recently, but already the older students recognized him for his good looks, his faultless manners, and his generosity. Despite his obvious charm, however, "young Nehru," as he was called, didn't appear to be much of a talker. He sat alone, a spectator rather than a participant.

Behind his graceful manner, Jawaharlal Nehru was keeping his opinions to himself. His new acquaintances surmised that he might be shy. However, turbulent questions were under discussion, questions which concerned whether or not India was going to stay in the British Empire or would try to become a self-governing nation. The students were anxious to size him up on the vital subject of "home rule," as they called it. Jawaharlal's reputation for reading and scholarship had preceded him at the university, but no one had yet had a chance to hear where he stood in relation to politics. If he had ideas on such matters, he must be nurturing them in private, for he seldom mentioned them.

The door to the meeting room swung open and the last of the students entered briskly, clutching a packet of newspapers. Without stopping to take off his greatcoat, or even to unwind his muffler, the latecomer declared, "Well, boys, I've got news for you. What we feared would happen has now come to pass. I can tell you that the Indian National Congress has split right down the middle. The December meeting of the party broke up in disorder."

The young man interrupted his report for a moment to remove his gloves. Meanwhile, his keen eyes swept his audience, trying to measure what effect his announcement might have had. As soon as he had come in, the boys had ceased conversing and turned in his direction; but they didn't react immediately to what he said. He added, as if to spur on the tense and silent group, "Well, what do you think? The Congress isn't a very strong party, is it, if its leaders can't reach agreement among themselves and their meetings break up in disorder?"

Knowing looks passed quickly, almost furtively, from one to another of the students, but not a single voice was raised. The boys felt on the spot and not one of them was prepared to be the first to speak. Mostly, they wanted to wait until they heard how their companions reacted before they expressed their own views.

The speaker walked over to the coatrack. Deliberately, he set his silver-topped cane in the umbrella stand and flicked a few drops of moisture from his collar. He hung up his hat, his coat, and muffler before he returned to the company by the fire. Then he slapped his newspapers on the table with an air of final challenge. "Here they are," he said. "Come and get them. You'd better see the story yourselves."

Eagerly, the young men fell upon the newspapers. Hastily, they dealt out the sheets. Since there were not enough copies for everyone, the students clustered together near the lamps and several boys scanned the headlines over the shoulders of their companions. Someone quickly volunteered to read aloud for the benefit of those who couldn't get near enough to see a paper for themselves.

Ordinarily, the young men would have reserved some doubts regarding the interpretation of Indian news as it was printed in English newspapers. But they could hardly question the facts of a case, and it was precisely the facts they needed. They read avidly.

"The Indian National Congress opened its annual meeting at Surat on December twenty-sixth in the afternoon," the London papers reported. "However, order could not be maintained and the meeting had to be postponed until the following day." When they heard that bit of news, the Cambridge students nodded, as if they could have guessed that such an occurrence was likely to have taken place. The confrontation of Gopal Krishna Gokhale and Lokmanya Tilak had been a long time coming and tension had been destined to reach its climax at the annual meeting of the Congress.

Both men were dynamic leaders and both commanded loyal followers. Both of them believed in democracy for India; and yet, their immediate goals for their country differed radically. Gokhale was urging representation for Indians. Tilak was advocating nothing less than complete independence. "Swaraj [self-government] is my birthright and I will have it!" he had once proclaimed determinedly. He must have said something of the same sort at Surat. At any rate, he was an impassioned orator and his audience would have taken sides quickly. The meetings he addressed were often turbulent.

"When the meeting was resumed on the next day," the newspapers stated, "Mr. Tilak mounted the platform and demanded the right to speak. He was shouted down and ordered to his seat. He refused to move, and even though his opponent, Mr. Gokhale, sprang to his defense, violence ensued. Missiles of various descriptions were thrown, furniture broken, and the meeting closed . . . not to be resumed."

Except for the voice of the one student who was reading aloud, the room at Cambridge was hushed. The reader continued steadily, "This incident has forced an open break in the Congress, a break which has long been foreseen; between the so-called Moderates, led by Mr. Gokhale, and the Extremist group, led by Mr. Tilak."

The reading ceased. These limited statements, so tantalizing to the Indians assembled there, formed the substance of the news report. For a few seconds, silence prevailed in the meeting room, a silence so profound that one could hear the wheels of carriages passing in the street outside. A student of determined Moderate opinions ventured to remark, "Well, that put Tilak in his place. That's where his talk of rebellion and revolution has landed him. If anyone asks me, I think he got exactly what he deserved."

The boy standing next to the speaker swung round and confronted his colleague immediately. "Yes, but just remember that it wasn't an outsider who was put in his place. It was an Indian. And, more important than that, because of the disorder, the Congress Party meeting was never held at all. We're no farther along the road to self-government than we were a year ago."

At this point the dapper young man who had brought in the newspapers took his turn and the rest of the students were forced to listen politely. "Actually, I think we're a lot farther along the road to self-government than we were a year ago," he said. "Now, at least, we know where we stand. The issues have been spelled out and the methods are clear. You can choose to work for reform with Gokhale or fight a revolution with Tilak."

"Those two methods obviously can't exist together in the same movement," the speaker continued in polished and academic phrases. "It may seem that at the moment we have two independence movements. In fact, we do have two movements, disregarding any other minor parties for the time being. But the Congress Party is bigger than either of the factions. When it reorganizes, it will *have* to choose one goal or the other and it is my view that it will be stronger for having had to make the choice."

After a few moments of thought, a tall, swarthy Sikh from the northwest province of the Punjab took up the argument earnestly. He leaned against the mantel and stroked his beard as he observed in somewhat forbidding tones, "It will be hard for the Indian National Congress to follow Gokhale and keep peace in the country. Tilak is powerful and he is a revolutionary. He's a man of action and he's not content with simply attending meetings and listening to speeches. He's already got himself a following. I'll wager he won't stop short of anything except *swaraj* itself."

The student stopped momentarily and then went on deliberately, "Tilak has attracted quite sizable support," he said. "Not all of those Congress Party members at Surat were supporters of Gokhale. If they had been, the meetings wouldn't have broken up in the way they did. What about our own group?" he asked pointedly. "I'd guess that we wouldn't be one hundred percent behind Gokhale and his slow reforms, either."

"I'm not so sure," one of his colleagues replied. "You have to remember that India is ruled by Great Britain at the present time. There are English soldiers on our soil and those soldiers take orders not from us but from the King. The best policy may be to go slow for the time being. I, for one, would be content with reform if it kept the country stable. I'd rather have that than revolution and bloodshed."

Cries of "Hear! Hear!" greeted the young man's moderate stand, but immediately a student of dissenting opinion leapt to his feet. He was from the province of Bengal, where Tilak was most popular. He spoke urgently.

"Consider the man's program," he insisted. "What does Tilak say? He says, first of all, 'Don't buy British goods.' Doesn't that make sense when we can produce our own cotton cloth, our own steel for railroad cars, our own pots and pans? He says to buy things produced in India. What else does he say? He says that education must be improved. That doesn't sound very warlike."

"Yes, that's all very well," countered another student, "but Tilak is also saying, 'Don't work for the British, either.'

That sounds like pretty drastic advice. If his program is effective, you may be sure the British are not going to take it peaceably. Tilak will see what becomes of his ideas soon enough. If he's lucky, he'll land in jail. If not, he'll be shot. Revolution is a bloody business. Right now the odds are against us with the British army camped on our plains. If we have to fight, we won't stand a chance. Remember what happened in 1857."

There was no immediate reply to that comment. The boys began to fidget. A few excused themselves quietly and left. It may have been that some of them had a premonition of the violence that was in store for their country. They may have sensed that clashes between the British and Indians were imminent in Bengal. Perhaps they foresaw that Tilak was going to be imprisoned for challenging the imperial government. Whatever they supposed was going to happen, however, the students had been shocked by reference to the mutiny. They did not like to be reminded of their country's weak, subservient position.

A young man who had sat at a corner table got up, walked back and forth at the front of the room for a moment, and then summarized the conclusions of most of his fellows succinctly when he said, "However much our sympathies may suggest otherwise, my friends, I'm afraid that if we want to survive, we can't afford to be anything else excepting Moderates at the present time."

This view was widely held, but all the same it did not provide a wholly acceptable alternative to action for vivacious young nationalists. Maybe only a few of the boys were ready to toss in their lots with Tilak, but a poignant sense of pride in India and an awareness of their patriotic duty had been aroused by his appearance on the scene. It was not without some qualms of conscience that they could reject him and his program entirely. As the Cambridge group began to disperse that evening, quite a few of the young men privately harbored feelings of personal disquiet with such an ineffective stand.

While the other students got ready to leave, Jawaharlal Nehru stood alone, wrapped in thought. What he had read and what he had heard during the evening had transported him immediately, thousands of miles, to India, to Allahabad, and to the discussions that had gone on in his father's house since the times he could first remember. How friendly all of his father's acquaintances had outwardly appeared to be toward the British; but, on the other hand, how delighted most of them had been when one of their own countrymen had been able to get the better of a situation involving an Englishman! Yet, they were not revolutionaries, and in matters of politics Motilal Nehru was a practical man. He abhorred disorder. As Jawaharlal pictured the conference hall at Surat, he knew that Motilal must have been sitting with the Moderates. Of course his father would have thought that that was the place where he belonged.

A few of the young men lingered by the fire and settled themselves for games of chess; but, after several minutes of private conversation, the majority moved toward the coatrack to select their wraps and umbrellas. Most of the boys were already at the door before one of them noticed Jawaharlal standing alone and called back to him, half in jest, "And what would have been your position if you had been present at Surat, Mr. Nehru?"

"I would have been with the Extremists," Jawaharlal answered without a moment's hesitation, "and I would have protested against the treatment of Mr. Tilak."

The speed with which young Nehru answered surprised his companion and stopped the crowd near the door. There was also something in the tone of voice the young man used which suggested that he was not jesting. His questioner eyed him suspiciously. "Come, come," he said in mocking tones, "That hardly sounds appropriate for one of your status and social position."

Jawaharlal's temper was short, and his expressive eyes flared angrily. "There is nothing in a man's nationality or his social position which should set him apart from any other man basically," he asserted shortly. "A person has to consider the good for the greatest number and be ready to act upon it, whatever position he maintains in life."

His fellow students were startled by this outburst, but they were not too shaken to be realistic. "Safety doesn't lie with the Extremists," one of them reminded Jawaharlal, "—not these days."

Jawaharlal looked his colleague straight in the eye. "Safety is not my motto," he declared. "The split in the Congress Party was inevitable, and, to my way of thinking, the sooner it came, the better. The Moderates will be put in their place. The time has come to rally for swaraj."

Later, Jawaharlal thought about the way he acted that evening and it seemed to him that he had been hotheaded and must have sounded more than a trifle conceited. But at the moment he had felt courageous and had let his opinions carry him where they would.

The young men near the fire looked up from their games and listened to the comments from the other part of the room. After a second's reflection one of the older students spoke to young Nehru authoritatively. "Your father wouldn't be at all pleased to hear you say that," he said. "He's no Extremist, and you know it. He's a Moderate through and through; and he probably backed Gokhale's program at Surat."

Jawaharlal's pale cheeks blazed again. "Fathers and sons can go different ways," he replied hotly. "If my father is well pleased with his own actions, then he may have cause to be displeased with mine."

The young Nehru liked the determined sound of these words. When he had been a little boy, he had played at freeing India from her adversaries single-handedly, and he enjoyed the same dramatic sense of power now. But he stopped and looked at his mannerly friends, gathered around him, who had been struck dumb by the implications of what he had just said.

It was a rare and shameful thing for an Indian son to flaunt his father's wishes in such matters. The import of the words he had spoken so resolutely in the presence of his comrades came home to Jawaharlal. His flamboyance ebbed. He was suddenly contrite. "Talk is cheap," he said, trying to cover his embarrassment.

Jawaharlal turned away and went to get his coat. He blushed to think of what had transpired and he vowed that he would say no more in that room on the subject of his convictions. But his remarks had touched a sensitive spot with his companions. Students who had been within earshot had been made to consider not only their ideas about the future of their country but some of the personal consequences that might result from holding those opinions. In a way, they admired young Nehru for his boldness. They eyed him curiously as he bundled himself up. When he rejoined them, those who were on their way out stepped aside somewhat bashfully and let him precede them down the stairs.

Outside, the night was rainy and chill. A cloud of soft coal smoke shrouded the university towers. The light of the street lamps shone murkily through the fog. The normal sounds of busy life in the town were hushed.

The boys were lonely and loath to return to their lodgings. They stood huddled together on the stone steps, reluctant to bid one another good night. They pulled their scarves close about their necks to keep out the cold, but they did not hurry away. The evening's discussion was still in their minds.

Jawaharlal realized that inasmuch as it was his reaction that had produced the present atmosphere, he had involuntarily become the center of the group. He grasped for some way to dispel the gloom that now hovered over his colleagues. He fell back upon cordial, familiar ways. "Come on, fellows," he suggested, placing a hand upon the shoulder of his nearest associate. "Tomorrow is another day and none of us knows what fate has in store for him. I propose we go up to London and have some fun while there is still time."

Once the winds of freedom began to blow, there was no shelter from their force. Good and able men had set out for India from England during three long centuries, men who had served their company and their empire well: engineers, teachers, and doctors, along with governors and colonels, men who had helped to build the schools, the railroads, and the irrigation canals of the subcontinent; men who had mapped the rivers and settled land claims, who had seen famine and faced death in a strange land, but who nevertheless looked back fondly when their ships left Bombay, individuals about whom an Indian could say, "I never knew his like. I loved him as a father." Good and able Englishmen would continue to set out toward India for a while yet, along with the selfish, bigoted, and prejudiced few who had always formed part of the ranks, but none of them would ever find the same receptivity on the part of Indians to the work they came to do. As soon as citizens are convinced that their country should be free, anything that stands in the way of that, however well-meaning or justifiable at the time, is regarded as an obstacle. As Jawaharlal Nehru said: "Political changes produce certain results, but the essential changes are in the spirit and outlook of a nation." Men of empire were no longer welcome in India.

Tilak's revolution of the early 1900's did not succeed, however. It did not succeed in the short run because Tilak was arrested, subsequently tried, and imprisoned by the British; and it did not succeed in the long run because public-spirited men who supported the Indian National Congress were not ready for revolution. They were much more attracted to the gradual reformist program of Gokhale, and after Surat the Congress entered into a long series of negotiations with His Majesty's Government on the subject of extending Indian representation on the Governor-General's Council in India. In 1909 it was a triumph for the Moderates within the party when they were able to get an increase in the number of places available for Indians on that Council, even though it was stated that the body would "continue to be so constituted as to ensure its constant and uninterrupted power to fulfill the . . . obligations that it owes and *must always owe* to His Majesty's Government and to the Imperial Parliament."

The time had not yet come for rebellion. The spirit of Indian independence had been awakened. To some extent, ardor had been aroused; but, as yet, there was neither a leader capable of uniting all parties nor a force; and there was always a lingering hope on the part of Indians that England would somehow see the error of her ways and make amends before it was too late.

So, in the summer of 1912, when young Jawaharlal

Nehru went back to India, he found a scene that appeared to have changed very little. Nan was twelve. A second daughter, Krishna, had been born to Motilal and Swarup Rani Nehru while their son had been away at school; but, otherwise, life at Anand Bhawan was lived in very much the same indulgent manner as it had been before Jawaharlal had gone to England.

Motilal Nehru remained the acknowledged head of the High Court in Allahabad. His work was lucrative but onerous. Jawaharlal had decided to prepare himself for a career in law too, and he had been admitted to the bar just before his return to India. Therefore, it was with increased parental pride that Motilal could welcome his son. He planned on a few more years of arduous labor and then he hoped to transfer his famous practice to the polished, intelligent Jawaharlal.

To further set the stage for a rich and secure life, in February, 1916, Jawaharlal Nehru married beautiful, gracious Kamala Kaul. According to Indian custom, she was chosen for him, but Motilal, with his usual good taste, chose well. Kamala was also of Kashmiri descent. She was the daughter of a prosperous businessman. At the time of her marriage she was seventeen, tall and slim. Her upbringing had not been Westernized, as Jawaharlal's had been, but even before their sumptuous wedding in Delhi she visited Anand Bhawan to be tutored and to learn the ways of the stylish household she was about to join.

Though she lacked education and world awareness at the time of her marriage, Kamala brought a lovely gentleness to the household in Allahabad. During the early years of her married life with Jawaharlal, she concerned herself with family affairs. As he came to know her better, the deep sincerity of this woman impressed itself upon her husband,

and when he was in difficulty he described himself returning to Kamala "as to a sure haven." Their only child, a daughter, Indira, was born on November 19, 1917.

He was well enough liked by others, but Jawaharlal's own judgment of himself was that he was a misfit in Indian surroundings during the years that immediately followed his return from England. Compared with the dash and excitement of London, where he had been living, he found Allahabad stuffy. Among other things, he had acquired a genuine love for lectures, the theater, and travel while he had been in Europe. The daily Indian round of home, the law courts, and his club was less stimulating to him. He had never been able to overcome his shyness completely, either, and public appearances in court were difficult for him. Despite the diversions provided by his wife and family, he felt bored and somehow out of touch with affairs.

In politics, Jawaharlal was groping for his place. On the one hand, the young lawyer was anxious to be up and doing; but, on the other hand, he lacked the confidence necessary to plunge to the forefront immediately, and his party was dominated by Moderates. The enthusiasm that had been aroused by Tilak had diminished.

Jawaharlal did attend Congress Party meetings with his father, and he was impressed by a man named Mohandas Gandhi, whom he met there. Gandhi had been amazingly successful at organizing Indians to demand their political rights in South Africa, but he, too, had just come home, and it was too early to predict whether or not he could do anything on the Indian scene. When Tilak was released from jail, he immediately sent out a fresh call for volunteers to help organize groups to work for home rule. Jawaharlal responded and such activities provided an outlet for his energies for a while; but, basically, his associations were still limited and nothing except his own impatience with his position would have indicated that he was waiting for a bigger challenge.

Then, on April 13, 1919, there occurred an event which presaged change in the lives of the Nehrus, as it did in the future of every Indian citizen and in the outlook for all Englishmen who served His Majesty's Government in India. With the clarity of the shot that had once been fired at Concord, Massachusetts, on another April day long before, an incident involving Indians and Englishmen at a park called Jallianwala Bagh rocked the country from its calm. Hostilities that had been simmering for generations erupted overnight. The pace of change quickened. People were forced to take sides. The delightful but protected existence at Anand Bhawan came to an end.

At the close of World War I, Woodrow Wilson had enunciated on behalf of the Allies the principle of "self-determination" for subject nations. His doctrine had been greeted with rejoicing on the part of Indians because they regarded it as a recognition of their country's right to independence. Moreover, in the Montagu Declaration of 1917, Great Britain had nobly pledged herself to confer self-government upon India eventually. Indians had rejoiced. Nevertheless, when the war was safely over, His Majesty's Government had actually granted very few concessions in the direction of home rule and had passed instead, a series of punitive bills that gave the government very severe powers with which to suppress political activity. Gradually, the country had taken on something of the appearance of a police state administered in the name of the Crown.

By the spring of 1919, a sense of foreboding and suspicion had replaced the earlier optimism of Indian nationalists. This was true of staid and moderate men of intellect as well as rowdy activists and firebrands, Muslims as well as Hindus. Those who perceived what was happening were suspicious. They held meetings to protest the hateful "Rowlatt Bills," as the punitive measures were called. Mohandas Gandhi went so far as to call upon members of the Congress Party to disobey the new laws. The real center of opposition to British authority was in the north, however, in the province of the Punjab, where enmity between Hindus and Muslims had been acute from the time of the Mogul conquest, and over which, since 1857, England had kept watch with a firm but wary hand.

Baisakhi, the Hindu New Year's Day, fell upon April 13 in 1919. Despite a ban on public gatherings of any sort, approximately twenty thousand people poured into the city of Amritsar in the Punjab. Some came for merrymaking, some for speechmaking; and the natural place for them to congregate was a park called Jallianwala Bagh, which was enclosed on three sides by buildings and on the fourth by wall, with only one exit wide enough for more than a few persons at a time. At three o'clock in the afternoon, when the crowd was at its peak, a contingent of British soldiers marched into the park and ordered the people to disperse. Since the soldiers were blocking the one exit, the assembly could not disperse. Orders were then given to fire. By the officer's own report, firing ceased only when ammunition was exhausted. The dead numbered in the hundreds; the wounded in the thousands.

The firing at Jallianwala Bagh marked the beginning of a long and painful period of martial law in the Punjab. For several weeks the province was almost entirely cut off from the rest of India. Rumors of floggings and executions filtered through to people on the outside. In return for vengeful crimes committed by Indians, outrageous punishments were said to have been levied upon the innocent as well as the guilty. Normal movement of trade and service was impossible. Englishmen on His Majesty's business were the only ones permitted to go in or out of the area.

Indians were terror-stricken. In his autobiography, which was published many years afterward, Jawaharlal Nehru wrote in remembrance of those days: "Helplessly and impotently, we who were outside [the Punjab] waited for scraps of news and bitterness filled our hearts." The hold of the British army began to tighten upon the rest of the country. In the speech he delivered as President-elect of the Indian National Congress in 1919, Motilal Nehru reviewed events before a shocked and hostile audience, concluding: "Our country is flooded with sorrow . . . O, for our land, woe."

There had always been good men, kind men, men who thought of themselves as God-fearing and righteous, among His Majesty's servants in India. There had been cruel men too, men who described the business of government as "getting out of one hole after another," men who swaggered and bullied, some who were swift and ruthless in the dispensation of justice, who did not shrink from "cutting a native in half," if they saw fit, men who believed that the one who used the most force in the beginning would prove to have used the least in the end. It was unfortunate that the men in charge of Amritsar and the Punjab in 1919, Generals Dyer and O'Dwyer, showed more signs of belonging to the second group than to the first.

But if such things had happened in India before and Indians had not been very much bothered by them, why were they so upset this time? The answer is that never before had there been a group of organized, articulate men in India who were ready to make justice their business and who believed that it was their right to control their own destinies. The British had promised that they would work in the direction of self-government for India, and they had ignored their promise. They had gone further than that. Their local officers had shown that some of them, at least, were willing to hold on at any cost. The time was ripe for protest.

And yet, it didn't happen all at once. The freedom movement was maturing, but it was going to be a while before it was fully organized and daring. The action that the Congress Party took was legalistic, befitting a party dominated by lawyers and other professional men. It sent a commission to investigate and to report on the Punjab atrocities.

Jawaharlal was dispatched to serve as an assistant to that commission, and when he entered the Punjab, he was shaken. Day after day he and the commissioners were besieged by witnesses who clamored to be heard, people who had seen so much suffering that simply relating their experiences brought relief, men and women who longed for some sort of miraculous return to order and stability. Personally, young Nehru was given the job of measuring and mapping the bloodstained walls of Jallianwala Bagh. In the end, he edited the report for publication. And meanwhile, the new and intimate contact with injustice and its consequences worked like leaven in his conscience.

③ he wakes *

Across the scorching plains of India's northern Punjab a crowded railway train screamed its urgent way. The hot, dusty passengers tossed back and forth. The young lawyer in a first-class compartment lurched from side to side. The rhythm of the train was so erratic that he found it almost impossible to read the book that lay open in his hands; but this was of little consequence, for, actually, Jawaharlal Nehru's attention was drawn to the other men who sat in the compartment, and his mind was absorbed by their conversation.

They were all older men than he. His own father, Motilal Nehru, was the most talkative and outspoken among them. Alongside him was C. R. Das, a lawyer from Bengal. Accom-

---

* Since no records exist of Jawaharlal's responses in the garden, these have been presumed. The woman's story, however, is taken from the records of The Congress Inquiry Committee.

panying these Hindus were two distinguished Muslims and a strange-mannered little man—Gandhi—who looked rather out of place that afternoon in the company of the others, for he was dressed in peasant clothes, while the rest of his friends wore English suits.

Compared with C. R. Das, or with the Muslim members of the party, Gandhi was a relative newcomer to Congress work. No one knew him very well, but his reactions to events were thought by many to be naïve and unpredictable. After studying his behavior at meetings, however, Jawaharlal knew that it would be wrong to judge Gandhi solely by appearance or in advance. When confronted with an actual problem, the man's insight was startling and his opinions were worth hearing.

"I realize that nothing can justify the murders which Indians have committed, their shameful attacks upon defenseless people, the burning and the stealing which have taken place during the last few months," Jawaharlal heard his father say, "but I do believe all of this was set off by the calculated, cold-blooded shooting on the part of the English. It was the order to fire on those innocent people at Jallianwala Bagh that released this river of blood."

Motilal Nehru sat heavily, his hands upon his knees. His face was clouded, his spontaneous laughter stilled; and his heavy jowls were set in resentment. He frowned and stared out of the window for minutes at a time, as if trying somehow to escape the burden of his thoughts.

"We can investigate on behalf of the Congress Party and we shall record what we learn and make sure that it gets talked about. That, of course, is why we have come," Jawaharlal's father continued at length. "Yet, if Punjabis have not been too intimidated to speak up and tell us the truth, I am sure that every shred of evidence will bear me out in my conclusion that the English are at fault."

Hearing these words, Gandhi shifted his position uneasily, as if he were disquieted by Motilal Nehru's sentiments, although he did not divert his attention from the speaker. The other men sighed and nodded in agreement. The elder Nehru went on. "By their acts," he concluded forcefully, "the English have now proved beyond a shadow of a doubt that they hold us in contempt. They don't believe Indians to be their equals at all, but merely members of an inferior race."

Again, the majority of Motilal Nehru's colleagues looked as if they agreed with him. Discussion moved heatedly, with one person and then the next ready to verify or to extend their friend's line of reasoning. Though he spoke more mildly than the others, even Gandhi expressed his belief in the soundness of the position Motilal had taken.

Jawaharlal's book dropped unregarded to his lap and he listened in horror. His father's words seemed incredible. He and everyone else who had heard reports of conditions in the Punjab hated to be told that they were true. To Indians, as well as to most of the rest of the world, it came as a shock to learn that in trying to suppress the idea of freedom, the English had been so ruthless. But it was even more terrible to suppose, as Motilal Nehru apparently did, that that cruelty had been, in part, the by-product of discrimination.

Despite his political inclinations, up to this point in his life Jawaharlal Nehru had been taught to admire the English and he had respected them as guardians of decency and fair play. He had been sent to school in England with the expectation that there he would acquire superior knowledge, ethics, and philosophy. He had grown to love the country.

To some extent he had voluntarily adopted an English rather than an Indian way of life, and he was aware that this had affected his outlook when he had come home. He had been back in Allahabad for only a few years and both his manners and his approach to affairs were still more like those of an upper-class Englishman than those of an Indian. But at this point was he to be told that he was regarded as inferior just because he had been born in India rather than in England?

The idea was hardly thinkable; yet, in what other way could the young lawyer reconcile the lofty regard he held for England and the English people with what they seemed to have perpetrated in his own country? If accounts were to be relied upon, any one of the recent actions taken by British officers was cause enough for him to realign his affections. Whether it was painful or not, eventually he supposed he would have to face the truth, but how was he to know what truth actually was?

Like the other men, throughout most of the train journey Jawaharlal continued to reflect upon the implications of Britain's behavior in the Punjab. Still, he did not go so far as to raise any questions about them with his father, nor did he hazard expressing any questions aloud. It was not that he was ashamed of his loyalties in any way or really intimidated by his companions, but he was aware that for the time being at least he was regarded as a somewhat junior member of the party and he felt it was appropriate to conduct himself as a guest while he learned what he could.

The Indian National Congress had chosen an official committee to investigate matters in the Punjab as soon after Baisakhi as travel permits could be obtained. Motilal Nehru had been selected to serve as chairman of that group. With the exception of Jawaharlal, the men in the compartment that day were members who had been appointed to the committee, which had the title of the Congress Inquiry Committee.

Jawaharlal had been asked to come along as an assistant, to organize the office records, to help edit the report, and to do whatever else might be required so that the committee could get through its work as fast as possible. Two months had already passed since the day of the massacre. The British government was about to publish a résumé of what had happened, and the Congress Party was more than anxious to have the Indian side of the story available for comparison.

On the morning after their arrival in Amritsar, the Congress Inquiry Committee set up offices. First of all, they summoned eyewitnesses of the Jallianwala Bagh incident to testify. Later, they appealed to the men who had been charged with defying martial law to appear if they were able to do so.

In all, the testimony of seventeen hundred witnesses was taken down. Over six hundred statements were selected for publication. Jawaharlal did not work as an interviewer; but, as had been anticipated, most of the office routines and the editing of the final report fell to him. As soon as committee procedures were well established, Motilal Nehru was recalled to Allahabad to fulfill his duties as President-elect of the Indian National Congress for the year. When he left, he turned over much of his responsibility to C. R. Das and Gandhi; so, it turned out that Jawaharlal was associated most closely with them, although the young man also asked to attend committee meetings.

Both of his superiors had a profound influence upon Jawaharlal and his thinking. C. R. Das, the lawyer, was scrupulously fair and just. His work was scholarly, of a type that appealed to young Nehru intellectually. Gandhi, on the other hand, was a man of drive and action. These attributes, combined with his deep humanity, kept him on the go and led him to out-of-the-way places. While in the Punjab, he decided to call upon victims at their homes, in hospitals and jails. He established contact with people who had felt completely cut off from friends and families outside. In some instances, he managed to arrange immediate help for them, using the offices of the Congress Party and relief funds which private citizens placed at his disposal. Jawaharlal was impressed at the difference this made. As a result of one man's effort, the name of the Congress Party was linked in the minds of Punjabi villagers with a person who would go out of his way to listen, who cared and got results.

The committee had been left with a tremendous volume of work to do in a very short time. Temporarily, at least, young Nehru tried to overlook the central question of British motives in relation to India. Along with C. R. Das, he was inclined to believe that whatever transpired in the future (and it certainly looked as if trouble were brewing), action had better be informed by a full and honest appraisal of things as they stood. He consciously tried to keep from forming hasty judgments. He struggled to maintain an objective position in relation to the sensational report. Even under pressure, he went about his work deliberately and quietly.

Gradually, the center of investigations moved to Jallianwala Bagh itself. As Motilal Nehru had said, the imprisonments, the skirmishes, and the recriminations that had taken place elsewhere were "like waves emanating from that pool of suffering." It was in the public garden at the heart of the city of Amritsar where violence had been sparked. In India's future, "the Punjab" and "Amritsar," but more especially "Jallianwala Bagh," would be rallying cries for revenge.

Early one morning Jawaharlal Nehru set out for Jallianwala Bagh to work on diagrams and sketches of the park which were to be included in the final report. A servant accompanied him to carry his equipment, and as soon as the two men left their lodgings, a few people from along the street joined them and followed inquisitively. They entered the public garden by the main gate and mounted the low hill from which the English soldiers had fired.

Considering the Baisakhi incident and its repercussions, the park seemed strangely quiet to Jawaharlal that morning. At the far end of the lawn a small boy was grazing his cows. In another section, a woman was preparing for worship at an old shrine. Otherwise, the place was deserted.

Jawaharlal Nehru walked briskly across the stretch of open lawn and began to measure and record the length of the line of houses that formed one of the boundaries to Jallianwala Bagh. Bit by bit, he and his assistant worked their way along, while he measured and examined the walls, searching for any outlet that could possibly have been used by the crowd when trying to escape. He found a single gate, no wider than an ordinary door, through which hundreds must have pressed in terror. He wrote down the dimensions of the gate and turned the corner, intending to survey the buildings nearest the shrine.

As the young assistant to the Congress Inquiry Committee approached the shrine, the woman who knelt there began to sob. While Jawaharlal had been inspecting the houses, she had completed her worship and unbound her hair. She now crouched upon her haunches in the position of a mourner and swayed back and forth rhythmically. Her eyes were half closed and young Nehru could see that her face was swollen from crying. She wailed in the strange, tormented tones Indian women have used since time immemorial to express their grief.

If the sight of misery had not become as familiar to him as it had during his stay in the Punjab, Jawaharlal Nehru might have been deeply disturbed by the outbreak of the woman's lament. As it was, he stopped his note taking only for an instant and glanced in the direction of the shrine; but as soon as he realized what the woman was doing, he went on with his work.

Through her tears, the mourner recognized the young man whose job it was to survey the garden. His appearance had become familiar to most of the people around Amritsar and he may have been pointed out to her as the son of the head of the Congress Party investigating committee. She hesitated only for a moment, then stumbled to her feet and rushed toward him. As soon as she reached him, she dropped to her knees and raised her hands in supplication.

Jawaharlal was surprised and somewhat bothered by this unexpected turn of events. He guessed the implications of the woman's presence, but he was not sure just how he should treat her. "Listen to me. Help me, Sahib," she began.

The men around him eyed the young Congress Party member closely, curious as to what he would do. The woman was upset. She had something she wanted to say. She'd come to the park alone, in all probability to grieve for a relative who had died there. Should he ask her to follow him to the office? Jawaharlal wondered. But if she had learned about the Congress Inquiry Committee, why hadn't she made an appointment to talk with one of its members before this?

The young lawyer quickly turned the matter over in his

mind. This was a woman, a woman of humble circumstances, judging from her looks. He didn't have to be told
that a woman, especially a woman of this demeanor,
wouldn't dare to present herself before committee men of
status. It was only a chance meeting, such as this one in the
park, which would provoke her to speak to a person such as
himself. He also saw that there was a bundle of provisions
at the shrine—more than she needed for morning worship.
Her clothes were crumpled. He supposed that she must have
spent the night there alone. But where had she come from?
Didn't she know that the officers had forbidden citizens to
grieve in public?

Young Nehru was as curious as his companions. He
was inclined to give the intruder a chance to speak even
though he had not been authorized to take down testimony
on behalf of the committee. He looked closely at the face
which was raised to his. The woman touched her forehead in
the dust as a gesture of humility. She pleaded for sympathy.
She insisted that she wanted only for him to listen, to have
him answer her questions, to receive his blessing. That was
all. He would have had to be very hard-hearted if in the end
he had decided to turn aside.

The firsthand story Jawaharlal Nehru heard then was
long and tragic. It was the story of a Hindu couple and their
only son who had come into town to celebrate the Baisakhi
holiday. They had stopped in the park. The little boy had
been given a toy whirligig, purchased by his father from a
vendor. He had found a companion, a Muslim child, with
whom to play. The children had run and skipped together,
while the mother and father had sat on the grass.

"There were many, many people in the park," the
mother explained brokenly, "all of them in small groups.
Some were Hindus and some were Muslims. We were all of

us very happy together that day. It was as if we were brothers. Young men shouted, *'Hindu-Mussalman ki jai!* Victory to Hindus and Muslims together!' The little children copied them. The Muslim boy put his hat on my son, Raman, and said that made him a Muslim. The two boys laughed and laughed. Oh, how they laughed together."

The mother went on. She described how more and more people had crowded into the park. There had been a decorated platform at one end, from which a man had addressed the assembly. He had ordered the crowd to wait because, he said, a great orator was coming to make a speech. The little family had not understood what the speechmaking was going to be about but they had mingled with the rest of the crowd and had waited.

"All of a sudden, there was a commotion over by the gate," the woman said. "I thought the great one must have arrived. We wanted to see him. My husband put Raman on his shoulders so that he was able to see better than we could. 'Soldiers, Dada!' he cried excitedly. We were surprised. There were some shots. We were afraid and started to run.

"We tried to run for the gate," the woman explained, "but our son held us back. He squirmed and he pounded his father's chest with his bare feet. He wanted us to take his Muslim friend too. I pulled the child by the hand. Then we ran for the wall because it was closer."

At this point Jawaharlal's informant paused, as if gathering strength to go on. The little group of bystanders stared at her. Out of respect for her position, Jawaharlal tried to keep his eyes fixed on the ground; but, try as he would, his gaze returned to the woman's face. He, along with the rest of his companions, was captured by the tale.

"We heard more shooting," the woman continued in short, jerky phrases. "I was terrified and drew my scarf over my head. The people behind us began to push. We were caught in the crowd. My husband still had Raman on his shoulders. We could not move very fast. We got to the wall, but the bullets spattered around us. People were shrieking like jackals. My son did not understand anything that was happening. His father hoisted him off his shoulders and reached back his hand for his friend. Then it was all over. Raman fell, warm and soft as a pigeon. He was dead."

Gripped by that memory, the poor woman raised herself onto her haunches and began to rock back and forth slowly. "We protected him with our own bodies," she said softly. "We crouched by the wall and let others pass over us. We sheltered the little Muslim too so that he would not be killed. We did not dare to move till the shooting was done. After that, we let the child go and told him to find his mother. But how could he have found her in that place?"

The young Hindu mother rested again momentarily, but then continued. "The garden was a awash with agony. I took my scarf from my head to wrap Raman and we started home. Our home is a long way from here," she explained tiredly. "The stars had come out by the time we got there, but in every compound we had passed, we had heard sounds of mourning."

Jawaharlal could not bring himself to break away immediately. For some time the woman wept quietly and wiped her tears with the end of a towel that had been wrapped around her offerings. At last she looked up at the young man and asked, "What is the meaning of all this? Tell me what is the meaning of storms that rise without warning and flood our land with suffering? What can poor people do to calm the rulers who will this?"

Jawaharlal placed his hand comfortingly on the woman's shoulder, but he did not answer her questions immediately.

Had he known what answers to give, he could hardly have expressed them. He was too overcome by feelings that had been roused and shown in a new light by this encounter.

To explain to a grieving woman that there was a conflict of ideas between men who believed in empire and champions of freedom did not seem to be enough. Neither did Jawaharlal think that he really could say why there had been a sudden change of heart on the part of the British, one that resulted in such drastic and cruel policies. What he did know, but even this he had no simple words to describe, was that there *was* a conflict and in it apparently people such as herself, Raman, or his own baby, Indira, could be caught without warning. They needed a voice on their behalf. They needed protection; but, above all, they needed action.

Old questions regarding England and British behavior stirred afresh in Jawaharlal's mind; but new answers regarding his position and the role of the Congress Party formed on the edge of his consciousness. He seethed with rage at the thought of the injustices that were being inflicted upon innocent people. He saw, with dreadful clarity, that Great Britain, or at least His Majesty's Government, was not going to yield much in the way of independence to India until it was forced to do so. For all practical purposes, the two countries were already at war. Henceforward, he supposed, Indians could expect to be treated as members of an enemy nation; but, so far as he was concerned, if England were going to treat India as an enemy nation, then something besides moderacy and fact-finding was called for. The time had passed for excusing the rulers. Someone had to stand up and resist!

✧

In 1920 there were three hundred and six million people in India and most of them lived in villages. By and large,

India had always been a land of villages; and the villagers who gave allegiance to George V in 1920 did not look very different from the villagers of Akbar's time, or even Asoka's. Probably one out of six of them could read and write; one out of twelve may have traveled farther than to the nearest town. Most of them lived in huts built of mud and straw and roofed with thatch. They tilled their land with crude wooden plows, yet somehow managed to harvest enough to keep themselves alive and, in addition, to raise crops that filled the ships, fed the mills, and stocked the warehouses of a prosperous, far-flung empire. Out of the villages of India poured rice and wheat, tea and spice, coffee and rubber, silk and jute, cotton and coconut, wool and sugarcane—in the early days for the profit of the East India Company and later for corporations under the protection of Britain's imperial government. For over three hundred years the rising standard of living in far-off England depended to some extent upon the steady production of India's villagers.

The villages of India were similar, whether they clung to mountain slopes or nestled on the seacoast, and it was the village way of life that united India's varied peoples. Factories had been established during the years of British rule and towns had sprung up because the men who worked in factories needed to live near them. But even such workmen thought of themselves as belonging to villages rather than to towns. They maintained the habits they had acquired in their villages. Often their families remained in the villages, instead of coming to the towns; and, consequently, townsfolk returned to their village homes for all important occasions: holidays, weddings, births, and funerals.

In contrast to that of a villager, or to that of a man who lived in a town, the life of a city dweller in India had always been quite distinct. City people had often become the elect of empires. They were more or less self-sufficient in their own surroundings and they had preferred not to concern themselves with the affairs of peasants. As the country developed, city people, including poor city people, had had access to schools, to newspapers, to hospitals, and to travel. These opportunities had removed them even further from the position of their village brethren. In 1920, most city folk knew nothing or very little about the countryside and they tended to scoff at rural people.

Ideas about independence took hold first among the city folk of India. Until 1920, the Indian National Congress and other nationalistic organizations, including the Muslim League, which was led by the erudite, sophisticated Mohammed Ali Jinnah, were drawn from the well-to-do and educated classes. The men who joined them were fired by injustice, it is true. They were righteously indignant and excited, too, at the prospect of home rule; but, except perhaps for Mohandas Gandhi, such privileged advocates of freedom did not put much stock in the notion that village people mattered in their struggle. They did not suppose that eventually India's destiny might be decided in mud huts rather than in the halls of parliament. By and large, they were diplomats and lawyers rather than fervent patriots and spokesmen for the common man. They considered themselves to be their country's representatives engaged in negotiations instead of battle on behalf of independence.

As a safe but symbolic act of defiance against the British Raj,* the Indian National Congress chose to meet at Amritsar in 1919. Motilal Nehru presided. Although moved by the turn events had taken at Jallianwala Bagh, he was as poised and dignified as he had always been when he appeared be-

---

* This is the term which Indians commonly used at that time to refer to the British government in India. It means "British rule."

fore an audience. He opened the party meetings with an eloquent speech in which he denounced the cruelty of the Punjab atrocities, and the delegates listened sedately.

The Jallianwala Bagh massacre and its aftermath had produced a remarkable unity among the Indian people and within the Congress Party. Delegates had come to Amritsar with a heavy sense of responsibility. In the main, however, they modeled their behavior upon that of their president. They dressed in morning coats and top hats and conducted themselves formally. The feelings they expressed were no doubt sincere and well-meaning, but couched in gentle and restrained terms.

Whether intentionally or by accident, the actions of His Majesty's Government played into the hands of that august assembly. A storm of criticism of the government's policy for India was sweeping Great Britain, criticism directed mainly against Generals Dyer and O'Dwyer. The officers were subject to discipline by Parliament, and for a while it looked as if they might have to forfeit their careers. As a gesture of good faith, Parliament reaffirmed its commitment to preparing India for eventual self-government. As a step in that direction, Britain proposed that certain departments of the government, such as health, transportation, and education, be placed in the hands of Indian ministers immediately, although other matters, such as defense and foreign relations, would remain under British control.

To Moderates within the Indian National Congress, such an offer had all the appeal of a victory. Actually, the delegates at Amritsar were relieved by Britain's action and, being appeased for the time being, they did not plan to protest. Acceptance of the British proposals was favored by nearly all influential party members. Even Gandhi sounded as if he were willing to agree to the terms that had been offered and he urged others to do so. "The Government went mad at the time," he said, referring to the Punjab. "We went mad also at the time. I say, do not return madness with madness, but return madness with sanity." His counsel was heeded. The tone of the annual session turned out to be mild.

Jawaharlal Nehru was enraged. He openly criticized the stand the Congress Party adopted at Amritsar. He quarreled with his father over the substance of Britain's offer, and he announced that he was sick of waiting for a change of opinion among party leaders. He turned directly to Gandhi as someone who might have sympathy for his nonconformist point of view and he begged to be set to work immediately on behalf of freedom.

Gandhi responded by offering Jawaharlal a job helping to organize the Satyagraha Society. Gandhi shared Jawaharlal's view that, in the long run, independence would never be achieved without resistance, and he hoped that the society was going to form the nucleus of the resistance forces. These were not forces in the usual sense of the term, since the members did not bear arms, but the Satyagraha Society did enlist and train young men for protests of a nonviolent kind. It looked as if it could provide the right spot for young Nehru, since he was certainly bucking and tugging at the ropes of tradition.

Jawaharlal joined the Satyagraha Society enthusiastically and threw himself into training with a will. However, to Motilal Nehru, the society smacked too much of rebellion and danger. He objected to his son's association with it and said so in no uncertain terms. The tranquil domestic routines of Anand Bhawan were upset. Jawaharlal's little sister Krishna was twelve at the time, but the conflict was vivid in her mind when, as an adult, she wrote in her autobiography:

"There were long discussions and sometimes heated words.
. . . These were most unhappy days for all of us, especially
for Mother and Kamala, who could not bear to see father
and son torn by politics and endless arguments. The atmosphere was tense all the time and one hardly dared to utter a
word for fear of rousing Father's anger or irritating Jawahar."

Things reached such a state in the Nehru household
that Gandhi was summoned to Allahabad to discuss matters.
After conversations with Motilal, Gandhi wisely advised Jawaharlal to be more patient, to go more slowly, and not run
the risk of alienating his father completely. Jawaharlal
agreed, but not very happily.

"Yes, India is quiet," an English governor had remarked
in another decade, but his words would have been equally
applicable in 1920: "As quiet as gunpowder." Beneath a calm
surface, turbulent forces were at work. Jawaharlal Nehru
was not the only determined young nationalist who was torn
between an urge for action and restraint. Gandhi, to whom
such people appealed for leadership, was desperately trying
to cement the good feeling that had sprung up between the
Congress Party and the Muslim League following Jallianwala Bagh. Meanwhile, Motilal Nehru and other high-rank-
ing party officials were committed to the position the Indian
National Congress had accepted at Amritsar; while England,
instead of making good on her promises, was strengthening
ties with the maharajas, the native princes empowered by
His Majesty's Government to rule at least half the subcontinent on its behalf.

All parties to the conflict were taking measure of one
another as it were, and an uneasy silence was maintained
among them. On the face of things, it appeared that Congress had done all it was going to do for the time being. His

Majesty's Government was satisfied with having granted a concession to home rule although it actually preferred to maintain its own pace and not take the activities of Indian politicians too seriously.

At the time, it hardly seemed as if much of anything more in the way of British action was called for. After all, many a governor reasoned, the Indians who were most vocal about freedom were in the minority and they obviously found it difficult to reach agreement even among themselves. If such a group became obstreperous, it could be silenced by simply packing the leaders off to jail. That would put an end to their organizing!

Probably these sentiments were never shared by more than a handful of Englishmen at any one time, inside India or outside; nevertheless, such views were aired and even printed. There was a measure of truth in them. "If it makes them feel any better," British officers would say over drinks at their clubs, "it's all right for Parliament to hand over the work of a few departments to the Indians; but there's no real connection between men like Mohammed Ali Jinnah, the Nehrus, or Gandhi for that matter, and the vast majority of the people in the country. The villagers are safe."

4 *the promise*

Surrounded by law books, Jawaharlal Nehru sat at his desk. It was a cruelly hot day and activities in the city outside had come almost to a standstill. The streets of Allahabad were nearly deserted. The shutters of the mansion at Anand Bhawan had been closed to keep out the heat. The house was quiet, since everyone else in the Nehru family was away. The servants were resting. For some time the young lawyer read and made notes without being disturbed.

Presently, however, Jawaharlal's work was interrupted by voices from the garden. He put down his pencil and listened. Apparently a servant was trying to turn away some visitor who was demanding to see the master of the house. Jawaharlal could hear the two men arguing by the gate. The servant indicated politely that Jawaharlal was the only one home. He was busy and had left orders not to be disturbed.

"But my business will take only a second, a very small fraction of his time," the visitor insisted.

The voices grew louder. It was impossible for him to read any longer. Jawaharlal snapped his book shut and fretted at the distraction; but then something the intruder was saying caught his ear. He paid closer attention. The visitor was maintaining that he *had* to talk to one of the Nehrus, that he urgently needed to be in touch with the leadership of the Congress Party. There was something he had for them to do, someone they must meet. Young Nehru became curious as to just what lay behind such a request. He decided that he had better talk to the fellow in the garden, after all.

Nehru stood at the top of the wide marble steps of Anand Bhawan and looked down at a somewhat disheveled figure on the gravel path. The two men greeted one another. Jawaharlal noted with pleasure that, despite his look of poverty, the newcomer was free of flattery and obsequiousness in his approach to a member of a wealthy household.

"My name is Ramachandra," the visitor announced simply and somewhat arrogantly.

"Yes," Jawaharlal replied, acknowledging his visitor in a reserved but friendly way. "What do you have to say?"

Ramachandra took time to explain who he was. He had been born in India, he said, but he had left the country when he had been very young. He had worked as a laborer in the Fiji Islands. He was not well educated; but, after his return to India, he had adopted the habits of a sadhu, a holy man. He now wandered around among the peasants, reciting the Hindu scriptures, and he lived on charity.

Jawaharlal had heard this kind of story a hundred times before. In summer and winter, for food or money, such men came daily to the Nehrus' door. However, the rest of Rama-

chandra's speech was different. He did not ask for alms. The
request he put before young Nehru was a new one.

"Believe me, I do not want money. I do not want food,"
he said. "On the ghats of the Jumna river I have assembled
two hundred men. They are peasant farmers who have come
into town from outlying districts. They are landless, all of
them, and are tenant farmers on the land they till; but they
are the men who grow the rice that you city people eat.
Their own livelihoods depend upon the mercies of their landlords and the unscrupulous moneylenders, from whom they
are forced to borrow money so that they can buy seed. The
landlords and the moneylenders demand outrageous rents
and interest fees. The debts of the farmers are staggering.
Their lot is hardly better than that of slaves."

Ramachandra obviously had sympathy for his peasants.
He described their situation with feeling, gesticulating forcefully. "These peasants on the ghats will not stand for such
treatment any longer," he asserted, waving his arms. "They
are determined to change their condition. They trust me. I
have taught them how to discuss their problems. I have prepared them to resist," he emphasized. "They are organized.
They have marched to Allahabad to petition the authorities.
It is important that someone from the Congress Party meet
them. You should come and talk with these men."

Jawaharlal sighed. Was there to be no end to the tales
of woe to which he would be asked to listen? If India spent
all of its time complaining, it would never get moving and
win the battle for independence. He was disgusted with the
nature of Ramachandra's errand after all. "It is too hot for
anyone to go out now," he protested, moving back into the
cool shadow of the veranda.

"All very well. You can come in the evening," Ramachandra conceded, although he indicated that he regarded the heat as a poor excuse for Jawaharlal to have given him. He showed some impatience with the young gentleman who stood in the doorway of Anand Bhawan. He stepped forward on the path. "Where do you expect your ideas of freedom to lead?" he asked Jawaharlal pointedly. "What good will independence do the Indian farmer if he has no land left to plow? The Congress Party had better watch out. While they talk about fighting the British, the peasants will be up in arms against the landlords, and justifiably."

Jawaharlal stiffened. What was this man talking about? The lot of the peasants was hard. He knew that. But there was a more basic hardship that affected the people of India. Every man, woman, and child was deprived of a voice in his government. Until at least that evil was corrected, the Congress or any other party couldn't afford to be sidetracked in a dispute between a few landlords and their clients. Ramachandra's men had better understand that and not let themselves get stirred up prematurely. Their kind of rebellion had no place in India at the moment.

"I will come in the evening," Jawaharlal announced to Ramachandra, "and I will have some other men from the Congress Party with me." Despite the urgency of the situation, he agreed to the visit reluctantly. He had a distaste for the noise and squalor of the riverbanks. So had his friends, who were no more used to it than he. But, one way or another, a spokesman for the Congress Party had to appear and explain to the peasants that it was no time to stir up a fuss over a side issue. If Motilal were not available, Jawaharlal would have to find another man to do the job.

To the surprise of the young lawyer and his friends, the group that received them at the river's edge appeared to be an orderly one. Ramachandra and a few of the peasants met

the Congress Party delegation at the main street where they
left their car. Without ceremony, they led them on foot
through narrow, twisting lanes to the edge of the Jumna.
There on the ghats, where the people of the city came daily
to wash and bathe and scatter the ashes of the dead, the
peasants had set up camp.

Jawaharlal found the men already assembled for a
meeting. Low wicker stools had been placed on a terrace
above the crowd and to these the Congress representatives
were ushered. Lanterns had been lighted. The farmers were
huddled together rather tightly and they crowded close to
their guests; but any jostling, any unseemly behavior was immediately checked by Ramachandra.

In the deepening twilight, Jawaharlal looked out over
the people massed around him. He tried to make out what
type of men they were and what manner of mischief they
had devised. Judging by first appearances, the audience was
curious and alert, but not rebellious, as he had feared. On
the contrary, the demeanor of the men revealed an almost
childlike dependence upon Ramachandra, their leader, as
well as a hospitable concern for their visitors.

Ramachandra opened the meeting by chanting prayers.
Then, to introduce the evening's discussion, he told the men
that by marching to Allahabad they had already advanced
their cause. Their petitions were not going to be made in
vain, he assured them. Young Jawaharlal Nehru, son of the
great and honored Pandit Motilal Nehru, president of the
Congress Party, had come to see them. He had heard about
their grievances and, once he understood the nature of their
demands, he would surely help them.

As he listened, Jawaharlal realized with alarm that following Ramachandra's introduction, he himself was expected to address the ragged crowd. He had not yet fully out-

grown his boyhood shyness and, except when he had to appear in the courtroom, he tried to avoid making speeches. Tonight he had not planned on giving a talk but had intended for one of his more experienced companions to act as spokesman.

When Ramachandra sat down, young Nehru rose from his stool self-consciously, thinking hard about what he should say. The first sentences with which he greeted his unfamiliar hosts sounded cold and formal. He wondered whether he should go on.

However unsure of himself the young man might have felt inside, he nevertheless appeared as a tower of strength to the people at his feet. The peasants waited attentively, with patience and respect. Jawaharlal was encouraged and somewhat flattered by their deference. He supposed that, whatever their motives, the peasants were not going to criticize *his rhetoric.* Therefore, he addressed them in simple, straightforward terms. "First of all, before I can help you at all, I must know the nature of your difficulties," he said to them. "Do not be afraid. Speak up."

The men replied eagerly. Their grievances sprang from a single cause, they explained. In the United Provinces, where they lived, the rights to control land and to collect taxes were in the hands of a few big landlords. The moneylenders were in alliance with the landlords. The peasants who worked the land found themselves entirely at the mercy of these two groups. Rents were high and taxes heavy. The farmers borrowed money and their debts mounted. Their families faced constant insecurity, not knowing whether they would be able to make ends meet or when they might be deprived of their claims.

Their position had worsened through the years. But, unlike their grandfathers, who had been content to till the land before them, the farmers who had marched to Allahabad demonstrated that they had no intention of accepting hardship conditions. "We cannot endure such a situation any longer," their spokesman declared. "We have come to protest." Rising from the audience and confronting Jawaharlal directly, one of their leaders asked whether, as a lawyer and a member of the Congress Party, he would support them and press their case against the landlords.

Jawaharlal was faced with a difficult choice. He looked around at his Congress Party friends uncomfortably. Here were two hundred restless men. The grievances they described were real, but he was sure that this was not the time for a discussion of land problems. He supposed he had to make that clear, whether or not the peasants wanted to hear what he had to say. For an instant he wondered how they were going to react to such a message. He hesitated.

As the young man turned matters over in his mind, his audience became suspicious. These were men who had endured lifelong servitude, and they had made petitions before. They were people to whom the grain of sympathy in one of their superiors was readily discernible from the chaff of indifference. Since Ramachandra had brought him to the ghats, they had assumed that Jawaharlal Nehru believed in the justice of their undertaking. He had asked for a hearing. Could it be that he hadn't believed what he had heard, or that he didn't want to have anything more to do with them? The longer he waited without speaking, the more bold they became and the more anxious to win him over.

"Come and have a look at our fields," one of the farmers called out. "Come and see the way we're forced to live. You'll find out that what we say is true."

The peasants glanced at one another with amusement. The crude invitation, which had been tossed out partly as a challenge, was immediately echoed by at least a hundred voices. "Come! Yes, come," the farmers insisted. "Come to our villages. We will show you everything. You can see for yourself what life is like."

When, in a firm but kindly way, Jawaharlal declined these invitations, the peasants teased and cajoled. No admonition from their guest or from Ramachandra seemed to dissuade them from a resolve to have the young aristocrat come and see the conditions they had tried to explain. The meeting on the Jumna ghat took on a more lively aspect. Men made hasty plans. Within a few minutes, a committee of peasants brought forward an itinerary for a tour. They offered the hospitality of their village homes and guest houses. In fact, they refused to release Jawaharlal to return to his car. They clung to him and to his friends until he and one or two others agreed to go out to the rural areas before another week had passed.

The homes of Ramachandra's peasants lay far beyond the reach of roads. Jawaharlal had promised to spend three days in the villages. He walked through the dust at the hottest time of the year. He slept in a mud hut. He ate the food the farmers ate; and he saw, as the peasants had promised, the conditions he had heard reported on the riverbank in Allahabad.

At the time, the fact that he had kept his word and come mattered more than anything else Jawaharlal Nehru might have tried to do for the peasants of the United Provinces. People in his position almost never visited the countryside. Consequently, he was received with honor. The villagers made his tour the excuse for a celebration. They welcomed him splendidly and shared what they had with him willingly. When they found that he listened to their grievances after all, they lost no time in seeking his counsel and advice.

For his part, Jawaharlal found that it was easier to discuss matters with the farmers in their homes and fields than it had been in Allahabad. In day-by-day conversations, he could question peasants intimately about their land, their families, and their crops. During marches across the countryside, he had a chance to observe firsthand what they were doing and assess their motives. Contrary to what he had suspected, he was dealing with no fly-by-night group of revolutionaries. He was simply confronted with honest, hard-working folk who had been sorely tried and yet had managed to survive for a very long time on very little. Their homes were shabby, their children undernourished. The sight of their poverty was appalling and it was a wonder that people who had had to live in such circumstances could muster any hope at all.

India was a land of villages and the villages were very much the same from Kashmir in the north to the tip of Cape Comorin in the south. Jawaharlal Nehru reminded himself of this as he moved from village to village on his tour. The vast majority of his fellow Indians were similar to the peasants he was meeting in his own province, generous and resourceful people, yet long oppressed and now almost destitute. As a doctor strips away bandages one by one, finally revealing a naked sore, Jawaharlal felt that at last he could perceive the condition of his countrymen. He found them subject not only to foreign rule but to other circumstances close to home that prevented them from having anything like an adequate existence.

How miraculous was the decision of these farmers to resist! What strength, what power, the young man realized, if the determination of such people could be joined in some way to the independence movement. Their fortitude would be an asset, but they must not be exploited. He now understood that self-government alone was hardly a sufficient objective to offer them. Once India achieved her independence, she must immediately apply herself to creating a better life in the villages. Only in that way could she ever hope to repay her millions of peasants for all the long years of neglect and hardship they had endured.

As he traveled from house to house and village to village, Jawaharlal addressed groups of farmers at every stop. He was moved by what was happening to him and in that setting shyness dropped away. Words came to him readily and he undertook to explain to the peasants the link, as he saw it, between independence and the fulfillment of their desires. He sensed that their minds were stirring with the message. Reports of what he said got around. Other farmers came asking for explanations. The idea of achieving a better life through independence was taking root.

Where telephones, radios, and highways did not yet exist, the age-old cry of *Sita Ram* was used to call remote villages and news was carried by runners. On Jawaharlal Nehru's last day in the villages, families from distant places started traveling before sunup in order to reach the house where he was staying. By late afternoon, throngs of peasants were arriving at young Nehru's hut. They straggled in on foot and by bullock cart, bringing with them grandmothers and grandfathers, children and babies.

Jawaharlal had mixed feelings as he watched the villagers assemble. It was not a handsome crowd. By and large, the people he went out to greet were disease-ridden, hungry, and ignorant. He couldn't help but bitterly resent their condition, and he abhorred lives that were so driven by labor, so deprived of change. He would never be able to get used to the squalor of some of the homes from which they had come.

At the same time, however, the young man knew that he felt more at ease than he had at any other time in his life. Despite the conditions under which they lived, these people bore themselves with a grace that was admirable and they had proffered their friendship to him most generously. Their devoted attentions to their guest had been heartwarming. He had been treated as one of them. When he now thought of the city and the stylish life he lived there, it did not seem at all satisfying to him in the way that it had before.

In the evening Jawaharlal spoke to the villagers enthusiastically, but as realistically as he could. Although he wanted to help them, it was important that they not expect miracles; and he tried to give them a picture of what they might reasonably anticipate would happen over the next few months and years. Petitions were of little use any longer, he told them, and they could hardly hope to discover quick solutions to such deep problems as poverty, landownership, education, or health. There wouldn't be much in the way of progress so long as the British government was in power, but neither would independence bring immediate relief. Still, if they held firmly to their resolve, and strove with others for what was right, they might see swaraj and the changes it could bring. But no one could do very much for them right away, he repeated.

This was not a comforting message to leave with friends. At sight of their kindly faces, Jawaharlal felt moved to provide some further token of assurance that the villagers could remember when the going was hard for them. He considered himself, too, and what was in store once he returned to the city and home. It wasn't going to be easy to convince his family to permit him to do so, but he knew he must return to places such as this and bring others with him. So far as this one group of peasants was concerned, of course, they always had Ramachandra. "Keep up your courage," he said. "You have started on a long journey; but remember, you do not walk alone."

That statement, too, seemed hardly enough to sustain the farmers and their families through their trials. What faith could they have in the world outside, which most of them had never seen? How did they know whether he would come back? Swaraj was a noble effort, but it was going to be a long time before its effects were visible in their lives. Yet, they had to believe that, even if they did not see him, he had not forgotten them. If the future turned out as he dared to think it might, then Jawaharlal Nehru owed an immense debt of gratitude to these people for the lessons they had taught him.

In India, the taking of a vow is a sacred obligation, whether it is given to a person or as a pledge for a cause. Jawaharlal had never paid much attention to the practice before, attuned as he had been to the customs of the West. That night, however, in front of the villagers, when he wanted to offer them some lasting token of his friendship, the words came naturally to his lips. "I promise," he declared to them, "I promise," he repeated in clear and ringing terms, "that I will strive unceasingly for India's freedom so that my countrymen may never again be subjected to the miseries and humiliations that are your lot." That was the most that he could offer them; but he knew that it was sincere and promised to change not only their own lives, but his too thereafter.

The pledge was taken far from Anand Bhawan and the meeting halls of the Congress Party. The people assembled on the village field actually represented only a few of the many millions who made up the nation of India. They had met under the stars and their lanterns cast a feeble light compared with the brilliance of cities. But, at the taking of his vow, how they cheered for Jawaharlal! *"Jawaharlal ki jai,"* the villagers shouted. "Victory, victory to Jawaharlal." Their voices surged with hope.

part 2 *1920–1947*

The year 1920 was a turning point in India's destiny. In December the constitution of the Indian National Congress was changed to read: "The object of the Indian National Congress is the attainment of Swaraj by the people of India by all legitimate and peaceful means."

If, as many Britishers avowed, this was a forthright declaration of war, it was a unique one. Independence was to be achieved, but "by legitimate and peaceful means." Swaraj was to be won by whom? Not by an army but "by the people of India," by assorted crowds of the impoverished and the illiterate mixed with the erudite and wealthy, presumably by Muslims, Hindus, and Buddhists, with the help of farmers and maharajas, through the combined efforts of those who profited handsomely from English rule and those who disdained it. All were expected to join in this mighty effort, and in the name of whom? In the name of the Indian National

Congress, a party founded by one of the ruling caste it was
determined to overthrow, up to this time a party of moderate intellectuals, now having chosen Mohandas Gandhi, a
saint and mystic, as president, but also harboring young in-
surgents like Jawaharlal Nehru. Could any one leader unite
such forces? Was there a chance they'd win?

At the moment, it was Gandhi who held the key to answering these questions; and, luckily, he was a man uniquely
fitted for his task. However much one might disagree with
him on matters of policy, he was so fair and generous that it
was almost impossible to hate him. Therefore, he had the
ability to hold together diverse and quarrelsome forces. His
simple habits automatically made him one with common
people. In addition, his South African experience had
equipped him with a rare tool to use on their behalf. That
tool was *satyagraha*.

Satyagraha can be translated as "soul force." It is sometimes defined as "the power of love." As Gandhi explained
what he himself meant by satyagraha, he said it involved believing that enemies are reasonable people, engaging in constructive activity rather than fighting, and resisting evil by
suffering. In the hands of a less-qualified person, nonviolence
might have been weak and ineffectual, but Gandhi had
forged it into a strong routine. He was not a military person,
but he was well-organized and as strict as a general. When
he spoke of loving an enemy, he knew exactly what he intended to do, how, and under what circumstances. He could
live satyagraha and he could preach it. He was a man to be
watched and to be reckoned with.

Perhaps the Congress Party couldn't win; but Gandhi
had a very deep faith in the goodness of human beings, and
he thought it had a chance, using the nonviolent methods he
prescribed. He recognized that Britain had produced proud

monarchs and empire builders in the past; but, alongside them, men of stature and learning, persons of conscience, persons of goodwill, thoughtful people, kindly people, parliamentarians and civil servants who were known to be scrupulously fair and willing to listen to reason. If Indians felt they had to resist, and they were willing to suffer for what they believed, Gandhi expected Englishmen would respond with sympathy and understanding. Regardless of official pronouncements, he simply didn't believe that British officers would be so inhuman as to fire repeatedly on unarmed crowds. In the long run, they were sure to recognize and appreciate "legitimate and peaceful means."

Besides, Englishmen had certainly read the lessons of history. Gandhi didn't think that it occurred to many of them that the British Empire was going to last forever in its present form. His Majesty's Government was already committed to dyarchy, or "dual rule," and English administrators were actually training Indians so that they would be able to take over the posts that Englishmen had held in India. He admitted that there were obvious differences of opinion between representatives of the two countries, but he interpreted them to be centered on the question of *when* England would go and not *whether* it would stay.

Given the mood of India's leaders, however, and the obstinacy of English policy, taking into account the fact that the classes and religions of the subcontinent had never been successfully combined before, the stage was set for a drama of epic dimensions. It was a time of marked tension, when every word was fraught with implication, when future strategists and columnists would see in the turn of a phrase, the nod of a head, the presence or absence of a certain delegate, an act of momentous significance. In India, during the hot months that precede the monsoon, temperatures on the central plains reach ninety, then one hundred, and sometimes one hundred and twenty before, with a horrendous crash and lightning charge, the rains come, whipping the forest with fury, tearing at the land. Destruction follows, but the life-giving cycle is again renewed. In 1920, the climate on the national scene was comparable to that over the Ganges plain before a monsoon. The storm clouds were rolling up. Everyone prayed that when the deluge broke, it would not be prolonged and that it would bring relief.

From the party statement of 1920 flowed immediate and irreversible consequences. The annual session changed the look of the Congress. Gandhi had a wonderful way of endearing himself to his followers, and Indians love to say, as they look back on the Nagpur meeting of that year, "That was the first *Gandhi Congress,*" meaning it was the first when Gandhi's ideas on what to do and how to do it were uppermost in everyone's thinking.

He began with the little things. Gone were the morning coats and top hats. Suits of homespun, hand-woven *khadi,* a rough cotton cloth which symbolized India's ability to supply its own basic needs, replaced clothes of foreign design. Women were in evidence at the sessions. Muslims and Hindus, sweepers and persons of higher castes, mingled freely on the benches of the delegates. Speeches in English were kept to a minimum. Hindustani was the preferred language to use when addressing the chairman.

Most noticeable and surprising of all was the attitude which members of the party expressed toward resistance. Breaking laws and going to jail were talked about openly and as if they were honorable activities. So Gandhi thought they could be under the right circumstances, and a good substitute for guns. He exhorted Congressmen to defy regulations that had been passed without their consent, to defy

openly and passively; but, he warned them that, in all probability, His Majesty's Government would expect them to pay
the full consequences for defiance, and that punishments
would not be light. His stand was far from moderate. It
didn't sound as if a satyagrahi's life was going to be a com-
fortable one, but all the same, a majority of the Congress
Party declared that they would welcome opportunities to resist empire, and to suffer, if necessary, for swaraj. Such was
the rising tide of enthusiasm for their leader and his methods. A specific program of civil disobedience was devised.

Gandhi's ideas were indeed novel, but they were not un-
heard of. Peaceful resistance, nonviolence, or satyagraha had
its origins in all the great religious teachings of the world.
Moreover, the idea of nonviolence was especially appealing
to Indians because in ancient times, Asoka, the most es-
teemed of emperors, had renounced conquest on the eve of
victory when he saw the bloodshed it cost. Every schoolchild
had learned to repeat Asoka's story with affection and respect. In the twentieth century, under Gandhi's own leadership, the Indian community in South Africa had achieved remarkable results, using satyagraha as a weapon; while both
that effort and the one evolving in India owed much to the
philosophy and the example of an American who had lived
near Boston, Massachusetts, in the nineteenth century—
Henry David Thoreau.

"Two things are very near to me," Jawaharlal Nehru
said when defending himself before the Allahabad District
Board a few months later, "independence for this country of
ours and equality between man and man." It is not surprising that he was elated by the turn events had taken within
the party. Strangely enough, however, among the Moderates,
Motilal Nehru was the first to accept the leadership of Mohandas Gandhi and the principle of civil disobedience. In all

likelihood, if it had not been for the elder Nehru's support, Congress could never have united so quickly and completely behind such a radical effort; but, once the influential, eloquent Motilal opted for the platform, others of less liberal persuasion followed suit. He had announced his choice at a special assembly of the Congress Party held at Calcutta during October, 1920. By the time of the annual session, Gandhi's success had been assured.

The grand old patriarch of Anand Bhawan was nearly sixty when he dedicated his life to swaraj. He gave up his fabulous law practice at the zenith of his career. He, who had been the friend and darling of empire, became one of its most doughty opponents. The man who was used to fine living and who could boast that "rivers of champagne" had flowed between him and a certain English governor now exchanged his kitchens, his silver, and his tasteful cuisine for a simple diet interspersed with prison fare.

Hard as it was on some of his relatives, particularly his wife, and unaccountable as it seemed to a few of his colleagues, Motilal Nehru's adherence to swaraj and to satyagraha as a means of achieving it was sincere and steadfast. After his position became known, it was discovered that he had practiced sleeping on the floor to get an idea of what it would be like when and if he went to jail. Undoubtedly his new allegiance owed a lot not only to the logic of events but also to the fondness he had for Jawaharlal, as well as for Gandhi.

The long arguments that the older Nehru had held with Jawahar and the example of his son had had their effect. Yet, there was something relentlessly individualistic about Motilal. Whatever he did was executed in a grand manner. Soon after the Nagpur session of the Congress, an acquaintance who had not seen him for twelve years remarked at the change that had occurred in him. "Hardly!" was Motilal Nehru's reply. "I have been a rebel all my life. I must have been born a rebel."

Rebel or not, Motilal had made a complete break with his past and jeopardized his own future, as well as that of his family. He was exposed to ridicule by many of his former friends and colleagues at the law courts who did not appreciate austerity. As loyal as they were in their opposition to empire, very few of the former Moderates were willing to go the whole way with satyagraha until they had some proof of its effectiveness on their own soil and in their own time. Jawaharlal and his friends, who were known as "the young crowd in Congress," stood behind the Nagpur decisions one hundred percent, but conservatives saw in the new program the doom of swaraj.

Among Muslims, Mohammed Ali Jinnah was directly opposed to Gandhi and to civil disobedience, and his position carried a great deal of weight with his particular following. Like the elder Nehru, Mohammed Ali Jinnah was a lawyer with an outstanding reputation, well-educated and brilliant. He too was a man of sophisticated tastes, an admirer of the West. He was a prominent Muslim, but up to this time he had been a member of the Congress Party and had been proclaimed as the "advocate of Hindu-Muslim unity." However, civil disobedience, Gandhi and his zealous fervor, and more especially the way of life now advocated by the Congress Party were anathema to him. Accept them he could not.

Jinnah withdrew from the Indian National Congress after the Nagpur session of 1920. He left India and lived in semiretirement in England for a while. He was a forceful lecturer and writer, known for his sharp and biting sarcasm. He gave a bitter tongue-lashing to members of his faith who stayed behind and offered their allegiance to the Congress Party. Despite him, many courageous Muslims did continue to work for swaraj within the framework the Congress provided, but Jinnah condemned them publicly, and the strength of his allegations frightened others who might have joined in the effort.

Personally, Jawaharlal Nehru described himself as "living in a kind of intoxication" throughout the year 1921. In his own thinking it was almost impossible to separate the marvelous man Gandhi from the Congress Party program, and so he went all out in his enthusiasm for both man and program. In accordance with Gandhi's strict religious teachings, the young aristocrat immediately reduced his material wants and simplified the business of living. He gave up smoking. He began to read deeply in the history of his country and the Hindu scriptures. Since Gandhi recommended that every Congress Party member learn to spin as a reminder of the dignity of hand labor, and insisted that his followers wear khadi, Jawaharlal became an expert spinner and dressed himself in homespun. These were the outward changes. Inwardly, Jawaharlal Nehru was in tune with the new program and he received from it, as well as from his deepening friendship with village people, the confidence and optimism for which he had been searching. He was prepared to argue, to teach, and to proclaim the ideas of freedom with ardor. He immersed himself in politics.

The younger Nehru was appointed General Secretary of the Indian National Congress in the United Provinces. In that capacity, he organized branches of the party in outlying districts and addressed many meetings. The village people saw a lot of him, but he was almost never at home. He caught only glimpses of Kamala and tiny Indira. Afterward, he blushed to recall how few times he had even thought of those two, captured as he had been by the demands of the moment; but he could hardly have neglected them entirely, because both of them became devoted to him.

The year 1921 turned out to be Jawaharlal's busiest up to that time. Enthusiasm ran high among members of the party. Basically, the civil disobedience directives of the Congress were extremely simple and personal; but they spread like wildfire and the results were surprising.

During November, His Majesty's Government announced that His Royal Highness, the Prince of Wales, would pay a state visit to India. Gandhi called for a nationwide *hartal,* a nonviolent protest, upon the occasion of the Prince's tour. Congress Party members avoided the ceremonies and encouraged others to do so in the name of independence. When the prince arrived, the streets were nearly empty. The parade grounds were deserted.

As hard as they tried, the government could find no means with which to enliven the occasion. Public officials became harried and enraged. Without a shot's being fired, members of the Indian National Congress saw the effect of their massed strength and endurance. They had delivered their first major affront to the prestige of the Crown. They were heartened.

Retaliation followed. There was a wave of arrests and imprisonments. It is estimated that within six weeks thirty thousand Indians were sent to jail on one pretext or another with sentences ranging from a few months to several years. Motilal and Jawaharlal Nehru were among those imprisoned, Motilal for membership in the Indian National Congress, which was declared illegal, and Jawaharlal for publicly engaging in the work of the party.

Excitement over satyagraha rose to fever pitch. Volunteers of all faiths applied to the Congress Party. It looked as though a new era of Hindu-Muslim friendship might be at hand.

Fortunately, Jawaharlal's jail sentence was not long. After a few weeks he was out and able to throw himself into political activities again. He was in constant demand as a speaker. He organized strikes against shops that sold foreign cloth. He marched on picket lines. He got merchants to pledge that they would sell only Indian-made goods. He encouraged local production of khadi. In fact, he worked with such ardor that it is no wonder he was seized by His Majesty's Government a second time and sentenced to eighteen months' imprisonment.

Civil disobedience now experienced setbacks. Gandhi was put in jail. There were riots between Hindus and Muslims in the south, and there was a small but significant skirmish between angry civil resisters and the police in a northern village. Immediately, from his prison cell, Gandhi called a halt to protest. He said that any outbreak of violence indicated to him that his forces were not ready and he wouldn't continue to lead them until he was assured that they were prepared to take their punishment and die, if need be, without striking back.

Although Gandhi's decision to suspend civil disobedience was hard for Congress Party members to accept when they were getting results, there is no doubt but that the British government breathed more easily as a consequence. There had been nothing at all predictable about the recent tactics of the Congress Party. The Raj had never known in what place or in what form resistance would be offered. The unprecedented efforts of volunteers like Jawaharlal Nehru on a widespread front had taxed English patience almost to the limit. With respectful but guarded praise, Lord Lloyd, then Governor of Bombay, described that first application of satyagraha as "the most colossal experiment in world history; and," he added significantly, "it came within an inch of succeeding."

From the point of view of the resisters, they were willing to take the punishment they had coming to them, but imprisonment was a sordid ordeal. During the early days of his stay in jail, Jawaharlal was assigned to barracks where he lived with murderers and thieves. Food was poor. News was censored. Sanitary conditions were almost lacking. It took fortitude to remind himself that by enduring such conditions he was advancing the cause of freedom, and to repeat Henry David Thoreau's statement which Gandhi considered the cornerstone of civil disobedience: "Under a government which imprisons any unjustly, the true place for a just man is also in prison."

Yet, imprisoned or free, Jawaharlal's own good humor abounded—so much so that his high spirits became an inspiration to his family and companions. When they were low or discouraged, they almost always found him to be on top of things. Long after they were tired out, he was still going. If members of the household cried when he was led away to jail, Jawahar managed to smile or to wave a last good-bye from the gate. His letters, even to little Indira, were witty and playful. Though he did not court danger heedlessly, the young man seemed to thrive on it. At this time in his life, when the future was so uncertain, he appeared stronger after every challenge. He never recoiled. He had his ups and downs, of course, but he steadfastly refused to become embittered. Instead, he tried to use events as a lever for better understanding, probing, and ultimately enduring the complex and relentless opposition.

Early in 1923, Jawaharlal Nehru was freed from Lucknow District Jail, and the family (who worried about him

more than he worried about himself) were relieved; but
soon thereafter he was handed a prison sentence of a different
kind and for new reasons. The circumstances surrounding
his case revealed some of the most astounding conditions ex-
isting in India. In order to comprehend what had happened
to him, Jawaharlal had to take a long view of history indeed! As he himself said, there were times when he had to
pinch himself to be reminded that he was living in the twentieth century.

When Akbar had reigned, he had made agreements
with the princes of certain states to rule on his behalf. His
arrangements with these petty monarchs had varied from
place to place, depending upon the amount of favor he had
wished to bestow. Some princes had been rewarded in coin,
others in prestige; but in all cases, their rule was absolute,
their word was law.

The British accorded the same recognition to local
princes. Maharajas and the sons of maharajas were permitted to rule and to levy taxes on their own behalf, provided
they kept order within their boundaries and turned over a
set amount to the king's purse. Some of these princes were
enormously wealthy but few among them were acquainted
with modern ideas of social justice. They were actually feudal chieftains whose peasants worked their land in order to
support the palace and to provide tribute for the king. The
Princely States of India were like fairy-tale kingdoms. And,
just as has always happened in fairy tales, there were wicked
kings as well as kindly ones who sat upon the jeweled thrones,
and the gulf between them and their subjects was wide.

As the winds of freedom continued to blow in the
1920's, ideas of independence swept out of the cities, across
the countryside of India, and over the frontiers of the maha-

rajas' kingdoms. The populace awakened and demanded to be heard. Tradition was challenged. There were disturbances in the Princely States. In some instances, local rule had to be supplanted temporarily by English officers who came in at the request of maharajas to help keep law and order.

In the Princely State of Nabha, which lay not far from Delhi, a British administrator was in power. To prevent disorder, he had forbade meetings of any sort, even for religious purposes. He had gone so far as to prohibit holiday celebrations and carnivals. The religious community of Sikhs, who constituted a large group within the population of Nabha, resented being confined. They continued to march to the scene of worship and to perform their ceremonies anyway, regardless of the governor's orders. In response, the governor ordered the police to engage the Sikhs and beat them soundly, hoping to discourage their rebellious behavior once and for all.

Jawaharlal Nehru read accounts of what had happened in Nabha. Something was stirring, he knew. Characteristically, he decided to go and see for himself what was happening. In the company of two friends, he journeyed to Jaito, in the state of Nabha, covering the last leg of his journey by bullock cart. He arrived at the border at about the time a Sikh procession was scheduled to pass on its way to worship.

As soon as the procession arrived at Jaito, it was stopped. The worshipers were not attacked, but Jawaharlal Nehru was drawn from the crowd and a paper delivered to him and to his two companions, ordering them to leave Nabha without delay. It seemed to make no difference to the officers that the young men they had singled out were not actually taking part in the procession. Neither were the officials prepared to wait until the departure of the next train to be rid of the trio. It was as if Jawaharlal and his friends were expected to vanish into thin air. Since they had no way of doing this, they were arrested and locked up.

Toward evening of that day, Jawaharlal and his companions, whose names were unknown to the authorities at the time they arrested them, were handcuffed, chained together, and marched through the street to the railroad station. For a while the young men hoped this was the prelude to the end of their adventures in Nabha. However, the train upon which they were placed was bound not for the border, but for the capital of Nabha. There they were promptly dispatched to the main jail, where they were housed in a common cell.

Chains and handcuffs were not removed from the three men until late the following day. Their jail cell was small and damp, scarcely high enough for anyone to stand upright. They were forced to sleep side by side on the floor. Jawaharlal remembered waking at night because a rat scuttled across his face. In such conditions he and the other prisoners were kept while their cases were heard, first on the count that originated in Jaito, and secondly on the charge of conspiracy. The courtroom proceedings were so inept and devious that Jawaharlal was enraged. In the end, all three men received two-year sentences but were not allowed to see copies of their judgment. In terms of the law, the proceedings were hardly worthy of the name.

On the evening after their judgment had been delivered, while they were soberly reviewing their fate, Jawaharlal and his companions were summoned to the office of the jail superintendent and shown a superior order from the British administrator which suspended their sentences. They were directed to leave Nabha and not return without special permission. They were immediately escorted to the railway station and released there. As it happened, the station was locked, but they boarded the first train that came by. It was bound for Ambala, and they proceeded from there to Delhi.

In the total drama of the independence movement, the Nabha incident was only a brief scene, but in Jawaharlal's life it loomed large. First of all, he and his two friends contracted typhoid fever during their twelve-day sojourn in jail. Jawaharlal's turned out to be the lightest of the three cases, but he was in bed at Anand Bhawan for a month and recovered slowly. However, the main legacy of his stay in Nabha was the impression he acquired of what life was like in a territory "beyond the rule of law." If such treatment could be meted out to him, a rather well-known young man of prestige, having recourse to courts of wider opinion, what must be accorded to residents of the area who had no resort to wider counsel? The Nabha incident fanned his antagonism to feudalism and increased his eagerness to release his fellow human beings from all vestiges of bondage.

The cleanliness, the order, and the affectionate care with which he was tended at Anand Bhawan were welcome. There was so much that was compelling to do, so many pressing tasks which plagued him ordinarily, that when he began to recover, it was good for Jawaharlal to rest and to relax in wholesome surroundings. Yet, the Anand Bhawan to which he was confined was a rather different place from the home he had known during his childhood. Nan's wedding to Ranjit Pandit, which had taken place in the spring of 1921, was the last grand celebration in the splendid compound. Nan, who had become Vijaya Lakshmi Pandit, had gone to live with her husband in Calcutta, and a definite regime of simplicity had been imposed upon the household.

The number of servants had been reduced. This in itself called for a difficult adjustment from people who had been used to luxury; but harder still was the lack of privacy that prevailed after Motilal and Jawaharlal entered politics. If the men happened to be out of jail, meetings went on at the house until all hours. No regular schedule of recreation or entertainment could be planned. No one knew how many satyagrahis were going to arrive at a time, when, or with what special needs. Police raids occurred fairly regularly, but without warning. Much of the handsome furniture and silver had been carted away and sold to pay fines.

It was no easy matter to try and support a family under such circumstances. Since all party work was on a voluntary basis, Motilal Nehru had to accept a few law cases in order to cover the financial needs of his household. Jawaharlal chafed at his continued dependence on his father, but Motilal reasoned that since he was the one who could more easily be spared for professional activity, money matters should be his responsibility. It was better that Jawaharlal give his complete attention to the independence movement.

In 1923, Jawaharlal Nehru was elected chairman of the Allahabad municipality, a post similar to that of mayor. He looked forward to the work, since it was directly related to the daily needs of citizens in his own city; but he soon found that for one reason or another, the procedures and reforms he proposed were not given a friendly hearing. Some of his ideas were rejected for political reasons, others because of inefficiency in the departments, or because they ran counter to tradition. He was frustrated at every turn and, at last, his spirits waned. He admitted he wanted to move a good deal faster than the Congress Party seemed to be going. All things considered, he longed for an open break with England which would force the pace of change.

This was a difficult period in every way at Anand Bhawan. Whenever their menfolk were hard pressed or in conflict, some of the worry rubbed off on Swarup Rani, Krishna, or Kamala. Yet, despite the hardships, from 1920 onward a more loving relationship developed between Jawaharlal and his family than they had ever had before.

To those who knew her, Kamala was like an opening flower. Her sheltered background had not prepared her for the rough-and-tumble circumstances of the freedom struggle; but it had given her a spontaneous sympathy for oppression and suffering. She now applied her keen intelligence to ferreting out the deeper implications of the inconsistencies she noted in daily life. She tried to understand at least the basic elements of the ideas that drove Jawaharlal at such a pace, and she took her own stand in relation to them. If she felt deprived or upset, she wouldn't say so. Whatever was hard for her was harder for her husband, she reasoned; and when he was challenged, she quietly went about making the adjustments that were necessary in her own life and that of Indira.

Kamala became such a lovely, steadfast accompaniment to the new way of life at Anand Bhawan that it was an especially painful shock for the family to discover that she was suffering from tuberculosis. When the doctors examined her, they insisted that her case was so serious that she could not recover in the midst of such turmoil. They recommended that she travel to Switzerland and enter a sanatorium there.

Jawaharlal sailed with Kamala, leaving his country with a heavy heart. His wife was frail; so too was the prognosis for India, and he wondered whether either of them would survive. After Gandhi had withdrawn the first civil disobedience campaign, there had been grumblings of discontent among the membership of the Congress Party. The Moderates had found plenty to complain about in regard to the program. Resistance could be kept up only in a sporadic way. Satyagraha now looked more like a series of specific ordeals and trials than an organized, vital force.

No clear line of progress toward freedom was discernible at the time. An English scholar later wrote:

> *India [in the 1920's was moving] forward like a sailing ship beating up in narrow waters and a moderate wind and a strong tide. Seen from six thousand feet above her, the tiny ship seemed to gain on almost every tack and slowly pass one marked reef or buoyed mud flat after another. But from the deck it was not so easy to discern progress, and every time the ship came about there seemed to be hesitation and contradiction, so that she would hang in the wind with sails flapping. . . . It looked from close quarters as though both captain and crew were thoroughly confused about the whole affair.*

Yes, Jawaharlal departed with a heavy heart indeed!

Young Nehru was visiting Europe after an absence of fourteen years. Back to the Continent at last—to the theater, the discussions, and the mountains he loved. He had gone home as an eager but timid graduate, capable but unsure for himself. He was coming back as a strong, assertive adult who was making a place for himself in national affairs. His convictions, the part he had played in politics, and his association with the new and dynamic thinking of India were going to open many doors to him. He would be invited to meet and discuss the prospects of India's independence with some of the most forward thinkers of the day. However grim the picture he carried of what he had just seen, proof was waiting for him that his country had begun to matter in the eyes of the world.

In the stimulating atmosphere of the European capitals, Jawaharlal's mind and spirit were enlivened. Even while Kamala was most seriously ill and he chose to spend many days at her bedside, he read and managed to work in short trips to Geneva so that he could see what was going on there at the League of Nations. In all, he and his wife stayed on the Continent for over a year, much longer than they had expected; but as soon as Kamala was well enough, she accompanied her husband to England, Italy, France, and Germany. Wherever they went, they were entertained by people who were keenly interested in the future of India, and they were besieged by inquiries on the potential and the techniques of the Congress Party.

Kamala improved but she could not maintain Jawaharlal's pace. In order to permit him to keep his busy schedule, Krishna came from India to take care of her. Jawaharlal then could accept an invitation to serve as the Indian representative at meetings of the League Against Imperialism, where he had a chance to become acquainted with men from Java, China, Africa, and the Middle East.

About this time, his father joined him. They went off to Russia to witness the tenth anniversary celebrations of the Russian revolution. As a result of their travel, and stimulated by wide-ranging experiences, both of them were reinvigorated. Jawaharlal, especially, began to feel an irresistible urge to return to Allahabad and get back to work as soon as possible.

In preparation young Nehru began to put together some of his thoughts about peasants, villages, and progress; and to combine them with the notions he had heard Gandhi express and with what he had learned during his stay in Europe. He was sure that it was not too early to talk about the kind of country India was going to be once it achieved independence. He knew that whatever course it plied toward freedom, the Congress Party had to consider economic justice for its people, as well as political justice; and so, he was sure that he was on the right track when he considered the relationship between democracy and development of the country's resources.

Jawaharlal was anxious to test out his newly formulated theories on the membership of the Congress Party and to get their reactions. Therefore, as soon as Kamala was able to make the trip, he took her with him and sailed for home, going by way of Ceylon. But his real destination was Madras, and he intended to arrive at Christmas, 1927, in time for the annual sessions of the Indian National Congress.

Jawaharlal Nehru returned to his country in the prime of condition. His outlook upon problems had widened. His faith had been reaffirmed that India's cause was just, and he had learned that her approach was attracting attention. His quick and broadening mind had perceived that freedom was important not only because it was right and timely, but because in achieving it, India had a role to play as a leader among subject nations. He fully understood the form of the economic organization he wanted the country to adopt as an independent nation. It must incorporate the best features of the Russian experiment and much from England and the United States. Immediate steps had to be taken in the direction of assuring such a framework and he had prepared resolutions to present at the annual session of Congress; resolutions on independence itself, on the position of India in relation to Europe, and on economic conditions at home.

In and out of jail, at the forefront of the Indian national struggle through the decade of the 1920's, Gandhi had shown himself to be a masterful leader. There was no one more capable of galvanizing enthusiasm and inspiring confidence when the time came for resistance, but Gandhi's emphasis was more on short-term objectives than on the long-range program of the party. He put a lot of stress on per-

sonal discipline and insisted that not by speeches but only by
self-sacrifice would home rule be achieved. Undeniably, he
was right, so far as freedom itself was concerned; but he
could be a formidable opponent to anyone who chose to shift
the focus of discussion to other issues.

Gandhi greeted Jawaharlal at Madras and he sat in on
the general sessions of the party; but, for some reason, he did
not pay much attention to young Nehru's motions at the
time they were put forward. It was only later, after they had
been passed and published, that Gandhi took them seriously,
and then they struck him as hasty and premature.

The older man questioned whether the time had arrived for anything as drastic as a call for a declaration of independence, which Jawaharlal was advocating. He shared
the young man's concern for world peace; but, at the moment, India was engaged in her own conflict with Great Britain, and that was far from being resolved. In relation to economic matters, he hadn't had time to give them much
thought on a national scale; yet, in any event, he doubted
whether the party could deliver on even a fraction of the
promises it had already made to the people of India; and,
until it did, he thought it foolhardy to involve itself any further. He explained his criticisms of the resolutions frankly to
Jawaharlal, yet rebuked him for his impetuousness and lack
of caution.

By contrast to their leaders, the youth and the peasants of
the country were ready and anxious to listen to Jawaharlal's
message. His vitality delighted the young people. They
cheered his appearances. His vision of a bold, new future appealed to farmers and factory workers as well. Taken as a
whole, the country accorded him a rousing welcome in 1927
and applauded his words. His popularity mounted and, as a
consequence, he was tempted to become more bold in his as-
sertions. He always spoke of satyagraha as the *way* to achieve

independence, but then he went a lot farther than anyone else dared to go in describing the country of the future. *Rash, socialistic,* and *hotheaded* were the terms his elders began to use to describe his ideas, as they eyed his work with skepticism.

Motilal was hardly the Moderate he had been ten years earlier; and yet, he could not say that his new allegiances endorsed the far-out notions advocated by his son after his European trip. The older man had a very high regard for Gandhi, and he was aware that Jawaharlal's behavior was distressing him. The threat of prison loomed large, and perhaps Motilal, better than Jawaharlal, realized what could happen if one goaded the imperial government too long. All things considered, he wished that the boy could be induced to go just a bit more slowly.

In spite of the best efforts made on his behalf, Jawaharlal took his way determinedly—talking, writing, and organizing. While he disagreed with him, Motilal Nehru also recognized that the young man was proving himself to be a real Nehru by sticking firmly to his points and acknowledging no interference. There was probably more than a touch of pride, as well as a premonition of sadness on his countenance as he watched his beloved Jawahar ride toward the furor of opposition. Still, he and Gandhi were deeply concerned for the safety of this "impetuous youngster," as they called him, who had so much to offer and whom they loved so much. At a time when he felt most separated from him, Motilal Nehru remarked to a relative who was staying at Anand Bhawan: "If Jawaharlal lives for ten years, he will change the face of India." He sighed. "Unfortunately, such men do not usually live long. They are consumed by the fire within them."

5 *bravely done*

There was disagreement in the Congress ranks, and that was an ill omen if there were to be an all-out effort to cast off foreign rule. In the spring of 1928 the party called a Constitutional Convention to establish the structure of government that would best serve a free India, but there at the conference table Mohandas Gandhi had ample proof that Jawaharlal Nehru was going too fast for the rest of the party. Discussions foundered on the question of whether or not India would accept the status of a British dominion when freedom was granted. The young Nehru and his following, which was becoming sizable, would accept nothing short of complete independence. The moderate elders present, led by Jawaharlal's father, wanted a report based upon recognition of India as a dominion under the empire.

The two groups temporarily lost sight of the fact that the establishment of a new nation is a step-by-step process and they appeared to be irreconcilable. The men could not reach agreement on the form of an independent government itself, let alone its platform. The young crowd was haughty and disdainful, but the elders remained intransigent. Heated words were exchanged. Gandhi was frankly worried and he blamed Jawaharlal. He vouchsafed that he could see only calamity ahead, unless young Nehru learned to be patient.

At the same time, a curious state of affairs existed in relation to the Congress Party, other national movements, and the British government. None of the Indian groups was yet powerful enough to bargain outright with the Crown, but all of them were too strong to be ignored. So, they and His Majesty's Government were involved in something that looked like a game, with each trying to outdare and to outsmart the other. Actually, they were biding their time and bidding for status.

Under the circumstances, it was not surprising that while the Congress Party was drawing up a master plan for the new republic of India, His Majesty's Government announced the appointment of a Royal Commission to review the comparatively insignificant question of whether or not Great Britain should continue to use Indian advisers for Indian affairs, as had been its practice since 1919. Sir John Simon was asked to head the Royal Commission, which became known popularly as "The Simon Commission." The commission was scheduled to come out for a look around India, then return to London and write a report.

The Viceroy wanted the purposes and the procedure of the Simon Commission to be made perfectly clear to Indians, particularly to those he recognized as the most vocal nationalists. Therefore, he summoned Mohandas Gandhi, Motilal Nehru, and Dr. M. A. Ansari, who was then president of the Congress Party, to his residence, in company with Mohammed Ali Jinnah of the Muslim League. He formally explained to these men the background of the commission's work, emphasizing that it was to be an "All-English" commission.

The Viceroy suggested that Indians would hardly expect to be represented on the commission since any recommendations they might make would be biased. The clear implication of the Viceroy's words was that it was time the nationalists understood that power was still in the hands of Great Britain and that she intended to exercise it. If changes were to be proposed for governing India, they were to be devised by Englishmen, not Indians.

What a challenge this presented to the Indian National Congress, and to any other group that presumed to represent even a fraction of India's citizens! England apparently did not fully understand that Indians, and more especially members of the Congress Party, were resolute when they talked of independence. So far as the Simon Commission was concerned, it was the old story of "decision without representation." Before they left the Viceroy's residence, the Congress Party leaders were well persuaded that circumstances demanded a display of nonviolent power and determination on a bigger scale than anything they had attempted before.

The Indian National Congress took action immediately. First of all, it voted to boycott the Simon Commission. Individual members of the Congress Party promised to withhold information from the commissioners, even when summoned. The party publicized its intent to ignore the deliberations of the commission and to disregard any report that would be written by them. Furthermore, Congress Party members agreed to disobey laws that would later be enacted upon recommendation of the Simon Commission. To call attention to their resolve in these matters, they laid plans for organizing mammoth demonstrations in the cities the commission intended to visit in the course of its tour.

Upon their arrival in India, members of the Simon Commission were met by a stubborn, defiant people. As had been the case during the earlier tour of the Prince of Wales, the people who lined the routes of the commissioners were hostile. But the ranks of Congressmen were better trained and organized than they had been in 1921. They could now flank the roadsides with solid lines of troops uniformed in khadi. Unashamedly, men of all castes and faiths assembled in public places, carrying black flags, shouting, "Simon, go home!" Their opposition was startling; their discipline remarkable. The impact of their numbers alone was significant.

Again the police went into action. One of the first cities to be visited by the commission was Lahore in the Punjab. There, among the front line of demonstrators, stood a well-known figure of the Congress Party, Lala Lajpat Rai. Whether to shield this man's face from view of the commission, whether to remove him forcibly from the spot, or whether in a nervous gesture intended to keep order among the onlookers, an English police officer advanced upon Lalaji, as he was familiarly called, and beat him across the chest with his baton. Lalaji offered no resistance. He was struck down and died a few days afterward. His doctors reported to the newspapers that his death had been caused by the beating.

The assault upon Lalaji touched off a wave of anger and fear all over India. Through the years that had passed since 1922, the people and their leaders had come to think that perhaps Gandhi had been right after all when he had withdrawn the first civil disobedience campaign because of violence. They hadn't been ready then, but Congress Party workers felt they were prepared for passive resistance now. Their jail terms and their punishments had given them fortitude and they could conduct themselves with remarkable calm. Had the British no respect at all for their point of view, and especially for their way of presenting it? The first flush of bravado and daring on the part of crusading Congress leaders had spent itself. No one expected independence to come immediately and all at once. But how long would officers continue to threaten harmless people? Were they still as callous as they had been at the time of Jallianwala Bagh?

The city of Lucknow was the capital of the United Provinces, where the Nehrus lived. It was a bigger city than Allahabad, with a population of approximately thirty thousand. The Simon Commission was scheduled to visit there at the end of November, only a few weeks after the assault upon Lala Lajpat Rai. Feeling against the British government and, more especially, against the commission was highly enflamed. Jawaharlal Nehru came forward and volunteered for the dangerous and unpopular job of organizing and directing the demonstrations in the provincial capital.

Upon the arrival of the Simon Commission in Lucknow, the government requested that there be no parades and no processions. This was done on the pretext that parades and processions interfered with traffic. To comply strictly with the wording of the request, Jawaharlal planned to have members assemble at the Congress Party offices and form into small groups, each with about sixteen volunteers and a leader. On the afternoon before the arrival of the delegation and again on the morning when the commission was scheduled to reach Lucknow, these small units would proceed by way of back alleys and lanes to assigned locations throughout the city.

In this way, without forming a large procession, several

groups of resisters could converge on one spot. Some were expected to meet at the park in front of the railroad station.
Others would take up positions along the route that would
be used by the Simon party. All volunteers were to wear
khadi. Each band was to carry a black flag but maintain silent, orderly lines of protest, no matter what provocation was
given them. Those were their orders.

On the afternoon before the commission was due to arrive in Lucknow, Jawaharlal Nehru took his place at the
head of a small unit of sixteen volunteers that was assembled
in front of the offices of the Indian National Congress. The
group set out along a prescribed route, a roundabout path
through back streets that led to the railway station. After an
agreed-upon interval of time had elapsed, the contingent was
to be followed by another band of party members, led by a
trusted friend of Jawaharlal's and a colleague of many years'
acquaintance, Govind Ballabh Pant. Subsequently, other
groups of men were to be dispatched from the offices to various parts of the city.

Jawaharlal and his men had moved scarcely two hundred
feet when they heard the clatter of horses' hooves behind
them. Turning, they beheld a contingent of British cavalry,
numbering well over thirty, bearing down upon their party
with upraised batons. Without reining in, the soldiers pressed
forward, intending to disperse the unit. Almost instantly
they were upon the volunteers.

Jawaharlal saw some of his followers downed immediately by the crashing hooves of the oncoming cavalry. Leaning out from their saddles, the soldiers slashed indiscrimina-
tely at the volunteers standing in the street on either side of
them. Several were knocked against nearby buildings. Others
stood fast, but a handful fled into the tiny shops that bor-
dered the lane. So intent upon their business were the sol-

diers that some jumped from their mounts and pursued the panic-stricken resisters into the recesses of the shops, wielding their powerful truncheons against any with whom they came in contact.

Because the cavalry had approached his group from the rear, Jawaharlal survived the initial attack. Before the horsemen reached the place where he stood, he had sufficient time to take cover. Instinctively he looked around for shelter, but he was not a coward. He knew his place was there, at the head of his unit. He had been as surprised as anyone else by what was happening; but, after all, there must be more to this than a chance encounter. It was perhaps a limited skirmish in the bigger battle for swaraj, but it was definitely part of that effort and there must be no retreat.

Through the open space that had been cleared of volunteers, a mounted cavalryman galloped straight for Jawaharlal Nehru. The officer's arm was upraised, his heavy stick ready to fall. Acting on impulse, Jawaharlal shielded his face and eyes. The truncheon came down with a resounding whack on his shoulder. He reeled but did not fall. The baton fell a second time, delivering a harder blow. Jawaharlal was stunned, but still managed to stay on his feet. The officer then pulled back, passed him by, and signaled for the cavalry to reassemble, forming a roadblock in the path of the volunteers.

Young Nehru straightened up and gathered his men together. They were all of them bruised. Some were very seriously wounded, bleeding and dirty. They had received word that the group led by Govind Ballabh Pant had been similarly set upon by another contingent of cavalry. Govind Ballabh Pant had been beaten.

So this was the way things stood. Perhaps they were being given a taste of what they could expect on the morrow,

Jawaharlal thought. In that case, he had better be sure that his own behavior and that of his contingents was a model, a model not of violence but of satyagraha at its best. He held hasty counsel with himself and decided to bring together the two units of Congress Party workers, his own and Pant's, in the narrow alleyway. That done, he would approach the officer who commanded the ranks of cavalry in front of him and request permission for the men to pass in orderly fashion.

Jawaharlal was denied permission to go ahead. He returned to his comrades. He suggested that they all take what care they could of themselves and one another and then sit down quietly in the street until such time as they were permitted to go on. He himself cared for those who had been most badly hurt, and making light of his injuries, moved about reassuringly, trying to get the men to smile and joke, hoping to restore their shattered confidence.

As ever, Jawaharlal's good spirits had an effect. The volunteers gradually settled down and he took his place in front of them. They waited together silently until they could get leave to proceed.

Slowly, ever so slowly, it seemed to the Congress volunteers, the minutes ticked past. Still no permission was given for them to go ahead. The minutes lengthened into hours. The wounded men were suffering, and Jawaharlal's back ached. He felt frustrated, but he turned the familiar lessons of satyagraha over in his mind. Be patient, he counseled himself as he considered the situation. We can do something more than suffer. We can refuse to give up.

The long autumn afternoon turned to dusk. The cavalrymen stood resolute. A group of rather important English officials assembled in an adjacent lane to survey the scene and to confer. Jawaharlal Nehru again demanded the right for his men to march ahead peacefully, but it was denied. Dusk deepened into night.

Suddenly, without prior warning or explanation, the officer who commanded the cavalry turned and beckoned for the volunteers to follow. Under cover of darkness, he and his unit escorted them along the route by which they had requested to go. With Jawaharlal walking staunchly at their head, the little band managed to make their way to the railroad station. Despite their wounds, they went the whole way with the cavalry before they dispersed.

Far more effectively than any other summons that might have been given, the attack on two small bands of Congress Party workers aroused the people of the countryside in the United Provinces. Within a few hours, reports of the assaults upon Jawaharlal Nehru, Govind Ballabh Pant, and their comrades spread through the city and out to the villages. The indignation that people had felt when they had heard about the attack upon Lala Lajpat Rai, whom most of them had never seen, was goaded almost beyond restraint by what had now been done to men of their own province and especially to Jawaharlal Nehru, whom the peasants loved. If he had been attacked, they would not rest.

By midnight, a host of village people were on their way to Lucknow. The roads were choked by bullock carts, by families on foot, and men on bicycles. What these people were going to do when they reached the city they did not know exactly; but they knew Lucknow was the place they wanted to be. How could one man hold out against an army, even if he had guns? they asked themselves. In all likelihood there was going to be trouble, and they wanted to be on hand where they were needed.

As soon as his unit had been cared for, Jawaharlal sent a message to his family in Allahabad. He said they would read in the morning papers that he had been beaten by troops in Lucknow, but they were not to be upset. It was true that he had been bruised, but he would recover. He intended to lead the marchers at dawn, as he had promised to do.

Motilal Nehru left Allahabad for Lucknow at twelve o'clock that night, traveling by car. He encountered some delays on the road, but he did arrive at the Lucknow offices of the Congress Party just before sunup, in time to see Jawaharlal and to embrace him before the demonstration. Although Motilal could hardly bear the thought of pain and danger affecting his family, it did not seem to occur either to himself or to Jawaharlal that they should alter the well-laid plans for the day. To resist was an obligation to the Congress Party and to swaraj. To lead the resistance was Jawaharlal's duty.

Quiet and sullen, villagers lined the streets that led to the Lucknow station. Not insensitive to the growing throng, the English army and police officers made preparations. Mounted soldiers, bearing long bamboo poles called *lathis,* took up positions at frequent intervals in front of the crowds. Between the cavalrymen stood police officers, almost shoulder to shoulder. Arranged like chessmen, the peasants and their guardians waited for dawn and then for the hour when the Simon Commission was scheduled to arrive.

According to plan, before the sun had risen, volunteers left the offices of the Indian National Congress. Contingents of sixteen marched by fours, with Jawaharlal Nehru in the lead. The units proceeded in the direction of the railway terminal.

Along the way, the volunteers met no interference at all. In orderly fashion they positioned themselves on the parade ground in front of the Lucknow station. Units arrived from other parts of the city. Similar groups of volunteers marched to their assigned locations on the route the Simon Commission would take from the station to the home of the governor.

The Congress Party units were made up of an assortment of men. There were both old and young; at the head of the ranks stood persons of learning and culture, but their followers included sweepers and laundrymen from the lowest castes. None of them had ever drilled in army formation. They were awkward and marched out of step. Many of the demonstrators walked barefoot. But, by the time the sun had risen on that November morning, hundreds of men in white homespun were packed onto the parade ground in front of the Lucknow station, black flags fluttering above their heads. They presented an imposing spectacle. Soldiers and policemen eyed them suspiciously. These ranks of Congress Party workers were of special interest both to the British officers and to the assembled villagers. Curiously, the peasants stared at "Gandhi's men" or "Jawaharlal's men," as they called them.

The village people wondered just how many of these same volunteers had been beaten on the previous afternoon, and whether all those who had been attacked were able to march. They saw bandages on the heads and shoulders of some of the men. They were sympathetic and stepped across to the ranks of volunteers in order to inquire about their welfare. Passing close to Jawaharlal Nehru, the peasants bent down to give him their blessing. Children pulled free of their parents and scampered back and forth in front of the demonstrators. In this way the crowd began to break up and move about.

Very soon, from the direction of the Lucknow bazaar came the clatter of horses' hooves on stone. Police and foot soldiers moved forward. From where he stood in advance of his volunteers, Jawaharlal saw the cavalry approaching, a long line of men and horses spreading across the open area in front of him.

Frightened, the onlookers began to scatter, but too late. Methodically, the soldiers set to work to clear the parade ground. With precision derived from training and combat, the horsemen struck. Children were hurled back into the crowd. Bystanders were pounded by flying hooves. The cavalry advanced as if over a field of battle, their ranks close together and undeterred.

The army moved headlong in the direction of the Congress Party lines. Jawaharlal braced himself and glanced sidewise at his men. This assault is meant for us, he thought. I hope we can withstand it.

For a perilous moment, the horses reared, their front feet poised and quivering above the heads of the volunteers. Then they lunged. The soldiers struck out with their lathis, aided by policemen wielding batons. Limbs were crushed in the confusion. Backs were broken and faces lacerated. The field became a mangled and horrid scene; but, for the most part, the satyagrahis maintained their original positions and, mercifully, no one hit back.

As the leader of such brave battalions, Jawaharlal had nothing but pride for his men and their endurance, but he was rent by indignation at the sight of the cruelty inflicted upon them. The drive for revenge was strong and he felt it. How simple it would be to pull down the rider he saw advancing in his direction! How easily he could unseat him, he realized; and wasn't there provocation for such an action?

But no! To strike at the moment would negate all that India was attempting to prove by its passive resistance. Violence would postpone swaraj and provoke conditions too pitiless to contemplate. He knew he had to last out even this; and, moreover, he had to believe that his opponents were sensible and capable of being moved by the sight of suffering the same as he.

Jawaharlal stared straight into the distorted faces of his attackers. "We have no quarrel with one another as men," he whispered to himself. "We are caught, all of us, by forces far bigger than any one of us has produced. In other circumstances, we might be friends." He breathed deeply. He held himself erect. He kept his hands at his sides. With set, determined features he took the onslaught.

The young leader was beset by blows. They fell upon his back, his head, his chest. He raised an arm to protect his face, and held his own during the prolonged encounter with cavalrymen and police. For several minutes he was singled out as a direct target for attack. The soldiers appeared to be relentless. Without realizing what was happening, Jawaharlal was separated from his companions. At sight of his danger, sympathetic volunteers at last rushed forward in order to divert attention from him and enable him to reenter the line, which they had re-formed a few feet away.

There was a whistle from an approaching train. The cavalry ceased its attack immediately and the officers hastily positioned their horses flank to flank in order to form a solid wall in front of the volunteers. Jawaharlal's men were commanded not to move or speak. Their leader and the few volunteers who still had strength enough to stand, remained resolutely at attention; but those who had been more seriously injured sat or lay in the dirt. The men who were wounded had to be ignored for the time being. It was in such hostile, threatening circumstances that the façade of order was maintained.

Jawaharlal heard the slow, laborious chugging of a railway engine as it pulled into the station. A few shouts resounded from the direction of the tracks. He could not make out whether or not shots had been fired, but there were no other evidences of trouble.

What fate, the youthful leader asked, had befallen Congress Party units in other places? He comforted himself temporarily with the thought that the army would probably not have risked bloodshed in a place where it might have been brought to the attention of the Commission or implicated its members. He turned his mind to the seven commissioners whose assignment had provoked this trouble. They were doing their duty as they saw it, he supposed. He could imagine they were perhaps a trifle cocky but otherwise well-meaning, well-mannered men. Surrounded by the securities of empire, they must now be settling themselves comfortably in the cars that would whisk them in safety to the governor's mansion.

Jawaharlal Nehru swept his eyes over the field around him where, by contrast, his satyagrahis lay gripped and writhing with pain. Their helplessness appalled him. He found it hard to tolerate. To his battered spirit returned the question: Where, to what end will this contest lead?

Similar to a picture that Gandhi had once described to him, young Nehru's image of his country at that moment was that of a weeping child. He would like to have held it in his arms. He would have been pleased to wipe away its tears and comfort its people, especially those who, without knowing the risks they would meet, had stumbled into this prolonged tussle with the British government. The conditions under which his men had to resist were terrifying and it looked as if the mettle of the enemy had only begun to be tested. He found the outlook discouraging.

At the same time, deep down inside, Jawaharlal Nehru

knew that he had hope, and for good reason. He studied the steadfast faces of the villagers and those of his unyielding companions. These people were not soldiers, he reminded himself. They were brothers. Standing in tattered shirts on bloodstained ground, they were united. Such was the nature of their struggle that they might achieve their goal only by passing across just such harsh and barren lands of suffering as this; but they were on the way together, and together they could not be turned back.

The morning's clash between volunteers and cavalry left a durable mark upon the independence movement and especially upon the Congress Party leadership. It was a serious and, for many families, a tragic occasion. Among others, Govind Ballabh Pant was so badly wounded that he was bedridden for months and always walked with a cane thereafter, although he gave long and distinguished service to his country. When Jawaharlal, stiff and bleeding, stumbled at last into the Lucknow offices of the Congress Party that day, Motilal wept at the sight of him. But when news of his marvelous stamina reached Gandhi, he wrote immediately:

My dear Jawahar:

>*My love to you. It was all done bravely. You have braver things ahead. May God spare you for many a long year to come and make you His chosen instrument for freeing India from the yoke. . . .*

The note which he wrote to Jawaharlal after the Lucknow march was typical of Gandhi. He could never be estranged for long. Because he held himself to very rigid standards, he could be as firm as a schoolmaster, as strict as an officer; but there was no jealousy in him, no smallness of any kind. He was the truest of friends. His untiring love, for individuals and for his country, had earned him the title *Ma-hatma*, Great Soul; but it was like him to insist upon being called *Bapu*, which means father, or merely *Gandhiji*, dear Gandhi.

Gandhiji worked from religious motives. He was devout and faithful, a pious man who led a restrained, contemplative life, which he would have preferred to spend in a quiet community, surrounded by people who held beliefs similar to his own. Yet, he had an uncanny way of knowing when and how to challenge the rest of society and its traditions, whether local traditions of caste or national traditions rooted in colonialism. His long spiritual meditations provided him with fresh and vivid insight. His humor was delightful. When he chose to drive home a point, his sense of timing was exact and his own behavior calculated. Despite his insistence upon nonviolence, he was a shrewd strategist, keen-witted and adroit in planning, precise in his attack.

Jawaharlal, on the other hand, was an intellectual. He liked to be thrust into the thick of things; but even when his body was engaged at an active task, his mind was roving in search of information, trying to ferret out reasons and devise new solutions for old problems. Unlike Gandhiji, he thought in big terms, always. In contrast to his friend who hoped to touch the spirit of every man, Jawaharlal Nehru espoused the causes of groups: peasants, factory workers, students, and residents of Princely States. As he grew older, his loyalties easily transcended even these classifications and he spoke on behalf of Indians, Asians, and World Citizens. Like his father, whatever he conceived was on a grand scale.

Because he considered problems common to large numbers of people, Jawaharlal Nehru defined goals that had wide applications in society. After his trip to Europe in the 1920's, he kept in touch with other developing countries and studied modern, up-to-date instruments of social planning. Fortunately, he had great skill not only in conceiving and designing but in launching enormous endeavors. He knew how to capture the imagination of his fellows and where their energies could be best applied. Common folk loved his fervor and his daring. Peasants appreciated his ability to explain even the most complex ideas in simple terms. He inspired students and innovators. He was the spirit of youth personified.

The independence movement needed both Mohandas Gandhi and Jawaharlal Nehru. For years they worked side by side within the Indian National Congress. Their points of view were distinctive but seldom divisive. On the contrary, their abilities seemed to complement one another. Neither of them relied solely upon any one particular faction for support. In the beginning, it was Gandhi who led and Jawaharlal who followed, but eventually the struggle for swaraj called for the best talents of both minds and spirits, and the interaction of the two produced miracles.

In December, 1928, the Indian National Congress took another long step forward on the journey toward freedom when, at the Calcutta session, they framed a resolution demanding independence within one year. This was an outright warning to His Majesty's Government, a warning couched in dignified phrases, but a warning nevertheless— and a threat. If swaraj were not granted, the party promised, England could expect India to resist by every means at her disposal. So far as numbers were concerned, it was not presumptuous to make such a promise, since the Indian National Congress clearly spoke for a majority of the people in the country. The only danger was that, on the fatal day, Congress might be faced with division in its own ranks.

To the Congress Moderates, including Gandhiji, swaraj

meant "self-government with dominion status." To the young crowd, dominion status symbolized continuing dependence upon the British Empire and they would have none of it. During the early part of the Calcutta session, Jawaharlal Nehru and a group of other youths, including a man by the name of Subhas Chandra Bose, tried to get the party to redefine swaraj as "complete independence." They admitted that their opposition was focused not upon whether it was *time* to declare independence, nor upon whether it was *fair* to provide Great Britain with a year of grace, but simply upon the *limited end* their elders had in view. They went about things in a temperate manner, but they were outvoted.

In spite of the presence of an ever-increasing membership of well-trained and articulate young people, the Moderates still insisted upon controlling the party. Their position was hard for Jawaharlal to appreciate, but he knew he had to work within the framework they provided. The Calcutta incident provoked further unpleasantness when, at the last moment, he decided to support the independence motion as it stood. Then his young comrades felt betrayed by him. He was clearly trying to find a formula by which to give youth a voice and placate his elders, but he had not yet hit upon a right and lasting way.

Nineteen twenty-nine was a decisive year. Great Britain had been offered a chance to prove her good intentions by making some tangible move in the direction of withdrawal. Meanwhile, if His Majesty's Government declined to take advantage of the opportunity it had been given, the Congress Party had to be prepared for all-out resistance, a campaign of civil disobedience that would be unified, widespread, and prolonged.

In the best of circumstances, it would have been difficult

to hold the reins of power on either side. His Majesty's highest representative in India at the time was Lord Irwin, the Viceroy. On behalf of Indian nationalists, Motilal Nehru was serving as president of the Indian National Congress. His son was his second-in-command, having been chosen in response to the upsurge of youthful opinion in the party, even though it was known that he disagreed completely with the official interpretation of swaraj. Because of his affection for Jawaharlal, as well as for political reasons, Motilal Nehru felt compelled to try every possible means to win a concession from England before the year expired.

In the person of Lord Irwin, Indian nationalists had an ally. If he could not wrest a promise of immediate and complete independence for India from his government, he would at least have them go as far as it was legitimate in that direction. He persuaded Parliament to reaffirm its earlier promise of eventual self-government and dominion status for India, which in itself was no easy task, and he summoned political leaders of all shades of opinion to plan a Round Table Conference where they could discuss ways and means of reaching those goals peaceably and soon. Jawaharlal was somewhat suspicious of the outcome of such a venture, but Motilal Nehru accepted the Viceroy's invitation and Gandhiji attended the meeting also.

Nationalist leaders were heartened by their session with Lord Irwin; yet, alas, he had offered more than his government was prepared to deliver. The Indian question was reintroduced and debated long and hard in Parliament. Members went back on their recent positions and demanded His Majesty withdraw support from the Viceroy. As soon as this happened, Congress Party members and, especially, Congress Party leaders were put on the alert. The forthcoming break between England and India was apparent and imminent.

In view of the national crisis, the choice of a president for the Congress Party during the year 1930 was crucial. On the surface, it looked as if no one but Gandhi could possibly mobilize the forces that were needed; but three names were actually put forward: Mohandas Gandhi, Vallabhbhai Patel (who was both a shrewd negotiator and a firm, dependable advocate of nonviolence), and Jawaharlal Nehru. Balloting took place in August, well in advance of the annual session. Gandhiji won a clear majority.

Gandhiji thought about this circumstance. He meditated upon his election; and, to the surprise of everyone, he said he refused to serve. In an act of unprecedented selflessness, he made an outright gift of his votes to Jawaharlal and persuaded Patel to do the same. They met with their electors individually and convinced them to rewrite their ballots. Thus, it was announced that young Nehru had been unanimously chosen to serve as president of the Indian National Congress during the decisive year.

Jawaharlal Nehru was astonished and dismayed. "I did not come to the presidency of the Indian National Congress by the main entrance or even a side entrance," he said. "I appeared suddenly by a trap door." His pride was wounded. His sense of fair play was aroused, and at first he had no intention of accepting the office. But Gandhi was adamant. "No," he maintained. "No, I will not serve!"

Gandhi left his religious community and went on a countrywide tour in order to define his position to the Indian people. In his speeches, his strategy became apparent. "The battle of the future has to be fought by younger men and women," Gandhiji stated. "It is but meet that they be led by one of themselves.

"Some fear in the transference of power from the old to the young the doom of Congress," he went on to say. *"I do not,*" he declared courageously before his Moderate colleagues. "In bravery Jawaharlal Nehru is not to be surpassed. Who can excel him in the love of the country? 'He is rash and impetuous,' say some. If he has the dash and rashness of a warrior, he has also the prudence of a statesman. He is pure as crystal, he is truthful beyond suspicion. The nation will be safe in his hands."

The Mahatma had spoken. It was obvious that he would not retract his decision. As far as Jawaharlal himself was concerned, Gandhiji was sure that the love they had for one another was too deep and lasting for any antagonism to be caused by this turn of events. He perceived that Jawaharlal's support was made up of vigorous and talented young men with farseeing minds. They would bring new life to the independence movement. They were the hope of the nation; and, as he had said, they deserved to be led by one of their own kind.

Moreover, Jawaharlal had ably demonstrated to the older man his faith in nonviolence. His enthusiasm for the cause was contagious. It looked as if he had the ability both to engineer independence for India and to achieve a new state with modern purposes. Motilal's pride in Jawahar was not misplaced, Gandhiji felt. Wherever he appeared, he attracted vast crowds who hung upon his words. Whether the Moderates liked it or not, Jawaharlal Nehru spoke in the voice of the future.

6 *victory for jawaharlal*

The winter sky above the Punjab was clear and golden. Three hundred thousand people swarmed into the city of Lahore. They came from every province of India, from her cities, and from tiny villages. On the banks of the Ravi, at a park called Lajpat Rai Nagar, tents were raised to house these delegates to the annual session of the Indian National Congress. A volunteer corps of women, including Kamala and Krishna Nehru, had been organized to offer hospitality to the massive crowds. Children, including twelve-year-old Indira Nehru, had been recruited to act as pages and messengers. The streets of Lahore were decked with bunting. The red sandstone walls of the old Mogul fort provided a distinguished backdrop for the occasion. A triumphal arch was erected near the railway station. All was in readiness for president-elect Rashtrapati Jawaharlal Nehru.

The president-to-be of the Indian National Congress

rode through the streets of the gala city on a spirited white horse, followed by a herd of elephants, gorgeously caparisoned. "Young Nehru" had just turned forty and his lithe figure sat erect and commanding in the saddle. He wore garments made of khadi and upon his head was one of the jaunty caps that were becoming popular as part of the costume of members of the Congress Party. He was bedecked with garlands of marigolds, jasmine, and roses. At sight of the crowds that lined his path, his delicate face lighted with a smile. *"Jawaharlal ki jai!* Victory to Jawaharlal! *Rashtrapati ki jai!* Victory to the president!" his admirers yelled in jubilant accord.

In all of India could there have been a prouder heart than Motilal Nehru's on that day? He and Swarup Rani watched their son's parade from the rooftop of a building along the triumphal route. The old man looked every bit a statesman in his suit of fine white khadi, and he too wore a Congress cap atop his shock of silver hair, but his response to the occasion was reminiscent of the unrestrained and effusive joy of the old days at Anand Bhawan. Hesitations about Jawaharlal's policies were of minor consequence now. This was the first time in the history of the Indian National party that a son had succeeded his father as president. When "Jawahar" checked his horse in the street below and raised his hand to the retiring officer in salute, Motilal stepped to the edge of the parapet and, flinging wide his arms, let fall a shower of rose petals upon the Rashtrapati.

For Jawaharlal, this too was a joyous, yet sobering climax to recent activities. The weeks that had passed since his unexpected election had been arduous ones. As might have been expected, he had been called upon to play the role of mediator between the Moderates and the Extremists in his party. At the center of negotiations, however, had been his father and Gandhiji, who had tried unsuccessfully to wrest some timely agreement from the British government. But now the year of respite had expired. The time had come to consider the next steps to be taken by the party and it was Jawaharlal himself who held its highest office.

The young president well knew his most urgent task. It was to secure passage of a resolution that would spell out India's new position in relation to Great Britain and leave no doubt in anyone's mind but that the country intended to be completely independent. If he couldn't assure that much for his youthful followers he was probably doomed as an executive; but he had received indications that even that much would be a lot to ask of the Moderates in the party. A month earlier he had been asked to phrase the demands that the Congress Party would consider a minimum basis for discussion at a Round Table Conference. Hard as it had been for him to sanction, the first of the demands mentioned nothing more than dominion status for India. Unless and until he could get a new resolution passed at an annual session, not one of the Moderates within the party would ask for more than that.

Jawaharlal Nehru had grave doubts as to the fate of his views regarding complete independence when it should come time to place them before an annual assembly of the Congress. On this one matter, however, he had no intention of backing down. If he had to do so, he would yield on other aspects of his program. He recognized that when it came to all-out resistance, Gandhi rather than himself would be the one to mobilize civil disobedience. But, on the matter of independence itself, Jawaharlal Nehru would not renounce authority voluntarily. At its Lahore session, the Indian National Congress would either declare *purna swaraj*, complete independence, for India, or reject him as Rashtrapati.

A handsome scene was enacted when the incoming president accepted the mantle of leadership from his father. The huge *pandal* tent was jammed to overflowing. The crowd appeared in its most colorful dress, representing all the varied sects and provinces of the vast country of India. It was a vivid array of peoples who saw the garlanded figure of Jawaharlal on stage beside Motilal and heard the outgoing officer prophesy: "What the father is unable to accomplish, the son achieves."

To this annual session of the Congress Party had come tall, bearded Pathans from the northwest, who were reputed to be the hardiest of India's warriors. It was their first appearance at a political gathering of any kind. They were men of striking physique, Muslims, soldiers to whom superiority in arms had been an honor and a challenge. It was astounding that they should have marched to Lahore, and vowed to lay down their arms, and to give their lives for the Congress Party and its program. To further distinguish themselves, the Pathans had dyed their shirts a deep, blood red. "Redshirts" they were called, led by six-foot Khan Abdul Gaffar Khan. The Redshirts bid fair to be the sturdiest and in some ways the most loyal of all the new converts to swaraj; but their very appearance gave a martial character to the assembly, and their presence in the crowd accented the fact that there were many newcomers, people untutored in the ways of Congress, and as yet untried.

When Jawaharlal Nehru delivered his address before that motley crowd, he tried to keep foremost the overriding need to convince the audience of his point of view regarding independence. He referred only in passing to the circumstances by which he had come to office. He modestly expressed gratitude to the membership for "confidence in one who strangely lacks it in himself"; but, deliberately, he then put to one side all apprehensions regarding a future split in the party, or any division between the old and new membership, and used his eloquence to gain support for purna swaraj.

The Rashtrapati reviewed the position of India in a changing world in which imperialism had been outdated. He did that because he considered it essential for Indians to remind themselves frequently that they were part of an uprising of subject peoples which included most of Asia and much of Africa. Within the world setting, however, the president acknowledged that India itself would have to work out its own unique solutions to the problems it would acquire along with democracy. He pleaded with his countrymen, whether Hindu or Muslim, to prevent barriers of prejudice from arising to impede their progress; for, he asserted forthrightly, "If the Calcutta resolution holds, we have but one goal today, that of independence."

With unwavering determination, the young president took measure of his audience. They were listening, with quiet breath and eyes fixed upon the platform. Motilal and Gandhiji were there, both of them seasoned Congress Party members. The assembly also included, most noticeably, Khan Abdul Gaffar Khan and his army of Redshirts. There were eager, youthful activists in the crowd, as well as people of age and sobriety. Women and children were present who would be called upon to make vital sacrifices in the forthcoming struggle with Great Britain. To such an assortment of peoples, Jawaharlal's next statement had deep implications. "Independence for us," he announced, "means *complete* freedom from British domination and British imperialism."

Having taken the basic position, the Rashtrapati went on to argue it in persuasive terms. For those who would be impressed by his logic, he explained his personal reasons for demanding purna swaraj. So that no one would be left in any doubt as to the probable aftermath of a declaration of independence on the part of the Congress Party, he anticipated civil disobedience. He called upon those who held office under the British to leave their jobs immediately. He warned that the schools and law courts must be boycotted, and he asked authorization for the central Working Committee of the party to take whatever action would be necessary in an emergency. He turned sympathetically to consideration of the special problems of peasants, industrial laborers, and those of the Princely States; but he stressed again and again that the major challenge of the moment was India's conquest of power.

"We stand today for the fullest freedom," Jawaharlal proclaimed. "Let no one, least of all England, mistake or underrate the meaning and strength of our resolve."

"Solemnly, with full knowledge of consequences," he summarized, "we shall take our stand and there will be no turning back. A great nation cannot be thwarted for long," he assured his fellow citizens, "when once its mind is clear and resolved. If today we fail and tomorrow brings no success, the day after will follow and bring achievement."

The president of the Indian National Congress had declared himself. His deep determination regarding the matter of independence was apparent. The delivery of his address had been swift and captivating. His audience had been magnetized, but whether he had succeeded in solidly uniting his party was yet to be proven.

Feeling as strongly as he did, Jawaharlal was not in an enviable position. Among those attending the session was his fiery comrade from Bengal, Subhas Chandra Bose, who had brought with him an aggressive faction of delegates who advocated cutting all ties with Great Britain immediately and taking measures that were far more extreme than those of civil disobedience. On the other hand, there was a scattering of conservatives among the Moderates that included the famous Indian poetess Sarojini Naidu, who would be ready to respond to any bid for delay or negotiation on the part of the British. Gandhiji, with his highly personal but realistic point of view, could probably be counted upon to try and hold the party together. From now on, however, Jawaharlal could counsel and he could plead, privately or in closed sessions of the Working Committee; but, when in the president's chair, he would have to withhold his opinions and enable the majority to choose its course of action.

There was a huge volume of work to be accomplished at the annual session that year, whether or not the break with Great Britain was to be complete. Demands and requests for support had been received from several special interest groups within the party. There were, as always, petty differences over minor resolutions to be ironed out. Plans had to be discussed for spreading the Congress Party program farther into the rural areas, for establishing more effective local committees, and for working closely with the Muslim League. Nevertheless, the imminence of a great decision and its accompanying uncertainty pervaded the sessions. In view of possible events, the party had to be ready for any contingency, and special rules for succession had to be devised. Voting on subsidiary resolutions took a long time. There were hours of speechmaking and preparation.

Throughout these deliberations, Jawaharlal presided with tireless restraint. The party learned that their young Rashtrapati had a mind of his own, but he was also ready to accommodate others. During the open sessions of the Congress, when people who represented all shades of opinion asked to speak, he conducted affairs with an impartiality everyone commended. He was businesslike and mature in his dealings, but he somehow managed to be delightfully spontaneous, witty, and charming at the same time. In countless daily contacts with his fellow members, he consciously tried to build the personal confidence and support that were necessary if the party were to follow his resolve.

Whereas open meetings of the assembly were noisy but controlled, discussions in the Resolutions Committee of the Indian National Congress were turbulent and stormy during the Lahore session. It was at these gatherings, first of all, that the danger from convinced Extremists became manifest. Subhas Chandra Bose was a rebel, and he had very little patience with nonviolence. His passionate quest for his own freedom led him to recommend methods that were far in excess of anything yet considered by Congress. Like Jawaharlal, he had a strong personality combined with a penetrating and incisive intellect. He was a born leader, and he loved to command. With his vision and his sense of urgency it was touch and go as to whether he would be willing to wait for democratic processes to work.

The tactics employed by Subhas Bose were frightening to some of his colleagues but they had a useful effect. As they listened to his impassioned speeches in the Resolutions Committee, delegates began to compare this young man with Jawaharlal. They considered his bombastic statements alongside those they had heard voiced by the president; and, in light of such comparison, the Rashtrapati's words appeared to be more tempered and less drastic than they had sounded at the beginning of the session. An increasing number of delegates found themselves in agreement with Gandhiji's choice and sharing his sentiment that the nation would be safe in Jawaharlal's hands.

During the extended meetings of the Resolutions Committee, a formal proposition embodying the essence of Jawaharlal's demand for independence was formulated and made ready for consideration by the delegates. It was Gandhiji who asked to present the motion on the floor at an open session. As agreed upon beforehand, but carefully and with obvious sincerity, before an audience of thousands, he moved that: "Congress in pursuance of the resolution passed at its session at Calcutta last year declares that the word *Swaraj* shall mean *complete independence* and hopes that all Congressmen will henceforth devote their exclusive attention to the attainment of purna swaraj for India."

Jawaharlal smiled. There wasn't time just then to thank Gandhiji for what he had done, but the gratitude of the younger man was immediately evident in his behavior. For a few moments, he simply kept his gavel raised and let the crowds have their way. At least half the delegates were on their feet in a second and cheering. Others joined them. They cheered for Gandhiji, for the resolution, and for their Rashtrapati. With a lightness of heart he had not experienced for some time, young Nehru stood before them and watched the performance. When he let his gavel fall at last, he felt emboldened and ready for combat. He nodded to his father, who was sitting in the front row. Motilal rose to second the historic motion.

Discussion on the proposition was sharp and prolonged. Patiently, Jawaharlal listened to his opponents present their points of view. As he had expected, the conservatives pressed for a further delay before declaring independence. On the other hand, Subhas Chandra Bose challenged the resolution on purna swaraj because he said it did not go far enough. He offered an amendment of his own which would make the proposal much more radical and far-reaching in its consequences. He insisted that all relations with England should be resolutely and irrevocably severed.

Bose's attack on the British government was hard-hitting, bitter, and laced with hatred. With one eye on the speaker, Jawaharlal noted the changing reactions of his audience. From moment to moment he tried to assess the probable effect the discourse was going to have upon the final vote. As time wore on, it became more and more difficult for him to maintain the silence appropriate to office. He was honestly afraid that everything he wanted was going to be lost if the man were to keep on talking and it could be presumed that his ideas were in any way linked to those of the Rashtrapati.

In a firm, courageous manner, Gandhiji took it upon himself to answer Bose, praising his enterprise but rejecting his conclusions. Stolidly, he insisted that the resolution before the house be accepted or rejected exactly as it stood, without amendment. It was, he reasoned with the party, "the longest step we can take today."

For the young crowd who might have been impressed by Subhas Bose's vitality, there must be no doubt but that the new leadership of the Congress Party meant business. Therefore, Gandhiji outlined the steps that would be taken if independence were declared. Except for the unlikely possibility that the British would adopt the Congress position, the resolution, when passed, would bring to an end lives of security and well-being for members of the party. The subsequent civil disobedience program was going to call for hazardous, long-term commitments from millions of people. Suffering and imprisonment would likely become commonplace in India before it could be proved to the British government that not only had Indians decided to be free but that they had no intention of submitting to imperialism any longer.

This line of reasoning, Gandhiji hoped, would give substance to the resolution and be firm enough to elicit the support of even a man like Bose. However, at the risk of alienating the young Extremist, Gandhiji seized upon that moment to emphasize a point which he and Jawaharlal agreed upon completely as a tenet of behavior. India's quarrel, he alleged, was with a *government* and not with *individuals*. The Congress Party would tolerate no fanning of prejudice in any quarter. There was to be no malice or backbiting!

Gandhiji thought he knew exactly how Jawaharlal would have reacted to his colleague if he had not sat in the seat of the Rashtrapati, and he took it in hand to do the job for him. He turned upon Subhas Bose and the rebels and admonished them soundly for the position they were taking in relation to England and the English people. "It is time we realized," he scolded, "that some day we shall have to meet in conference with the people you call our enemy in order to establish independence." The warning was timely; and, as he resumed his place, the Mahatma reflected that there were others in that assembly, whether old or young, who could well take his words to heart.

Discussion on the independence resolution ended at ten o'clock on the night of December 31, 1929. Voting went on for another two hours. The air was tense inside the pandal. The delegates hardly stirred from their places until the last tally was taken.

The hopes of the president were more than fulfilled. His resolution was carried in the end. A majority of the party expressed themselves in favor of making an immediate and complete declaration of independence. The vote was not unanimous, but it was decisive and there was no significant dissent. The final count reflected a clear picture of unity, and the call to action was definite. Both Moderates and Extremists were defeated.

In spite of the ominous overtones of the step they had taken, the membership of the Congress Party were relieved and exhilarated; yet, not one among them was any more elated than their president. By the passage of that motion, he considered himself to have received his real election and a vote of confidence. Jawaharlal Nehru had been the first to propose an independence resolution, as a delegate, two years before, at Madras. His resolution had passed, but he had been chastised by the leadership for his action. Since then, he had faced strong opposition. He had been elevated to the office of Rashtrapati against the wishes of the Moderates. Only now had the membership acknowledged his lead. At last he had triumphed, not because he bore the name Nehru, nor because he was Gandhi's choice; but because the time had come for purna swaraj, and he was to be its instrument.

The crowd went wild with excitement. In the midst of their rejoicing, a body of strong-armed Congressmen rushed onto the stage, grabbed their Rashtrapati, hoisted him above their heads, and, amidst the shouting, bore him out of the tent. There, on the banks of the swiftly flowing Ravi, they kindled a gigantic bonfire and at the stroke of midnight, Jawaharlal stepped up to raise the flag. It was a moving sight to see the broad stripes of green and white and saffron unfurl against the stars, with Gandhiji's spinning wheel embroidered at the center, signifying labor, the necessity and salvation of India.

Immediately, out of the mammoth crowd sprang the Redshirts to form a circle around the flagpole and the fire. Instantly, their feet began to tread the powerful steps of an age-old folk dance. *Crack* sounded the bamboo sticks that they carried and snapped against one another in time to their stamping. *Clap* echoed the hands of the spectators.

The dancers moved slowly at first, with steady, majestic

rhythm. Then they began to circle faster, gaining momentum, driving and twirling, their bamboos crashing. Around and around the fire they sped, pounding and twisting. When they paused and smacked their sticks together, they threw back their heads and shouted fiercely. Mighty, grotesque shadows were cast by their figures. Cheers were rung from their happy audience.

Acting on a sudden impulse, Jawaharlal Nehru leapt into the circle of swirling men. Grabbing a bamboo from one of the dancers, he too began to step and twist with the Redshirts. He was marvelously agile. He stooped. He stamped. He tossed his bamboo with the vigor of a frontiersman.

When the audience caught sight of the Rashtrapati's figure among the dancers, their voices swelled with admiration and with glee. Like the Redshirts, Jawaharlal tossed back his head and answered with powerful, lusty cries. On and on his figure raced, at the center of the jubilant performers, one with his admirers. Temporarily he cast aside all vestige of sober office. The new decade was to be hailed with merrymaking. As if the past had held no worry and the future promised no danger, the Rashtrapati leaped and laughed and shouted with his men.

On New Year's Day, 1930, delegates to the annual session of the Indian National Congress assembled again on the banks of the Ravi, this time to recite their pledge of freedom. At a simple ceremony, the young president of the Congress Party, Jawaharlal Nehru, read out the oath and the membership repeated:

> *We believe that it is the inalienable right of the Indian people, as of any other people, to have freedom and to en-*

joy the fruits of their toil and have the necessities of life, so that they may have full opportunities of growth. We believe also that if any government deprives a people of these rights and oppresses them the people have a further right to alter it or to abolish it. . . . We believe, therefore, that India must sever the British connection and attain purna swaraj.

We hold it to be a crime against man and God to submit any longer to a rule that has caused . . . disaster to our country. We recognize, however, that the most effective way of gaining our freedom is not through violence. We will therefore prepare ourselves by withdrawing, so far as we can, all voluntary association from the British Government, and will prepare for civil disobedience.

Independence Day was set for January 26. Scores of eager, able men came forward to help, men whose names became famous in the history of the freedom movement: Govind Ballabh Pant, Vallabhbhai Patel, Syed Mahmud, among others, Khan Abdul Gaffar Khan and Rajendra Prasad, to whom Jawaharlal entrusted the job of organizing the widespread celebrations. Congress Party members worked feverishly. Thanks to their efforts and those of their energetic president, the flag was raised in thousands of villages, hundreds where the Congress Party had been hitherto unknown. In the cities there were displays and parades complete with high-stepping musicians in khadi uniforms. The occasion attracted lots of publicity. Millions repeated the pledge. The day was memorable, announcing to the world at large that India had declared herself to be independent of British rule forever.

As soon as they had taken the vow, it was time for Indians who worked for the British government to resign. Jawaharlal and his father, who was well thought of in official circles, called upon civil servants to leave their jobs immediately. They responded in a body, thus severing yet another tie that had bound India to colonial rule. The public took notice. Men, women, and children began daily training for civil disobedience.

The task of highlighting civil disobedience was Gandhiji's. Without fanfare, he announced that on March 12 he would begin to march from his community at Ahmadabad to Dandi, on the shore of the Arabian Sea, a distance of two hundred and forty-one miles, with the avowed purpose of manufacturing salt when he arrived at the ocean's edge. This was his way of protesting the British salt tax, which was levied on all salt marketed in India. The salt tax had been a particularly oppressive form of levy in a hot country where salt was a vital ingredient of the diet. Gandhiji pointed out that salt was a commodity used by everyone, rich or poor; and so the salt tax symbolized the subjection of the entire citizenry to laws passed in London. He couldn't have picked a better way to emphasize the connection between empire and the daily life of the common man!

Before he started for Dandi, Gandhi selected seventy-eight hardy volunteers to accompany him, including Sarojini Naidu, whom he asked to walk beside him; but, as his march progressed, it assumed gigantic proportions; and, moreover, persons who could not join the demonstration found other ways to defy the salt laws. Those who lived on the seacoast began to manufacture and market their own salt, as Gandhiji had said he would do. In the interior of the country, citizens refused to pay the tax when they bought their salt in the marketplace. There were protests, boycotts, and processions. Very soon Gandhi was in a strong enough position to inform the Viceroy that, unless the salt tax were repealed, he and a band of resisters could take over the salt factory

Anand Bhawan (Abode of Joy), the old Nehru family home in Allahabad. It was renamed *Swaraj Bhawan* (Abode of Independence) in 1930, and was presented to Indian National Congress.

The young Nehru at Anand Bhawan.

Nehru in 1907, during student days at Trinity College, Cambridge.

Jawaharlal Nehru with Mahatma Gandhi in Bombay, 1946.

Meeting in 1961 with John F. Kennedy and Lyndon B. Johnson in the United States.

The mature man.

Jawaharlal and his grandchildren,
Rajiv and Sanjiv, in the Prime Min-
ister's garden in Delhi.
Information Service of India

at a place called Dharsana. Civil disobedience had been fully launched.

Retaliation was to be expected. On April 14, 1930, Rashtrapati Jawaharlal Nehru was arrested and sentenced by a British court to six months' imprisonment for breaking the salt laws. Since it was only a matter of time before Gandhiji was also imprisoned, the presidency of the Congress Party then passed back to Motilal Nehru.

With the loyal help of Kamala, who acted as secretary, and with the support of those members of the Working Committee who were free, Motilal undertook the immense job vacated by Jawaharlal; that of coordinating, interpreting, and safeguarding the activities of the Indian National Congress in the face of ever-increasing pressure from His Majesty's Government and troops. His assignment was lightened somewhat by the willing cooperation of the membership of the Congress Party, however. They responded in stirring fashion to every challenge.

Strikes, demonstrations, and marches took place all over the country when the Rashtrapati and Gandhiji were imprisoned. Following the lead given by the Nehru sisters, Gandhiji's wife, and Kamala, the housewives of India undertook to picket shops that were selling English goods. British officials immediately passed ordinances that forbade such picketing, but the ordinances were countered by instructions issued by the Working Committee of the Indian National Congress. Party workers were then arrested and taken to prison in droves. Demonstrators were beaten and fired upon.

It was at this time that the Redshirts made their most impressive stand. Their homeland on the northwest frontier could be reached only by way of the Khyber Pass. That strategic gateway had been a troublesome and contested outpost for centuries. When the British government refused to permit a Congress Party delegation to pass through it, Khan Abdul Gaffar Khan and his men quietly took possession of the pass to insure that it would be kept open. The British were astounded. Still, the Redshirts made it perfectly clear that they were demanding only their rights as citizens and they had no intention of capturing territory. They guarded the pass without weapons but in the inevitable clashes that followed with the British army, over two hundred Redshirts were shot, and others captured.

Khan Abdul Gaffar Khan, "The Frontier Gandhi," as he was called, insisted that the Redshirts were engaged in a battle that would be waged by principle, not guns, and they would prove it. When his men had been tried and sentenced, they walked before the firing squad proudly and with heads up, despite their traditional feelings about authority. Some of them were bound and shot from the mouths of cannons. They displayed courage which military men of any nationality could respect. A point was reached when the soldiers who were ordered to shoot upon the tribesmen would not raise their guns. Orders were repeated, but two platoons of the Indian army refused to comply.

From London and Delhi the situation in India looked serious indeed! The far northwest, where the Pathans were in the majority, had traditionally been the most difficult part of the country to control, and English officers who knew their history were uncomfortably reminded that the Mutiny of 1857 had started with the refusal of a few soldiers to follow command. Furthermore, it looked as if His Majesty's Government was now faced not with a party but with a nation in revolt. The Congress message seemed to be penetrating every nook and cranny of the subcontinent and people were on the move. White homespun caps were appearing everywhere. On the streets of Calcutta coolies were shouting, "Swaraj is on the way!" Sections of the government had been entirely crippled for lack of men. Ordinary day-to-day operations of the country could no longer be depended upon to function.

In order to get at what it took to be the source of the trouble, the British government in India declared the Working Committee of the Indian National Congress to be illegal in June, 1930. The offices of the party were raided and all officeholders who had not been imprisoned previously were arrested, including Motilal Nehru. But then, to everyone's surprise, the wives and daughters of Congressmen stepped into the positions vacated by their husbands and fathers. The work of the party continued and, moreover, civil disobedience spread.

The British Raj was mightily disturbed by this state of affairs. They secured neutral and respected Indians to act as go-betweens and requested a meeting between leaders of the Congress Party and representatives of His Majesty's Government. The immediate purpose of the meeting was to discuss suspension of civil disobedience as a prelude to further negotiations.

Jawaharlal Nehru, Motilal Nehru, and Dr. Syed Mahmud were escorted from jail under guard and taken by special train from Allahabad to Poona in order to join Gandhi and confer with His Majesty's representatives at Yeravada Prison. Their hopes were high; but contrary to what might have been supposed, the British government was not really prepared to make even temporary concessions which were acceptable. The meetings became deadlocked and the Congress leaders had to return to their cells.

The Nehrus and Dr. Mahmud crossed India by special train and under heavy guard. Although they were moved by night and the British authorities had made every effort to keep the journey a secret, enormous crowds assembled along the tracks to cheer the leaders on their way. Their refusal to accept appeasement had only elevated them in the esteem of their countrymen. Much to the dismay of their guardians, what had been devised as a quiet rendezvous turned out to be a rather extravagant and provocative occasion.

Jawaharlal Nehru and his father shared the same cell at Naini Prison. As always when he was in prison, the younger man maintained a strict regime of spinning, exercise, study, and writing. Despite privations, he stood up under the schedule very well; but the strenuous activity of the last few months, the bewildering responsibility, and anxiety were beginning to tell on Motilal. The father was determined to last out the struggle if he possibly could; but after his return from Poona, he became gravely ill. He pleaded with the authorities not to release him, as disagreeable and unhealthful as his surroundings might be. Yet, with public opinion as volatile as it was, the government well knew that it could not risk the possible consequences of having him die in jail; so they placed him in the care of a physician who took him to Mussoorie in the hills.

Jawaharlal's prison sentence expired on October 11, and he was discharged; although no one expected him to be out for long. The police dogged his footsteps. He traveled up to Mussoorie to have three days with his father and family. Then he returned to Allahabad and threw himself into the unfinished work of the Rashtrapati.

The moment had come, Jawaharlal had decided, for the peasants to refuse to pay their taxes. If they did this, it would deprive the British government of yet another major source of income from India and focus attention upon the villages. He hoped that such a protest would involve farmers from all over the country eventually, so it was essential that the action be well understood from the outset. He made arrangements for a conference of rural people to be convened in Allahabad immediately.

Jawaharlal addressed the conference, explaining to the peasants the reasons behind the "no-tax campaign" and its relation to swaraj. As he stepped down from the platform, the police van was waiting. He was arrested after exactly eight days of freedom and taken back to his old cell. It was the fifth time that he had been locked up and the sentence allotted to him this time was two and one-half years of rigorous imprisonment.

The peasants went home from the Allahabad conference with a fiery determination fanned by the loss of Jawaharlal. Since news was heavily controlled, they publicized the no-tax campaign by word of mouth and major events were proclaimed by beat of drum. Such crude methods of communication turned out to be effective, however, and resistance, which had been largely confined to the cities up to that time, began to spread noticeably among the countryfolk. With the help of the peasantry, Motilal Nehru organized nationwide celebrations on the occasion of Jawaharlal's forty-first birthday, even though he himself was too weak to leave his room.

Repression tightened upon the Indian subcontinent. Youth groups and local committees of the Congress Party were declared to be illegal and the attention of the government turned to the activities of women. In the Nehru family, Nan was with her children in Mussoorie. Krishna, who had already had a taste of prison life, was quietly nursing her ailing father and her mother. However, Kamala was free and active in politics. Consequently, it was she who was arrested and put in jail.

Jawaharlal read the news of his wife's arrest from a

newspaper that was brought to his cell, and he couldn't help but feel immensely proud. But circumstances were different for his father. Motilal was dying and knew it. The tactics of His Majesty's Government were becoming more ruthless. One by one he had seen his precious children snatched away. "Not Kamala," he cried this time. "They mustn't take Kamala. Prison will kill her."

Characteristically, Kamala Nehru accepted her prison sentence quietly, feeling that nothing else could prove so well to her country and to her husband the depth of her commitment to independence. During the months immediately preceding her arrest, she had helped to move the family into smaller quarters and to convert the old house, now called Swaraj Bhawan, into a hospital for civil resisters. Without previous training for such work, she had handled much of the correspondence for Congress Party headquarters. In defiance of Indian custom, she had organized women's groups and addressed them, urging them to take their full part in the freedom struggle. If prison were the consequence of such activity, she would take her punishment gladly. Before entering her cell, she made a statement to this effect, which considerably lifted the spirits of her fellow countrywomen and Satryagrahis.

Kamala was arrested on January 1, 1931. During Jawaharlal's year as Rashtrapati of the Indian National Congress the freedom struggle had been fully initiated. During those turbulent months the Congress Party had grown in numbers and deepened in its resolve. Its membership had widened so it could be said to include not only representatives of all major religious and social groups, but farmers and city dwellers, women as well as men. It had demonstrated to His Majesty's Government that what had started as a discussion group was in fact a national movement, dedicated to freedom. It commanded powerful forces. Moreover, citizens had become so devoted to its leaders that any government that mishandled those men would be faced with rebellion forthwith, and no major change in Indian policy could ever again be taken without first consulting India's own representatives.

National feeling, both in India and in England, urged that there be a respite in the struggle. The Viceroy expressed his willingness to negotiate. Kamala Nehru, who had been held almost as a hostage, was freed. On January 26, 1931, the first anniversary of Independence Day, Jawaharlal Nehru and Mohandas Gandhi were also released from prison, as were other members of the original Working Committee of the Indian National Congress. It was apparent that Great Britain expected these people to get together and to propose some form of settlement.

The Working Committee meetings of the party were held in Allahabad, in the new and more modest Anand Bhawan, to which the Nehrus had moved. Although somewhat fatigued by the vigorous campaigns of the last year, the men who attended the meetings were optimistic. In fact, they were anxious to discuss interim terms with Great Britain. The atmosphere of their deliberations was hopeful, even though overlaid with personal apprehension because of Motilal Nehru's long illness and weakened condition.

Refusing to give in, the sturdy old man had himself propped up in a chair so that he could receive the many visitors who came to see him. But he took no part in the deliberations of the Working Committee. His illness had so affected his throat that he could not speak. Occasionally he wrote messages, giving his opinion on the affairs at the moment, but most of the time he was silent, looking very much like an old and venerable monument set in the midst of a busy intersection.

One evening while Jawaharlal and Gandhi were beside him, Motilal Nehru scratched a final note and handed it to the older man. "I am going soon, Mahatmaji," it said, "and I shall not be here to see swaraj. But I know you have won it and will soon have it." These were his last words for the freedom movement. All his love and hope for India he bequeathed to the two, his beloved Jawahar and Gandhiji, who were left to carry on. He died on February 6, 1931.

If only the members of England's Parliament had been as eager for a settlement as were some of their representatives in India. Negotiations between British and Indian representatives dragged on interminably, first in India and later on in England. Meanwhile, the British government on the subcontinent had to crack down upon an aroused and restless population.

Ordinances were again passed outlawing Congress Party meetings at every level. Police raids were frequent and came without warning. Further ordinances put an end to peasant associations, to many types of local industry, to any circulation of news regarding political activities, to the movement of people from province to province, to certain schools, universities, hospitals, and even libraries. As Sir Samuel Hoare, Secretary of State for India, stated in the House of Commons: "I admit that the ordinances that we have approved are very drastic and severe. They cover almost every activity in Indian life."

A state of outright siege now existed between England and India. It was forbidden to fly the Indian flag. Civil disobedience had to be renewed. Mohandas Gandhi and Vallabhbhai Patel, who was the incoming president of the Indian National Congress, were held as state prisoners, without benefit of trial. Jawaharlal Nehru was again imprisoned. The length to which the army and the police were willing to go to keep order was evidenced by the fact that Jawaharlal's mother, Swarup Rani Nehru, was beaten in Allahabad during observances of National Week.

In retrospect, it appears that the winning of Indian freedom was a slow process and a heartless one; but, at the time, events moved with lightning speed and the British governors in India, who stood between the two opponents, were constantly faced with emergency situations. So new were the means that civil disobedience employed, so restricted was the news, so long were the delays involved in dealing with the British Parliament in London, and so wrapped up in his own activities was every individual who was on the spot in India, that people lived with heightened awareness of effort, with an increased perception of their ultimate importance and responsibilities. No wonder their behavior was excessive at times.

Jawaharlal Nehru moved like a whirlwind, whether he was in prison or out. During the days when he was free, he attended to the disposition of Motilal's estate, arranged urgent medical care for Kamala and for his mother, and presided at Krishna's wedding to Raja Hutheesing. While in jail, he wrote ceaselessly, both personal letters and articles. His first book, entitled *Glimpses of World History*, had been started in 1930. He had intended it as a series of letters to Indira, which could supplement her studies while he was away and her schooling was interrupted; but the letters were so delightful that it would have been a shame if other children couldn't have read them too. Jawaharlal's friends encouraged him to have the correspondence printed and put together as a history book that could be used the world around.

Jawaharlal Nehru had a talent for writing; and, under different circumstances, he might even have become an author. When he was not in office, he was still regarded as "the idea man" behind the freedom movement. He expressed his concerns so fully and he could so easily describe the ends he had in view that everyone always felt he knew exactly where the leader stood and, consequently, what the party was going to do. For the annual meeting of the Indian National Congress which was held in Karachi in 1931, Jawaharlal drafted a resolution on fundamental human rights which became a cornerstone of the modern, democratic state that was later built. He was so eloquent, and was so gifted in expressing ideas in human terms that he began to win acclaim from statesmen on either side of the political barrier. His Indian colleagues referred to him fondly as *Panditji,* which means "wise man whom we love."

It was remarkable that in the midst of such a life as Jawaharlal Nehru lived during the 1930's there should have been any time for laughter. Still, he garnered some of his happiest memories from that period. The sound of children's voices, the smell of flowers, the tenderness of life at home, and, especially, the companionship of his wife brought him added pleasure when he could enjoy them so seldom. During his three-day visit to Mussoorie in 1930, he romped and played with Nan's little girls as if he had not a care in the world. He took Kamala with him to Ceylon for ten days in 1931, where they mingled speechmaking, writing, and interviewing with holiday fun.

The eminent position Jawaharlal had attained easily became the butt of good-natured teasing. "Would *The Jewel of India* like to have a cup of tea?" his sisters would inquire jokingly, mocking a name he had been called in public; or they would announce, *"O Embodiment of Sacrifice,* you have a caller." These touches of affectionate humor helped to keep more serious matters in proportion. To soften the blow of parting, the family chose to celebrate the days when one or more of them should go to jail. The children strung garlands of flowers for the prisoners and everyone held his tears in check with gaiety.

But, it was hard to keep faith with one's friends and to believe in the eventual triumph of the freedom movement while India was exposed to the grinding hardships she was undergoing. In the early 1930's it became virtually impossible for the leaders of the Congress Party to keep in touch with one another. After the newest restraining ordinances were passed, Congress officers could have very little contact with the masses; and, as a consequence, civil disobedience could not be revitalized. Likewise, there was practically no opportunity for colleagues to witness, to praise, confirm, or even acknowledge the brave and selfless behavior of such men as Khan Abdul Gaffar Khan on the frontier, or to be informed of the daily personal testimony made by the populace on behalf of swaraj.

Years now gaped between one meeting of the Indian National Congress and the next. It could hardly be helped if the thinking of leading Congress Party members began to drift into widely divergent channels. Jawaharlal and Gandhiji had always written to one another frequently and in that way had striven to narrow the gulf that separated their thinking on certain vital issues. Still, when life was so circumscribed, it was hard for even these two who believed so resolutely in one another to keep in touch. It was hard, terribly hard!

7 alone

Sunlight glanced from the rooftops of the crowded city of Calcutta. Heat shimmered above the wide waters of the Hooghly River. Sweat dripped from the naked backs of the rickshaw pullers who plied their carts through narrow lanes. The sun's hot rays crept across the walls of gracious mansions and makeshift hovels. Dry winds swished through the bazaars, the offices, mills, and schools. Gradually, the streets emptied. Almost the only sounds were made by the water carriers as they ran back and forth, their wet feet slapping upon the pavement. Like a city under attack, the sprawling metropolis drew its shades and closed its shutters against the afternoon heat of May.

Jawaharlal Nehru mopped his brow. Hoping for some relief from the oppressive heat, he went to the door of his prison hut and stepped onto the narrow veranda. The tiny square of concrete before him was barren. Sunlight reflected

164

from the whitewashed walls of his dwelling. Smoke poured into his courtyard, bringing with it the unwelcome smell of soot and hot cooking fat. The prisoner frowned and looked at his watch. He could see that it would be several hours before the warder's key again turned in the lock of his gate or evening marked the end of another day spent in jail. He went back inside the cell and sat down on the wooden bed.

To a small area of pavement, cell, and wall, Jawaharlal was again confined. This was his seventh term of imprisonment and his sentence was for two years. Close to fourteen hundred days of his life had been spent in jail. By contrast, his hours of freedom seemed to have been infrequent and to have had an unreal quality. The only persons he now saw were his jailers and, occasionally, Kamala. His letters were opened. The news that he read was censored. His ties to the outside world were fragile.

Jawaharlal was proud that he had survived most of his jail sentences with good spirits. In its way, life behind bars had become familiar to him, rhythmic and tolerable. During his prison years he had experienced periods of satisfaction and delight, although he had never considered imprisonment as an end in itself. It was worthwhile only if it served some elevating purpose. The issues for which one went to prison were what made life bearable, he said, and it was by their connection with larger events that otherwise dreary days of solitude had been made radiant for him.

All of the many years he had been forced to spend in jail had not been spent alone and in isolation either. At times he had been imprisoned with his friends. The close confinement of prison quarters put a great strain on friendship, but it also provided new and gratifying ways to show one's regard for his fellow men. Jawaharlal was glad that he had had his father for a companion in Naini just before Mo-

tilal had died. He had nursed the old patriot constantly, as
he could never have done if they had been at home in
Anand Bhawan, and the memory of that intimate association was a comfort. He had taken care of other companions
as well, when they had fallen ill in jail. Nursing them had
given him an opportunity to feel he was useful to someone,
if only in a small way, and Jawaharlal sometimes wondered
whether it was he or a sick comrade who had derived the
most benefit from his attentions.

He had discovered another activity for himself in jail
too, something for which he would not have been able to
find time at home. During the long, unbroken winter nights
that he was forced to spend alone, he had learned the names
of the stars and their positions. Wherever he was detained,
and however lonely were his days, as soon as night fell, he
could stretch out on his back and wait for the constellations
to appear. They were like friends who visited him regularly
without having to wait for permission.

Despite his occupations, however, Jawaharlal was aware
that by and large he had been able to endure the privations
and indignities of prison life for as long as he had because of
the realization that the country was moving forward toward
true independence. "But today," he asked himself seriously
on that hot May afternoon, "who would dare to prophesy
when or if India will ever be victorious?" The old rallying
cries had a hollow ring.

Success should have come when India's citizens had
been united and optimistic, Jawaharlal reasoned. Then they
would have taken up the challenge of establishing democracy and developing industrially along with the rest of the
world. But since 1929, when the prestige of the Congress
Party had seemed to be at its peak and citizens had flocked

to join the freedom movement, the country had been severely tested. Civil disobedience had been countered by unbelievable repression. As a result, the party looked as if it had disintegrated. Its best men had been threatened, deprived of their livelihoods, or imprisoned. The freedom movement had slowed almost to a standstill.

Reluctantly, Jawaharlal thought of England and the men and women he knew there. He still maintained that the cruel policies that were being employed in India were unworthy of so tolerant a people, regardless of the party they had in power at Westminster. The inhumanity of such practices was indefensible, coming from as civilized a nation as Great Britain. The tragic waste which resulted from such tactics infuriated him.

Jawaharlal reacted so strongly in this matter that he had been unable to contain himself at his last trial. "Individuals sometimes misbehave," he had said to the court. "Officials also misbehave; crowds and mobs get excited and misbehave; all that is very regrettable. But it is a terrible thing," he had emphasized, his sentiment ill concealed by outward calm, "when brutality becomes a method of behavior." He should have known that he would not be permitted to finish that speech, he now told himself sternly. The only door left open for him, or for anyone else who was outspoken about present conditions in India, was the one that led to jail.

During his imprisonment in Alipore Jail, Calcutta, in the early summer of 1934, Jawaharlal Nehru was as disheartened and as discouraged as he could ever remember having been. He felt the confinement of his meager quarters acutely. His tiny hut became wretchedly hot at midday, and the odor that came to it from the jail kitchens was sickening. Although he had maintained his physical well-being during former periods of imprisonment, he had no appetite for food this time and he was losing weight rapidly. By the end of each day he was feverish.

The knowledge that he was not as strong as he had once been bothered Jawaharlal; but he also knew that the underlying reason for his condition was not a personal one, nor was it entirely a consequence of where he was housed or the excessive policies that were being employed by the government of Great Britain. The basic cause of his depression was a threat to swaraj that had arisen from the independence movement itself and through the utterances of no less a person than Gandhiji.

Beside Jawaharlal Nehru's bed there stood a rough table on which he had arranged the few possessions he had been allowed to bring to jail: his toilet articles, pen and ink, paper, one or two photographs, and some books. Spread over the top of these was a well-worn copy of a newspaper called *The Statesman*. The paper came to him a week late and the news that had moved him so profoundly was over a month old. The item that had attracted his attention was a short one, so brief that he had long since committed it to memory. Yet, it was so astonishing to him and so disturbing that he read it again and again, turning its implications over and over and over in his mind.

Acting on his own initiative, Gandhiji had decided to terminate all forms of civil disobedience. He had announced this fact in a communiqué issued from the religious community where he lived. He said he had received a letter from a fellow member of the Congress Party who had confessed that he would prefer to remain at his desk and continue his studies rather than go to jail. Gandhiji had replied resolutely that he saw no reason for keeping up resistance if his soldiers were so faltering and swaraj could not command their steadfast allegiance. Therefore, in his capacity as the acknowledged head of civil disobedience, he had called a halt to all forms of protest for the time being.

Even after prolonged acquaintance with the article, re-reading it bothered Jawaharlal. Confronted by his friend's decision, he felt disappointed, worried, and, at the moment, utterly powerless. Gandhiji's action had been taken when the day of victory seemed very far away indeed; but, to with-draw civil disobedience was the same as admitting defeat, he reasoned.

Did Gandhiji, or any other leader of the Congress Party, have the right to take upon himself the responsibility for sur-rendering? he asked. What other meaning could His Majes-ty's Government have possibly read into the statement and what indications beyond that did it have for Indians who, like himself, were undergoing sentences because of the parts they had played in the freedom movement? Perhaps some of them had lost hope of ever seeing swaraj, but everyone had not. What would happen to those brave souls who were waiting for the time when they would march ahead together once again? Wouldn't they feel betrayed by Gandhiji's deci-sion, Jawaharlal wondered, the same as he felt betrayed?

This was not the first time, however, that he had been upset by an action of Gandhiji's. No one with as vigorous opinions as Jawaharlal Nehru could always have found it easy to agree with the older man's convictions any more than Motilal had been able to give his immediate support to the radical program Gandhi had announced in 1920. Gandhiji's ideas were so novel that it took a while for even his closest friends to get used to them.

In regard to the manner in which he presented his ideas, Gandhiji also had a way of shocking people with state-ments that came unexpectedly, just as this latest one had

come, and sounded dogmatic. He had made such pronouncements on other subjects from time to time, without taking
into his confidence any of his comrades. That type of behavior had alienated him from Jawaharlal for brief periods, and
from other members of the Congress Party. When their
anger had cooled, however, they had accepted Gandhiji's
point of view because what he had advocated had always
seemed to be right for India fundamentally, and for the
achievement of independence. In fact, the younger man had
never been conscious of being as completely out of agreement with any other position which Gandhiji had taken or
as disturbed by the logic with which he had tried to support
a position as this time.

In the early days of the national movement, Jawaharlal
was convinced that the vigor of the Indian National Congress had depended almost entirely upon Gandhiji's inspiration. That selfless little man had infused people with courage and Congress Party members had willingly and enthusiastically followed his lead. Gandhiji and the party had
shared one objective, and the techniques of nonviolence,
upon which the Mahatma had insisted, had brought results.

In order to use his methods most effectively, Gandhiji's
example had been essential to the nation. Furthermore, Jawaharlal admitted fondly, no one else in the party had first
understood the toiling masses of India as well as Gandhiji
had nor had anyone else ever had as much compassion for
them. The Mahatma had been one with the poor and the
oppressed from the outset. He had sensed their innermost
strivings and he had served them commendably. But, Gandhiji's recent talks and, more so, his actions, had seemed to
Jawaharlal to be somewhat removed from the political reali-
ties that confronted India. Gandhiji's unique way of operat-

ing was hard to incorporate into a national party, and he did seem inflexible at times.

Gandhiji had based his decision to terminate civil disobedience upon his disappointment in a single follower. Is swaraj to be set aside because of one man? Jawaharlal pondered. It might be a good thing to withdraw civil disobedience *temporarily,* he agreed. India, including the peasants, and especially the members of the Congress Party were tired of harassment and insecurity. They needed a recess. They ought to have time to refresh themselves, to take stock of where they stood, and to reassemble their forces. If that were what Gandhiji had been aiming at, everyone would have understood his action, but he should have said so, Jawaharlal insisted.

In the long run, he questioned, could the Indian National Congress or the people it represented get anywhere at all in their efforts if, as Gandhiji now maintained, every individual who took up the cause had to renounce everything else? Of course not, he answered. Looked at from that point of view, Gandhiji's dogma would never enable them to achieve the goal they had set.

And what is the goal we hope to achieve? Jawaharlal considered, as he sat alone in his quiet cell. Independence first, but then a state that will guarantee a better life for *all* its citizens. Gandhiji had one method of combating social inequality, Jawaharlal reflected, but it was not the only way he, Jawaharlal Nehru, expected a new government to advocate. In addition to dedicated public servants, there must also be a constitution that would outlaw such practices as untouchability. There must be laws to assure human rights, and provisions for education that would increase men's understanding of one another. Education, of course, required the independent pursuit of knowledge by just such scholars as the one Gandhiji had criticized and because of whom he had withdrawn civil disobedience.

No matter how he approached social problems, though, that bespectacled, tireless man was a genius in his way, Jawaharlal admitted. Who else but Gandhiji would have thought of the salt tax as the focal point for mobilizing the country for resistance to colonial rule? Yet, *salt* had become a magic word when uttered by Gandhiji and around it he had rallied the entire population of India. His actions certainly produced results, too. When he had vowed to fast unto death for the cause of the Untouchables,* the rest of the Hindus had taken note of their grievances immediately.

And no one, not even Jawaharlal Nehru, could ever think of Gandhiji for long without smiling, the prisoner mused. The Mahatma's simple habits, his absolute sincerity, and his sense of humor disarmed both friends and enemies in time. He was scrupulously fair in his dealings with other people. If he, Jawaharlal, were to write to him and spell out his misgivings about the article that had appeared in *The Statesman*, he had no doubt but that Gandhiji would suggest that they go over his objections point by point in letters that they could publish, if necessary, and thus give people the benefit of both arguments when making up their own minds on the question.

Jawaharlal chuckled. Perhaps Gandhiji appeared to be rather otherworldly at times and hard to control as a member of a political party; but, if he were a tyrant, he was cer-

---

* The British government had offered to give Untouchables separate representation in limited elections. This looked like a triumph to many Indians; but Gandhi had felt so deeply that Untouchables should not be treated *separately* that he had vowed to "fast unto death" if the proposals were accepted.

tainly a lovable one. Other men talked about saintly lives, but Gandhiji actually tried to live one.

Returning to the larger problem of religion and its place in the India that was emerging, Jawaharlal questioned whether anyone should strive to build a nation entirely on a religious basis. He was sure that Gandhiji would agree with him that such a course would be undesirable if the state were to represent only one sect. Jawaharlal had listened to members of the Muslim League when they expounded the point of view that they needed a separate state for members of their religion, and he had to admit he didn't like the idea. In the end, it seemed to him that a state that rested on the beliefs of just one group would be narrow and restrictive, no matter how broad and tolerant it appeared to be in the beginning. People in such a state would tend to look inward, he thought, and to take care of members of their own faith, while, actually, events demanded that they look outward and consider men of all faiths.

Jawaharlal did not know what place India would occupy among the nations of the world once it had achieved independence, but he was sure of one thing. Free India would stand for the broadest kind of internationalism. He glanced through the pages of a second newspaper he had permission to receive from Europe. In that paper there were stories of unrest in France, of workers' riots, and of the formation of an antidemocratic government. A man named Hitler was upsetting Germany. Liberals and conservatives were in conflict in Spain. The world seemed to be moving toward a confrontation, perhaps a showdown, between the forces of democracy and reaction. When it came to a showdown, India had a vital role to play in world affairs, Jawaharlal was convinced. Yet, there was not one word about India in the newspaper. In order to assert its place, India had to rise and make itself heard in the councils of nations. Its freedom movement must not be stifled. The country somehow had to reach beyond its own frontiers and cease its preoccupation with internal matters.

The prisoner got up from his bed and stretched. He walked a few steps to the end of his room, then turned at the wall and walked back. Those were idealistic phrases he had voiced to himself, but they had the power to raise his flagging spirits somewhat and to make him feel related, if only in a limited way, to the rest of humanity.

Jawaharlal paused by the table and there his eyes fell upon the European news once again. His energy was so depleted that his shoulders drooped momentarily. "Who am I to consider the freedom of man?" he asked himself with a sigh. He looked about his minute cell. "For the time being, I am little better than a caged animal," he said. "By day I have only myself to talk to, and at night, the stars."

The strength he had received from thinking about India's place in the world did not leave him entirely, however. The prisoner stepped through the door of his hut and onto the patch of concrete. Above his prison walls he could see the tops of two flame-of-the-forest trees that stood in someone's garden nearby and they were in full and gorgeous bloom. While his eyes drank in the bouquet, a flock of green-gold parakeets fluttered from the foliage, their iridescent wings in vivid contrast to the crimson blossoms. The sight diverted Jawaharlal Nehru's attention from his own situation momentarily and helped to calm his troubled spirit. He stood and watched the parakeets until they had risen high over the treetops and were lost from sight above the city.

When the birds disappeared from his view, Jawaharlal

looked at his wristwatch once again. It was the time of day
when Gandhiji would be at prayer, he reflected. In his
mind's eye he could see the older man sitting cross-legged on
his mat, his eyes closed, deep in meditation. It had been a
long time since he had seen Gandhiji. How he would love to
have a few minutes' talk with him! Since he could not see
him, however, he must write. He had delayed the letter long
enough. He would get down to the task, he resolved, and if
he forced himself to put his thoughts on paper, he might feel
better.

Jawaharlal went inside and sat down at the table. He
got out his pen and began to compose his letter to Gandhiji.
"Dear Gandhiji," he wrote. "I accept the withdrawal of civil
disobedience, but the reasons which you gave for withdrawal
appear to me to be wrong. You have also made me question
the nature of our struggle and my place in it."

The prisoner had been right in thinking that his mind
would become clearer as he wrote. He reread the lines he
had set down and then found it easier to continue. "I am a
revolutionary, Gandhiji," he explained. "I work for far-
reaching changes, politically and socially, because I am convinced that no other changes can bring peace and satisfaction to our country and to the world. If the flag of India
is hauled down, or even trod upon, I will raise it again, if it
is humanly possible. And if the ideals which inspire our national struggle are right, they will triumph, whether you or I
live to witness their success."

The prisoner felt suddenly tired. He had intended to
say more, but he put his pen in its case. He was worn out
from the burden of isolation, and his body was limp. He
folded his arms on the makeshift desk and lay down his
head. Solitude and exhaustion threatened to engulf him.

Jawaharlal Nehru stiffened, as if with contempt at his

own weakness. Had he not learned, he asked himself sternly, that there were no resting places on the path he had chosen, and that success, when it came, would place even heavier burdens upon him? Besides, he was not alone. Gandhiji would never desert the cause of freedom, whether or not he continued to work within a political party. He raised his head and again took his pen from its case. His eye fell upon a faded picture of Kamala that lay on his desk. He picked it up. A smile flickered across his features. "There is also Kamala," he said to himself. "No matter what happens, we have one another."

At that moment a clashing and banging of pans started in the kitchens on the other side of his wall. Preparations for the evening meal must be in full swing, Jawaharlal surmised. "And there are also the warders," he acknowledged. "Not all of my jail keepers have been coarse and hardened men. Prison life reveals many inconsistencies in human behavior. There are many who would wish to treat me humanely and yet they are forced by circumstance to consider me an enemy."

The lowering sun now cast its long rays through the doorway. In the distance, his ear discerned a noisy crowd of workmen on their way home from the jute mills on the waterfront. *"Jawaharlal ki jai,"* they shouted as they passed the main gate of the prison. *"Bharat ki jai!* Victory to India!" They did this every night, perhaps to nettle the guards or maybe just to let their Jawaharlal know that he was not forgotten. In any event, he was grateful for the sound of their voices. They couldn't have guessed how much that meant to him in his confinement.

"There are also the people," he told himself. "They are waiting too, just as they have waited for centuries, patiently; some far more patiently than I."

With those words the prisoner tossed up his head defiantly. He could feel his confidence coming back. Enough time had been spent in despair. It was time he got on with what he had to say to Gandhiji.

In August, 1934, Jawaharlal Nehru was released from prison for a few days and then was able to mail his letter to Gandhiji. In that letter he had told Gandhiji honestly of the effect that the withdrawal of civil disobedience had had upon him and he had stated his own position in open and forceful terms. This was a long letter and an explicit one. Jawaharlal left no doubt in Gandhiji's mind as to how he felt or where he stood. "Perhaps some parts of this might pain you," he had written affectionately. "But you would not have me hide my heart from you."

Gandhiji's reply was equally forthright. At points the older man frankly criticized the youthful leader for certain aspects of his behavior, especially for always being in a hurry. "I cannot march quite as quick," Gandhiji said. Nevertheless, he would not allow a feeling of competition or estrangement to arise between himself and Jawaharlal. "After the explosion I want construction," he wrote. "Therefore, now, lest we do not meet, tell me exactly what you will have me do."

It was too bad that Jawaharlal was returned to jail almost immediately, so there was no opportunity for the two friends to speak to one another at that time. Within a month, Gandhiji had made another decision and had resigned from the Congress Party. He had realized that, admirable as its members were, his ways of working no longer meshed with those of the politicians, and he had come to the conclusion that his presence in the party was holding back progress. He was convinced, as he had said in 1929, that leadership should pass to younger men; and his resignation was a dramatic way of pointing this out.

In explaining his decision to his closest associates, Gandhiji declared again: "Jawaharlal is bound to be the rightful helmsman of the organization in the near future." "He is one who is much more than a comrade and a person whom no amount of political differences will ever separate from me," he said, as if speaking of a favored member of his family. Realizing the dreadful uncertainty that pervaded the country at the time, he insisted that people put their trust in Jawaharlal. "He is courage personified," he assured them.

Jawaharlal Nehru had need of courage, not only for the course he had set for India but for himself and his loved ones. In August, 1934, he was transferred to the jail in Allahabad because Kamala had been taken seriously ill and it was thought she might not recover. The government promised to release him completely if he would agree to refrain from political activity, but Kamala wouldn't hear of his doing that. Her condition improved slightly and she was moved to a sanatorium in the mountains. Jawaharlal was held in a prison nearby so that he could see her for an hour every few weeks. However, in May of the following year she had to be placed in a hospital in Switzerland. By then her body was so ravaged by tuberculosis that doctors had very little hope for her.

Jawaharlal was kept under armed guard in solitary quarters and was permitted to receive only occasional letters. These were trying months for him. Kindhearted persons, both in England and in India, pleaded with His Majesty's Government for the prisoner's release. New and powerful changes were in the making for India, they pointed out, and Jawaharlal Nehru was destined to play an important part in what was coming. His prolonged imprisonment at the time of his wife's illness seemed especially cruel and unnecessary. Worldwide sympathy had been expressed for him.

On September 5, 1935, His Majesty's Government relented. Jawaharlal Nehru was let go. He went immediately to Switzerland, where Indira joined him at her mother's bedside.

Suddenly Jawaharlal found himself in a strange world to which he could not readily adjust. Instead of the grim routine of prison life, he was free to go and come as he wished, to eat good food, and to sleep in a soft bed. There were books and flowers and people to talk to. He was far from the tempests of India and surrounded by the snowy, quiet Alps. He was treated as a prominent figure and his views were sought on many subjects. Letters and messages of sympathy poured in for him from virtually every nation. Yet, Kamala, upon whom he had relied so heavily for love and support when the going was hard, was about to leave him forever.

During the hot, worrisome days he had spent in jail in Calcutta, Jawaharlal Nehru had started to write his autobiography. He had thought that the activity might help him to look with perspective upon what was taking place in India, as well as elsewhere. He wanted to call it *Toward Freedom*. While he sat by Kamala's bedside in the fall of 1935, Jawaharlal read parts of his book to her and wrote the last lines on his manuscript. "I have a feeling that a chapter of my life is over," he said, "and another chapter will begin."

This was a true insight, for within a few months he was returning to India, having been notified that he had again been elected president of the Indian National Congress and would be allowed to convene an annual session, the first in several years. The tide of opposition to independence seemed to be turning in England. He would be greeted by colleagues who were renewed with hope. But he carried back with him a vase of ashes, which was all he had left of Kamala. She will never see the rest, he thought to himself sadly, nor will we write any more together in the book of life. Indira was enrolled in school in Europe. His sisters were married. Swarup Rani had become old and feeble. Anand Bhawan was going to be quiet.

The Rashtrapati arrived in India to preside at meetings of the Indian National Congress which were held in Lucknow in April, 1936. After eight years of preparation, which had started with the work of the Simon Commission, His Majesty's Government had passed "The Government of India Act," which allowed Indians to stand for election in the provinces. That kind of provincial representation was a long way from purna swaraj, but it did provide chances for rebuilding the Congress Party, for contact between party members and the people, and for showing Great Britain what Indians could do if they were given a chance to govern themselves. These were opportunities not to be missed. Jawaharlal Nehru and the Congress Party welcomed Britain's offer wholeheartedly.

During 1936–1937, the election year, Jawaharlal presented his program and the Congress Party candidates to the Indian people. To help win that election, he covered fifty thousand miles in less than five months. He traveled by plane, by car, by train, on horseback, by camel and elephant, with a bicycle, by river steamer and country boat, and on foot. He worked from twelve to eighteen hours a day, conferring, speaking, writing, and interviewing. He spoke to over ten million persons, addressing meetings of as many as ten or twenty thousand people at a time, often under unusual conditions, in fields and on noisy street corners, without benefit of microphones and loudspeakers. Colleagues marveled at his vigor, his fortitude, and his good spirits. Within a very brief time and almost single-handedly, it was "Panditji" who had reunited the tired country behind the national movement, the Congress Party, and its candidates.

Exactly as Gandhiji had predicted, Jawaharlal spoke directly to the conditions of those he met. He talked with poor farmers about the very things that were on their minds; redistribution of land, excessive taxes, crops, health, and schools. He assured workers that industry would expand if the Congress Party should ever come to power. Jobs would be created and better wages paid. The man's stance, which, despite hardship, was so vigorous, his eloquence, his ready smile, and his sympathy lifted people out of their daily circumstances, dignified them, and restored their confidence in their own worth. What he said, combined with the way he said it, produced an amazing transformation in his listeners.

And, just as his appearance strengthened others, Jawaharlal himself was buoyed by contact with the common folk of India. His journeys took him over large areas where he had never been before and brought him face to face with millions. The villages had much the same effect on him that they had had in 1920. He found that villagers still regarded themselves as the inheritors and transmitters of a great and noble past. The masses were eager to win and use their freedom. Democracy was on the move.

As long as he lived, Jawaharlal Nehru referred to that set of tours as his "Discovery of India." He wrote a book, inspired by his travels, to which he gave the title *Discovery of India*. It was a magnificent experience he had, the memory of which he always cherished. "I came back weary and like a tired child," he said honestly, "yearning for solace. That solace came to me in overflowing measure; thousands of hands were stretched out to me in love and sympathy; millions of silent voices carried their message of affection to my heart."

Through the gaunt years of suffering, young Nehru had become a remote and lonely figure in the eyes of his country-men. When they saw him after Kamala's death, they opened their hearts to him as they had done to no other leader. If they thought of Mohandas Gandhi as their father, Jawaharlal Nehru was their son. In return for almost superhuman and solitary efforts, he had earned the generous, undying love of India's millions. They showered him with affection and with pride. "How can I thank you men and women of India?" he asked, when the campaign was over. "How can I express in words feelings that are too deep for utterance?"

The results of the election were significant. Out of the eleven provinces in British India, the Indian National Congress won a clear majority in five and it secured a substantial vote in three others. By contrast, the Muslim League, the second-largest party, received only five percent of all the votes cast. After conferences with Great Britain, Congress Party governments were formed in eight provinces. Men who had waited a long time for a chance to govern now took the reins of power: Govind Ballabh Pant, Vallabhbhai Patel, Rajendra Prasad, and scores of other outstanding Congressmen. Nan Nehru, who was better known by her married name, Vijaya Lakshmi Pandit, became the first woman to hold the position of Minister in the history of India. She was to serve as Minister of Health in the United Provinces.

Members of the Congress Party were prepared to govern well, but their victory and its aftermath revealed unfinished tasks with which neither their president nor themselves had been concerned sufficiently. The first of these was brought out as soon as the votes were counted, in the flush of triumph. Looking at the tally, the Rashtrapati remarked, "It is clear that there are only two forces in India today, British imperialism and Indian nationalism as represented by the Congress." Smarting under defeat, the leader of the Muslim League, Mohammed Ali Jinnah replied, "No, there is a third party, the Muslims."

In order to appreciate the full import of what Jinnah meant, it is necessary to glance back at history. The vast majority of Muslims had come to the Indian subcontinent as conquerors at the end of the twelfth century, entering by way of the northwest, battling their way to Delhi, increasing their prestige over the years, acquiring lands and converts in Bengal to the east, and pushing to Hyderabad in the south. At its heights under Akbar, the Mogul Empire had been hailed for its splendor; yet it had won only the docile consent of its Hindu subjects. The populace was subdued but chafed under authority.

In the nineteenth century when an English queen, Victoria, became the acknowledged ruler of India, prestige returned to the Hindus. After the Mutiny of 1857, the last vestiges of Mogul power were stripped away. Whether or not the uprising had been a bid to reestablish their weakened empire, when it was over Muslims were deprived of opportunity and Hindus were encouraged through education, favor, and position. The pride of the descendants of former conquerors was trampled. They were made to feel despised.

Meanwhile, as the freedom movement emerged, apart from all considerations of democracy and welfare for the peasants, it had one clear and overriding aim, that of swaraj; and, however swaraj was interpreted, it required, first of all, that Indians win their freedom. Great Britain, with whatever good intentions, tried first to prevent and then to delay having that happen. However often such men as Jawaharlal

Nehru and certain English statesmen tried to emphasize the final goals of their enterprise (and they succeeded to an amazing degree in keeping those goals uppermost in people's thinking), the two nations were in conflict. It is to the credit of both sides that what was initiated in India on behalf of freedom was viewed so steadfastly as a *movement* and not a *struggle*.

Yet, a struggle it was; and, however ill-prepared Gandhi or Nehru might be to deal with such tactics, winning in that struggle meant "bidding for advantage," "spotting your enemy's weakness," and even "hitting when he was down." To those who chose to play the conflict as *battle*, the Hindu-Muslim antagonism was a ready-made weapon.

The Muslim League was founded in 1906, after George V, then Prince of Wales, had visited India and observed that the Indian National Congress was becoming quite powerful. From the outset, the League was a society of landed intellectuals with a common religious background. Actually, it could be viewed as having operated very much as a subgroup within the Congress Party until 1920. But when Gandhi took the freedom cause to the people, the leadership of the Muslim League finally withdrew its support. Gandhiji then offered to press the interests of Muslims when their spiritual leader, the Caliph, was deposed in Turkey; and many members of the Muslim League rejoined forces with the Indian National Congress. However, the reunion of the two groups was short-lived.

Fine and able Muslims were attracted to the Congress Party in large numbers throughout the 1920's and 1930's. They served its offices with distinction and found in its democratic principles no conflict with their religion; but the more conservative followers of Islam stood apart. All the same, the program of the Congress Party, which was designed to interpret the meaning of democracy to the poor and the oppressed, spread like wildfire among the peasants, regardless of religious affiliation.

Out of a population of about three hundred and eighty-eight million people in India in 1937, close to ninety million called themselves Muslims. In the total count at the time of the elections, fewer Muslims had voted for the Muslim League than for the Congress Party. Therefore, there was justification for Panditji's statement. A certain degree of pride in their achievements would also have been forgivable on the part of Congressmen; but the League had been alienated.

"Islam is in danger!" announced Mohammed Ali Jinnah, maintaining that a state of emergency existed between the Muslim League and the Indian National Congress. Jawaharlal countered by saying that the Muslim League was indeed in danger of losing its support unless it began to pay attention to the conditions under which the majority of Indian Muslims actually lived. In response to that challenge, at its annual session in 1937, the League drew up its first comprehensive program of economic and social improvement, and taking a leaf from Jawaharlal's book, Mohammed Ali Jinnah went to the villages with his message.

Whatever Jinnah chose to say at that moment, and even taking into account the fact that no elections at all had been permitted in the Princely States, it was still obvious that the right of the Congress Party to govern was unchallenged. Furthermore, Congress Party candidates enjoyed tremendous personal popularity at the moment. The party stepped into office confidently.

The appeal of the Congress Party had been universal before the elections. The changes they tried to effect gave no credence to the charge that they intended to discriminate along religious lines once they were in power. They were pledged to support land reform, to reduce taxes, and to provide new facilities for villagers. Moreover, they had promised to improve conditions in industry and to find jobs for those who were out of work. They devised special provisions for changing the status of women and for removing the taint of untouchability from Hindu practice. In fact, their program of reforms was so immense that under Panditji's guidance, a National Planning Committee had to be established to consider resources and to fix priorities for action.

Just as architects draw up plans for buildings, members of the National Planning Committee sat down to sketch on paper the design of an independent government in India. At the long-awaited sessions of that committee and its subsections, members of the Indian National Congress thought hard and long about the long-range purposes and possibilities of swaraj. Manufacturers, lawyers and bankers, educators and builders, as well as politicians, began to talk in very specific terms about how much money there was and how much was needed, about what they could do first and how, whether more food could be raised and the best way to distribute it. Working plans for a new state were formulated and published; and, best of all, this was done if not with the approval, at least with the permission, of the British who were still in power. The summit of freedom looked very close. Jawaharlal was jubilant!

Then came a war of worldwide dimensions and the dangerous, unresolved position of India was immediately exposed. The central authority of the country was the Viceroy, who acted on behalf of the King of England. When Great Britain declared war on Germany in 1939, Lord Linlithgow, the Viceroy, immediately declared war on behalf of India as well.

Jawaharlal Nehru received the news on September 3, 1939, while he was the guest of Generalissimo and Madame Chiang Kai-shek in China, where he had been called for conferences as the official representative of his party. He was summoned back to India immediately and left as soon as he could get transportation.

8 *world citizens*

The plane that was bringing Jawaharlal Nehru home approached the Ganges delta. Excitedly, he pressed his face against the window. Tea was being plucked from the gardens of Assam. Bengal was carpeted with rice. Heavily laden carts and brimful baskets were moving along the narrow roads and jungle footpaths that threaded the landscape. In the distance were the jutting smokestacks, the wharves, and white villas of Calcutta. He could not keep himself from smiling with pleasure. How varied and how lush was his land of India!

Panditji wished the plane did not take so long to land. He felt a familiar urge to set foot on just such village roads as he could see from above, or to glide on a country boat along the swollen streams. He was coming home, and it would be good to be among his people. What a welcome they would give him. "Panditji is back. He's back! He's back!" the children would shout, tugging at his hand. The villagers were going to gather at some likely spot and hear about his recent adventures. He would have fun talking to the men and women of India this time, for he brought news of faraway brothers and sisters, news for which they were eager.

The plane banked and climbed again. The wing obstructed his view from the window. Panditji turned and glanced back into the upholstered cabin. So returns the modern traveler, he thought. Not for me the slow sea voyage which took two years when the first emissaries moved back and forth between China and India. In these times the trip takes less than a day. I shall soon be there. He closed his eyes and with a characteristic gesture rested his chin on his right hand, while he thought back over the momentous journey he had taken.

It was the ordinary people of India, the peasants, who should be the first to hear his story, since the greetings he was bringing from China in 1939 were from millions of energetic, friendly people who worked terribly hard in the fields, the hospitals, the schools, and the workshops. They and their Nationalist leader, Chiang Kai-shek, were striving desperately to modernize their country. Everyone had a part in that great effort, whether rich or poor, old or young; and they all labored hard, Panditji remembered, yet willingly, and against fearful odds. We in India should sympathize with them, he told himself. We are strengthened by their friendship, and we can learn from their mistakes.

Jawaharlal Nehru opened his eyes and looked at a scribbled message that lay on his lap. His handsome brow then furrowed. He shook his head as if rousing himself from a daydream. But what China can give us right now is courage, he concluded soberly. We may not have much time before we too are attacked. India has been plunged into war.

War, he repeated. To romantic students and to former patriots he supposed war brought visions of bold and daring ventures, valor, and heroism. To statesmen in the twentieth century it meant hazardously protecting boundaries, keeping watch along a far-flung line of defenses, and trying to halt the atrocious advance of Nazism. Yet, what about those people? Panditji asked, peering down upon the thatched-roofed huts of the delta. What does war mean to our villagers, excepting recruitment and privation, the fear and threat of invasion?

No, it means more than that, he assured himself, because India itself means more than that in the scheme of things. Her village people, the ones to whom he was so anxious to speak, her masses understood that they were part of a larger struggle which was taking place between the forces of democracy and the forces of reaction. While they resisted imperialism at home they knew they upheld freedom and democracy elsewhere. Because they knew this, they spontaneously felt sympathy for China, Czechoslovakia, or Great Britain, for that matter. Through their own freedom movement, Indians had become educated as citizens of the world.

Citizens of the world, but in name only, Panditji had to admit. Until their right to independence was recognized, fully and irrevocably, no convocation of nations would ask their opinion or give much credence to their motives. For the time being they had to be viewed as pawns in a game played out by others. Undoubtedly the common people cared, Jawaharlal reflected. They cared about such things as the misery and persecution of Jews in Germany. They condemned the aggression of Japan against China; but how were they to show it? Until such time as they could exercise their own sovereignty, they were like hapless birds, caught in a storm, flying betwixt two mighty winds: their own inclination to rush to the defense of threatened democracy, and the force of colonialism that kept them in their places. Recognizing this, what course should they pursue?

The thoughtful passenger adjusted his seatbelt and prepared for landing. He speculated that by other conveyances other men were traveling with the same question on their minds, called as he had been to the emergency session of the Working Committee of the Congress Party. Jawaharlal knew the ones who would be coming, for, by and large, they were the comrades who over the years had borne the brunt of trial and office within the party. He felt he knew them, that is. He had certainly worked with them a long time; yet, he would not care to predict how they were going to react in this latest crisis—excepting, of course, for Gandhiji in whose house they would meet, and whose trust in the goodness of human beings would be undiminished even in face of the present challenge.

Rajendra Babu (Rajendra Prasad) was president of the Indian National Congress, and it was he who had called the meeting. Badshah Khan (Khan Abdul Gaffar Khan) would be there too. Undoubtedly, Sarojini Naidu was on her way from the south. She had been ill, but she would certainly be as witty and perspicacious as ever. Jairamdas Doulatram, Acharya Kripalani, and Vallabhbhai Patel were also coming. They were all staunch defenders of freedom, even though they differed radically in temperament. Maulana Abul Kalam Azad would undoubtedly lend his wisdom to the occasion as well. Maulana Azad was a fine scholar, a man of deep convictions, a Muslim but absolutely loyal to the Congress Party. "The Maulana" and Jawaharlal were fast friends. In Panditji's opinion, Azad dignified any cause he espoused. The deliberations would proceed more steadily because of his presence.

Those were the ones who now constituted the elected Working Committee; but there were others who would attend by invitation, Jawaharlal supposed. In all likelihood, Subhas Bose was coming. He was still amazingly popular with the Bengalis. Gandhiji would be there; and then there was himself to be considered. He could probably be regarded as the leader. It did not seem to matter any longer whether Jawaharlal Nehru was in or out of office. His responsibilities only deepened with the years.

Within forty-eight hours after Panditji had received Rajendra Babu's message at Chungtu, the Working Committee was in session in Gandhiji's hut at Wardha. The first action they took was one upon which they agreed easily. The issue they had gathered to discuss affected every man, woman, and child on the subcontinent. The ultimate question before them was whether India would go to war or not, if it would in fact accept the position foisted upon it by Lord Linlithgow or take a different stand. According to their way of looking at things, a decision on war demanded consensus, and it was imperative that the country speak unitedly. Therefore, if it were in any way possible, Mohammed Ali Jinnah had to be brought in on the discussions. As soon as his committee assembled, Rajendra Prasad was given permission to send a telegram to Jinnah, urging him to join the Working Committee while it was in session.

Jinnah replied that he had a previous engagement and could not accept the invitation. Alternatively, he proposed that Rajendra Babu meet him in Delhi after the meetings were over. However, since the purpose of having invited the head of the Muslim League in the first place was to benefit from his counsel during discussions and before decisions were reached, the committee found it difficult to see just how that end would be served by having Rajendra Babu go to Delhi. The president sent a second telegram explaining that, but by then further delay was unthinkable. If Jinnah were not willing to come immediately, the committee felt it had to go ahead on its own.

Mohammed Ali Jinnah was a difficult man to deal with. Why did he make it look as if he preferred to settle this matter in private with Rajendra Prasad rather than in the presence of the full committee? He was also a clever man. Was he consciously trying to stall or, even worse, cast himself and his party in a good light by waiting until positions were fixed and then choosing the alliance that would be most advantageous? Surely some such questions as these occurred to the various men on the Working Committee, but they would not be long detained. On the street corners of Delhi, at the newsstands of Paris, London, and Washington, in Moscow and in Chungking, people were clamoring for news about India and the war. "Has the Congress made a statement yet? What has it decided to do?" they were asking anxiously. It was necessary to act with all possible speed.

On the other hand, part of the seriousness upon this occasion, and a measure of frustration, rose from the fact that it was not the first time that the Working Committee had tried to lay before Great Britain its view of the war and India's contribution to the effort. The Congress Party had repeatedly emphasized the principles it felt should govern associations with England in the event of war and only a month earlier had requested His Majesty's Government to take their leadership into its confidence when making decisions that involved the role of India. Under the circumstances, it was hard for these people to bury their pride and to display understanding.

So the sessions did not get off to an easy start. The men were ripe to vent impatience and distrust of those responsible for the predicament in which they found themselves. It wasn't too difficult to find a scapegoat upon whom to pin the blame or to wish that things might have turned out otherwise from what they had. But Gandhiji would not tolerate expressions of ill feeling at such a decisive moment. He was willing to condemn the committee itself for harboring selfish motives and he roundly chastised even his closest friends for bigotry and peevishness. "We have no quarrel with people," he said. "It is with decisions of masters that we have come to deal." After his scolding, and under the restraining gavel of Rajendra Babu, the group began to settle down.

Meanwhile, Jawaharlal Nehru had sat with eyes downcast, refraining from comment. Attentive but withdrawn, he had heard, and yet he had seemed not to hear, the initial arguments going on around him. Before him still paraded his memories of Asia and pictures of Europe during recent, anguished years. He was a curious man, and ever since his experience at Jallianwala Bagh in 1919, he had somehow managed to receive firsthand appraisals of events as they happened. Therefore, he had made sure that he visited France when he was in Europe at the time of Kamala's death. He had seen the country just before Hitler's occupation of it. He and a friend had tramped across the battlefields of the Spanish Civil War some years before; and, most recently, he had been to China, where he had experienced five Japanese air raids in less than a fortnight. Impressions of such incidents and, more importantly, of the effect such incidents had upon human beings, were vivid in his mind.

"We have before us problems bigger than those of a lawyer's making," he broke forth at last in a commanding tone. "The world that we have known is dissolving before our very eyes. In this tragedy what part will India play? That is the question to which we must address ourselves."

"It is *our* peasants," he said with feeling, "who are being taxed from what little they have to support fighting in far-off England. It is *our* Maharajas who have offered to join in a fight in the name of freedom, while they enjoy the privileges of despots at home. Albeit the work to which the Congress Party originally applied itself is unfinished; and yet, Britain's Viceroy, without consulting a single Indian, has involved our country in war. Will we accept that treatment? No one of us can say just yet; but together we must say before we leave this room, and we'd better get down to business."

Startled eyes were turned in his direction. Panditji continued. "Let us think of the people in various countries," he said, "whether in Poland, France, England, Russia, or *Germany* with respect and full sympathy. It is the peoples of the world who will have the final say, not the governments which have misled them. We have an old quarrel with England, though not with the people of England. We have sympathy for them and we know too, it is for the ideals of freedom and democracy they fight."

Jawaharlal realized that he was asking a great deal of the men around him to have them view the crisis in such broad terms, when they had not yet achieved independence for their own country. In order to raise their spirits he emphasized that India, though thwarted, was not downed. "The path is difficult, yet there is a path," he said. "In spite of our difficulties, we are no weak nation today," he maintained. "A free India, with her vast resources, can be of great service to the world and to humanity. India will always make a difference. Fate has marked us for big things.

"We must hold together now, we must speak together,

and we must act together for the sake of India," he went on forcefully. "We must find a way to oppose fascism, but we cannot win freedom by surrendering our freedom in a struggle to achieve it. We must not bargain for our freedom now, but neither ignore it nor put it to one side. The question is not of India only, but of all the world and all those who have faith in the future of humanity and who are determined to rid the world of all causes of war and human exploitation."

The group listened. They listened carefully. They had heard their Jawahar speak before, graciously and ably, but never with such intensity; and when they thought about it, they had to admit that it was he, not they, who had lately walked through war-torn streets and while they had been preoccupied with domestic matters, it was Jawaharlal who had conversed with the leading minds in foreign nations. Without doubt, his insight and his example were forging a place for India in the eyes of other countries. So this was the message he brought back to them, to forget their bickering and take a world view of affairs.

"You're right, Jawahar," Maulana Azad agreed. "What he says is true," he confirmed, nodding to his colleagues. The words had sounded bold but persuasive to Rajendra Babu, Acharya Kripalani, and some of the rest of the committee. "He is a jewel, and a poet," Sarojini Naidu commented in reference to the speaker, "blest with a great humanity. Few of us may understand Jawaharlal; but we can at least dignify ourselves by following him." The meeting proceeded, but with a different tone.

Potentially the most disruptive issue was whether India would fight at all. On that question Gandhiji was in a touchy position. Pacifists the world around were looking to him for leadership and were begging him to do something that would avert total war. On the other hand, if he were to make a statement condoning war, it would immediately be used to advantage by the militarists. To a man like Badshah Khan, however, the answer was clear-cut. "Our aim is to win freedom," he said. "But we are equally pledged to serve humanity, and I do not understand why we should go and fight another's battle in order to attain our goal. Such freedom would be a farce. We have been condemning wars and their horrors, and now is the time to prove our sincerity."

It was a hard matter to decide. No one in that gathering, least of all Jawaharlal Nehru, was a coward or wished to step aside and let someone else fight his battles for him. They all recognized that under certain circumstances they would have to fight. Even the Mahatma had agreed that it was "better to fight than to be afraid." They were mightily tempted to go along with Great Britain and take up the sword by her side in a worldwide crusade for justice.

But just as peace was said to be indivisible, they recognized that freedom was also indivisible. The world could not long continue part free and part subject. The challenge exerted by Fascism and Nazism was also the challenge of colonialism. If freedom was to be established, not only Fascism and Nazism had to be resisted, but imperialism as well. When the question was asked, "Do we stand for freedom?" the Working Committee answered, "Yes, we do!" When asked where and under what circumstances, they replied, "In whatever country and whenever it is threatened. We resist any man, of whatever nationality, who would hold another subject!"

To the further question of whether or not India would follow the lead given it by Great Britain, the committee answered with a firm no. The men felt called upon to criticize the methods of Nazism and Fascism then rampant in Europe; but they also stated clearly that "the issue of war or peace for India must be decided by the Indian people, and no outside authority can be allowed to impose the decision upon them." The committee requested England to clarify its war aims and suggested that it free India as proof of its sincerity in pursuit of those aims. Yet, as forcefully as they asserted their rights, the group denied that they would permit the Congress Party to use such a decisive moment for bargaining or pushing an advantage with Great Britain. It was entirely in keeping with their methods that upon that occasion they should design a document which they regarded as a first step toward negotiations with His Majesty's Government but which they had no intentions of delivering as an ultimatum.

In the first place, the statement made by the Working Committee appealed to the Indian people to end their own conflicts and unite. It openly denounced the Indian princes who were willing to rush to the defense of democracy in Europe but unwilling to introduce social reforms in their own states. But, whatever the system of government and the action taken by the government under which they lived, the Indian National Congress made it equally plain that it had no quarrel with the *peoples* of the world. To the contrary, it stated: "In this war we do not look forward to the victory of one people over another, or to a dictated peace, but to the victory of real democracy in all countries, and a world freed from the nightmare of violence and imperialist oppression."

To England the Congress Party reasserted its friendliness with an assurance that India wanted to forget the past of conflict and stretch out her hand to help. It was like Gandhiji in particular to insist that the final word given by the Working Committee not be released to the press immediately, but held back until the Viceroy should have had a chance to read it and reply. The door must be left open for apologies, a change of heart, and perhaps an alliance.

No other document they ever set forth quite so adequately embraced the mind and mood of the Congress Party as a whole under Jawaharlal's guidance. He was asked to write the statement; however, after five days of continuous meetings, every phrase he suggested had been worked over and refined until the end product was acceptable to everyone. Each sentence could be readily understood and interpreted. In the end, the judicious mind of Jairamdas Doulatram was revealed in the paper. The precision of Vallabhbhai Patel was stamped upon the final work. The fervor of Subhas Bose was part of it, the skepticism of Acharya Kripalani. The Mahatma described what was produced as "a manifesto to the nations of the world." Through it the Congress Party addressed themselves to the most important topic of their times, yet with an eloquence and a point of view it had learned from Jawaharlal Nehru.

The final session of the committee lasted until very late. When Panditji read their statement to his friends for the last time before they departed, the momentous import of what they had done was brought home anew. "The Committee earnestly appeals to the Indian people to hold together, calm of purpose," they heard him say, "determined to achieve freedom for India within the larger freedom of the world." There they were, a mere handful, presuming to represent millions, and with the fate of millions more in their keeping. They had done their best, yet, in the scheme of things, they questioned whether they had done enough. It looked like so very little.

Regardless of what position they had taken, they knew the war was bound to be widespread, long, and terrible. Their fervor and their tolerance were going to be tested all over again. They wanted to believe that their offer to Great Britain to reopen the question might be accepted, but given the historic attitude of that country, there was hardly one of them but realized it was only a matter of time before he would be judged for the crime of putting his signature on such a testament and prison gates closed behind him. Even now, when Jawaharlal Nehru thought about the acquaintances he had made so recently in China, it was as if they were on the other side of a wall across which he could barely reach.

A silence, which was almost prayer, deepened in the still, plain room. Was it always going to be India's role to suffer mutely for the sake of humanity? the men wondered. It looks that way, some of them would have been tempted to answer. But no, only a little while longer at most, Jawaharlal would have maintained. I believe that. You can believe it too. The times are moving in new directions, and India has chosen to be one with the times. Our faces are set forward, not backward, and forward we shall march. Such was his enduring faith in the power of their undertaking!

Men may have to stop, but nations go on. There are times when persons are forced to step aside, but life itself does not slow down. It moves, gathering all the while new forces, fed by the circumstances of the moment. When those circumstances include an event of such significance as World War II, there are very few nooks or crannies of existence that are left unmolested; and, when the holocaust is over, affairs do not return again to where they were at the outset. The world has been remade and even the most keen observer, if he has not been an eyewitness to events, will be hard put to find a familiar landmark.

Jawaharlal Nehru was imprisoned twice during World War II, once for a period of thirteen months as a consequence of having personally resisted Britain's policies and the second time for nearly three years because he was a member of the Working Committee of the Congress Party at a time when the party was declared illegal. The dates of his imprisonment were from October, 1940, to December, 1941, and from August, 1942, to June, 1945. His first sentence was awarded soon after Germany had attacked Russia—not long before Japan's attack at Pearl Harbor and the subsequent occupation of Burma and islands in the Bay of Bengal. The worried leader chafed under detention and came out resolved to explore new ways by which India could in full freedom of conscience defend itself and contribute to winning a just and speedy peace. He was heartsick when he found there was still no chance of her participation in the war effort as an independent nation.

Indeed, the outlook for the allies was a discouraging one when Nehru was again impounded in 1942; and it was not until after victory had been achieved in North Africa, D-Day had passed in Normandy, and victory had come to Europe that he was released. Meanwhile, war had been waged on India's soil in Assam; Calcutta had served as a center for the United States Army in the East; and his comrade Subhas Bose had miraculously escaped and then died in an attempt to raise an army for India's liberation from abroad. The Bengal Famine of 1942–1943 had taken a toll of somewhere between two and three million Indian lives. It was the eve of a new age, announced by the blast of an atomic bomb exploded by the Americans at Hiroshima in Japan.

The outlook for freedom had changed too. Throughout the stormcast years of war, the possibility of India's independence had been raised repeatedly and considered paramount in the negotiations of the Allies. President Roosevelt and Generalissimo Chiang Kai-shek had applied constant pressure upon Winston Churchill, the Prime Minister of England, urging him to make an early settlement with members of the Congress Party. A mission headed by Sir Stafford Cripps had come out from England to India in 1942 to try and devise such a settlement, at the time when Panditji was free and eager to negotiate. However, such was the harvest of distrust, reaped from the contest between the Congress Party and His Majesty's Government, that England was suspicious of delegating full powers to the leadership of India at the time; and neither would Indians believe that England could be counted upon to make good on a promise of eventual independence given under the stress of war. Therefore, no date for freedom could be fixed.

At that point, even Gandhiji's patience was tried! Without proper reflection, thinking perhaps that in the hour of danger Britain would be most likely to come to terms, he began to agitate for the immediate withdrawal of Britain from India. Reprisal was swift and keen. The government immediately declared Congress Party activities illegal. Members of the Working Committee were arrested. There was talk of deporting them. Their whereabouts were kept secret. Gandhiji and Sarojini Naidu were taken to other places but the majority of the committee were housed together at Ahmednagar Fort for the duration of the war in Europe.

Meanwhile, the leadership of the Muslim League was active. At the outset of the war there was a good bit of talk about Mohammed Ali Jinnah and how he used the rejection of the Congress Party statement for his own advantage. How much of his conduct was intentional will have to wait for a more conclusive verdict from history, but it is true that after 1937 he had entered into open combat with the Congress

Party and had persuaded the Muslim League Council of the justice of that cause. Accordingly, he found himself able to wield tremendous personal power. The fact that Gandhiji especially, then Jawaharlal Nehru and his colleagues, began to defer to Jinnah's opinion increased his prestige, and in October, 1939, when members of the Congress Party resigned their ministries in protest against India's involvement in the war, Jinnah called upon Muslims to celebrate the occasion as a "Day of Deliverance."

It is understandable that Muslims would be concerned about their role in an independent state with a majority of Hindus, but Jinnah increased their worries by insisting that Muslims would not be treated fairly. In 1940 the Muslim League put forward the demand that at the time of independence "the areas in which Muslims are numerically in the majority should be grouped to constitute Independent States."

"When the Congress comes to power, the Hindus are bound to dominate," Jinnah said. It is a curious fact that for six years, from 1939 to 1945, the man responsible for answering this charge as president of the Indian National Congress was himself a Muslim, Maulana Azad. But Jinnah played repeatedly upon the theme of *separatism* in his speeches and in the resolutions he recommended to his party. By the time the Working Committee of the Indian National Congress emerged from prison, the Muslim League was a new kind of force to be reckoned with.

In prison a man has a long, long time to take stock of himself. During the time that stretched from 1940 to 1945, what could Jawaharlal say of his life and action? That for twenty years he had resisted empire with every ounce of his energy and all the devotion at his command. That he knew the Congress Party represented the will of India's people as a whole and was dedicated to their best interests; and that he could never fully express his personal gratitude to the party and its cause for the opportunity it had offered him to know and serve his country.

The situations that had obtained in the past, and particularly the line-up of power, were changing in India. Panditji recognized this. Even without the benefit of information and contact with his countrymen, he knew it must be so. Powerful and dramatic forces were affecting the scene, both internally and externally. But, in regard to the Muslims, if he had had any part in teaching them to demand their full share of life's benefits, he had done so because he had believed it was their right as much as his. If, in fact, it was a consequence of his actions that they had risen to assert themselves, he still had no regrets. He had confidence that when India attained her destiny, the present conflicts could be forgotten. By the time he walked out of Ahmednagar Fort on June 15, 1945, Panditji was well along in his fifties. He had become thin and was growing bald; but otherwise, he was as vigorous as ever, and just as ready to be on the move.

A month earlier Lord Wavell, the Viceroy, had gone to London. He had returned with the news that fresh steps would be taken to solve India's political problem. As a matter of fact, the Working Committee of the Congress Party had been released so that they would be available for meetings. A conference was to be held at Simla, the summer capital of the British government in India. To it were summoned leaders of both the Congress Party and the Muslim League, as well as representatives of other national groups and of His Majesty's Government.

The delegates to the Simla Conference were received cordially and the proposals the Viceroy presented were generous. His Majesty's Government did not feel that it could make the constitutional changes necessary to transfer power to India as a free and self-governing nation before the war was fully over, in Asia as well as in Europe, but it was willing to make concessions. First of all, His Majesty's representatives proposed that henceforward the Viceroy's closest advisers be Indians. They would constitute the members of his Executive Council, which was entrusted with consideration of the most significant decisions of the nation. Moreover, His Majesty's representatives were ready to recommend that the Viceroy be instructed to take his councilors' advice seriously and act upon it.

The setting up of an Indian Executive Council was a step in the direction of self-government that was acceptable to all national parties. All the same, when the time arrived to suggest names of persons who would serve on the Executive Council, Mohammed Ali Jinnah insisted that the Indian National Congress should restrict its nominations to Hindus. He naturally expected that the League would be empowered to choose Muslims. He did not acknowledge that there were other religious groups who could very well ask for representation, including the Sikhs, the Parsees, the Buddhists, and the Indian Christians. Neither did he in any way distinguish between so-called religious and governmental functions.

To have given in to such a demand would have gone against the most time-honored principles of the Indian National Congress. This was a *democratic*, as opposed to a *communal*, organization. Its leaders had taken into their keeping the interests of the entire country and they expected to make good on their promises. Therefore, they refused to turn their backs on anyone who might look to them for representation. They had no intention of having political issues settled solely on religious lines.

In like manner, His Majesty's Government declined to constitute an Executive Council on the bases suggested by Mr. Jinnah. Therefore, the Simla Conference was dissolved and further consideration of independence was shelved for the time being. But Simla remained as a landmark in Indian-British relations. It was the first time that negotiations on independence had failed not because of differences of opinion between India's representatives and those of the Crown but because of differences between one segment of Indian opinion and another. This was a bitter blow for the Congress Party and its leaders, especially for Maulana Azad, who considered himself no less a Muslim for the fact that he was not a separatist. The defeat of His Majesty's proposal at the hands of Mohammed Ali Jinnah was very hard for the Indian National Congress to take!

In August, 1945, representatives of the Labor Party came to power in Great Britain. Within a few weeks the Viceroy announced that general elections would be held in India, the first in several years. The idea behind such limited elections was outmoded, as everyone recognized; but at least the occasion provided opportunities for candidates to get out into the countryside and reestablish contact with their constituencies by campaigning. Once again, the Congress Party returned to the villages.

Once again too, Jawaharlal Nehru took to the air, the road, and the jungle footpath to reach his people. Armed with an election platform forged by the All-India Congress Committee, he tried to explain his party's view. "We regard it as our first duty to redeem our pledge of independence," he said. "Then it becomes our most urgent responsibility to tackle the causes of poverty and to raise the standards of our people. In international affairs, we stand for the establishment of a world federation of free nations. This election is a small test for us, a preparation for greater things to come."

Panditji reminded his listeners that the Congress Party stood for equal rights and opportunities among the citizens of India, whatever their religion or political persuasion. He implored people to support Congress Party candidates, thus putting the freedom and independence of the motherland ahead of communal considerations. On the strength of that appeal, his party secured an absolute majority of votes cast in all but three provinces of British India. They even won in the Punjab, where a majority of the citizens were Muslims.

Nehru, Patel, Pant, Azad, and Badshah Khan—all of them who had helped to interpret the Congress Party program during the campaigns—learned a lot from that experience. The war years had served to awaken a new generation of patriots and had implanted in them an unquenchable thirst for independence. Congress leaders found the country-side united in its demand for immediate freedom. The Indian Civil Service, the police, and the armed forces, groups that had not formerly aligned themselves with one side or the other, were ready to place their services at the disposal of patriots. It was obvious that however entrenched the empire had been, Britishers would be hard put to it to hold on to India much longer.

Meanwhile, feeling between Hindus and Muslims was near fever pitch. The propaganda aimed by the Muslim League had found its mark in the suspicions and rivalries engendered by past generations. It looked as if the none too easy accord that had prevailed between the two groups could be shattered in a second. On this count, too, it was apparent that the time had arrived for a decision by Great Britain and that there was not a moment to lose.

The Labor government of England took immediate action. On February 17, 1946, Britain radioed the news that a Cabinet Mission was being dispatched to India to discuss with Indian representatives the question of freedom. On March 15, Clement Attlee, then Prime Minister of England, made a speech in the House of Commons in which he reviewed the Indian situation and explained what the Cabinet Mission would try to achieve. He set forth exactly the terms upon which His Majesty's Government was prepared to negotiate. He sounded optimistic and sincere. It was a speech without precedent in the long association of England with India. It made a deep impression upon the people of India and heralded a new era of goodwill between the two nations.

Times had changed, Mr. Attlee admitted; and he suggested to those of his countrymen who wanted to hold on to India at any cost that it was better not to try to apply old methods to new situations. Faults had been committed by both sides, he said; but he thought one should look to the future rather than harp upon the failures of the past. The desire for freedom had grown ever stronger among Indians of all walks of life and in men of all faiths. It was fitting that they be soon entrusted with the management of their own affairs.

On the important issue of purna swaraj, the Prime Minister declared: "India herself must choose what will be her future Constitution. I hope that the Indian people may elect to remain within the British Commonwealth. But if she does so elect, it must be by her own free will. If she elects for independence, in our view she has a right to do so." As for the separatist demand of the Muslim League, he said that "minorities should be allowed to live free from fear. On the other hand, we cannot allow a minority to place a veto on the advance of the majority." In closing, he emphasized that his Cabinet Mission was going out to India in a positive mood, *resolved to succeed.*

Recognizing the deep concern of Indian Muslims for their own welfare in an independent nation, the Cabinet Mission proposed a unique solution to their problem. It suggested that states having a clear majority of Muslims be allowed to assume more responsibility than other states in an Indian federation. In fact, it would be left to them to decide how much they wished to rely upon the central government except in certain well-defined matters, such as foreign and military affairs.

The Muslim League had gone so far in its demand for a separate nation that it was hard for Mohammed Ali Jinnah to back down at that point; but, in the end, he did agree to the Cabinet Mission's proposal, admitting that a minority in a national state could hardly expect fairer treatment. Plans were then drawn up for an "Interim Government" of Indians who would serve the Viceroy until a Constitution could be ratified. By the end of the sessions, Englishmen and Indians, both Hindus and Muslims, appeared to be satisfied. Swaraj was dawning.

The events that followed came in rapid-fire succession. Maulana Azad laid aside the mantle of office after having served as president of the Indian National Congress for six years and Jawaharlal Nehru was chosen unanimously as his successor. The Constituent Assembly was scheduled to convene and start work on the Constitution. Then, at a press conference, in his dynamic way, the new Rashtrapati referred to the forthcoming assembly as the place where the future government of India would be decided, meaning where it would be given shape. Jinnah was enraged and he hastily called his councilors together.

Alerted, Panditji and the Working Committee of the

Congress Party reaffirmed their adherence to the plan put forward by the Cabinet Mission. Still, the Muslim League was not placated. It met and immediately decided to withdraw its support from the Interim Government. It went even further. It called upon Muslims throughout the country to employ "Direct Action" to achieve their separate nation. August 16 was set as the day for launching Direct Action and on that day Mohammed Ali Jinnah announced: "Today we bid farewell to constitutional methods."

What resulted was a wave of violence that started with an attack of Muslims upon the Hindus of Calcutta, but soon became a riot of killing that swept rapidly across Bengal, through Bihar, past Delhi, and into the Punjab, leaving vengeance and death in its wake. What took place on such a widespread scale could hardly have been foreseen. It could not be called a civil war, and yet many of its effects were the same.

Muslims had struck Hindus, but Hindus had struck back. Neighbor was now pitted against neighbor. Houses were looted and crops destroyed. The populace lived in fear. Innocent people were attacked in dark alleys. Children were kidnapped, places of worship desecrated. Thousands lay dead and hundreds of thousands more were wounded. Nothing like it had ever taken place on Indian soil before. It was more than the outcry of a minority. It was an epidemic of terror!

How could anyone accept such tactics? What victory could be sought by such devices, what solace gained? If Direct Action were the work of the Muslim League, it was ample proof that they were determined to have independence, but alone. If they had prepared for such violence, they must surely have felt that killing was their last resort. They could have seen no other way. And, if it had been Jinnah's words that touched it off, people who had faith that men of all religions, however severe and unapproachable they appeared, were at heart tender, human, and kind were convinced that he had not known, he could not have intended, the suffering that spread in the wake of his commands.

The substance of the Congress Party was brutally tried. Believing wholeheartedly that there *was* another way to settle affairs, they had to prove it. This, then, was to be their ultimate trial. Could they hold out for unity and act peaceably?

Here it must be said that they were helped immeasurably in their task by the British. If evidence of British friendship were only the number of lives they succeeded in saving at the time, then both the Congress Party and the Muslim League could have counted them loyal; for British officers, both military and civil, stayed at their jobs and did what they could, even when they knew their own days in India were numbered and they were called upon to function in the midst of appalling circumstances. Volunteers also came forward to help, it is true—representatives of service clubs and students, the Red Cross, and Indian scouts—but the fabric of society was held together by the English. It was they who provided guards for the streets at night, who made arrangements to bury the dead and put out fires, who conducted trials of criminals and kept food trains moving. For their aid in that emergency, India will be forever grateful. Whatever opinions the English held about independence, partition, or leadership, they still did not hit the enemy while he was down. Instead, they helped him to get up and recover his health and sanity as best he could.

And there was also Gandhiji, the man who many years before had decided to give his life to religion rather than politics, but whose love embraced men of all persuasions and whose methods were nonviolent. Now, while the task of the Raj was to restore and maintain order, he was its strongest ally. In his courageous way, he undertook to travel through the terror-ridden provinces on foot and in country boats. So he proceeded from village to village, exhorting the terrorists, comforting the stricken, and demonstrating exactly what he believed: that Hindus and Muslims could live in friendship.

From day to day and week to week Gandhi followed a path that took him through East Bengal and into Bihar while the rioting was worst. Like a saint of old, he traveled without any armor other than his faith; and, like a saint, he seemed to achieve miracles, for where he went, the people listened to him. They ceased fighting, laid down their weapons, and began to rebuild what they had destroyed. Not a man of either faith lifted a finger against him; and, after he had passed, people got on pretty well together, remembering the promises they had given him. Where he did not go, folk still took heart from knowing that he cared.

In former times, it had seemed to Congress Party members that freedom was worth the last full ounce of human effort. Now unity was worth even more. Congress leaders gave their utmost. In the face of dissent that amounted almost to a stalemate with the Muslim League, the Interim Government took office. Jawaharlal Nehru was sworn in as vice-president of the Executive Council, an office comparable to that of Prime Minister but with special responsibilities for foreign affairs. While the country seethed with conflict, Vallabhbhai Patel assumed the unwelcome office of Home Minister. When the time came to convene the Constituent Assembly, despite lack of cooperation from the Muslim League, Rajendra Prasad became its president. Convinced that even though he was a Muslim, he could be more useful inside the government than outside, Maulana Azad agreed to become Minister of Education.

During the months that followed, there was much done in India that would have been better left undone; much said that would have been better unsaid. In face of active opposition, the sessions of the Interim Government came nearly to a standstill and rioting continued. However, in the tangled web of circumstance that surrounded each event, it is possible to trace three strands of endeavor. The Congress Party stood resolutely by its view that the country was one and must be democratic. The Muslim League was bent upon achieving a separate nation, Pakistan; and the office of the Viceroy used its power to hold on to authority and arbitrate. When the Viceroy, Lord Wavell, felt at last that things had reached a point where he could no longer be effective, he resigned.

The subcontinent stood on the brink of anarchy. Yet, if after three hundred and fifty years of British rule, England's legacy to India was to be chaos, then Englishmen would be sorely ashamed. And, having stood for unity, they could not help but regard partition as a failure. So there was a temptation to hold on for a while longer; but even with the best of intentions, British presence could serve only to worsen the situation. The one remaining hope for a stable, undivided country lay in its exercise of freedom. Perhaps with the coming of independence the parties might bury their differences in the tasks of reconstruction. Then the majority would have a chance to prove that it could rule without prejudice. But on all counts, the time had definitely come for Great Britain to withdraw.

On February 20, 1947, Prime Minister Attlee announced to the British Parliament the intention of His Majesty's Government "to effect the peaceful transfer of power into responsible Indian hands by a date not later than June of 1948." That intention was greeted throughout the world as a bold and admirable step. The man chosen for the task was Admiral Lord Louis Mountbatten, who had been Supreme Allied Commander for Southeast Asia during World War II. He was handsome. He was just, but above all, he was speedy and efficient. If his job were to surrender into the hands of Indians the safekeeping of their own destinies, then that mission would be dispatched. England was going to leave India under this Viceroy. To see him was to know it.

9 | *the appointed day*

The handsome, energetic Mountbatten bent over his desk. He ran his finger down the list of afternoon appointments. "Ah, yes," he said aloud. "Nehru next."

It was Mountbatten's first day in office. He had arrived in Delhi the afternoon before. That morning trumpets had proclaimed the swearing-in of a new Viceroy. Resplendent in his white uniform, wearing the broad blue ribbon of the Order of the Garter, he had taken his oath before princes, envoys, and ministers. He had also wasted no time in getting off notes to Gandhi and Jinnah, asking them to come for talks. Later in the afternoon he would see Liaquat Ali Khan, member of the Muslim League and Minister of Finance in the Interim Government. But first on his list was Nehru. He had met the man briefly once before, and he looked forward to seeing him again.

Mountbatten and Nehru liked one another immediately. Luckily, they had common interests, boundless energy, and enthusiasm for life. They had steel courage and determination, too; and they were conscious that their acts bore import. But each seemed a bigger man, and more capable, standing beside the other. In all probability, wherever or whenever they might have been associated, Jawaharlal Nehru and Lord Louis Mountbatten would have been friends; and so they became. It was clear that though their tasks were formidable, they were going to enjoy working together and the results of their endeavors would be lustrous.

At the end of the appointment, standing in the doorway of the viceregal study, Mountbatten extended his hand. "Mr. Nehru," he said, "I want you to regard me not as the Last Viceroy winding up the British Raj; but as the first to lead the way to a new India."

Panditji stopped. He looked up suspiciously, and then he chuckled. Those words represented England as he liked to think of it and at its best. "Now I know what they mean when they speak of your charm as being dangerous," he commented to the Viceroy, turning on his heel. He was deeply moved.

But the fates of mighty nations cannot be settled in the conversations of friends. India was in agony, tottering on the rim of disaster. Reconciliation between the two major religious communities was unthinkable at the moment and a truce could hardly be depended upon to hold, even with Gandhiji's constant surveillance and ministry. English officers were beginning to lose heart for what looked like a thankless job. The Punjab was governed by emergency decree. Panditji's central administration was helpless.

Action was what was needed—bold and imaginative action that would command the attention of the country, that would produce effects that were more than temporary and restore good faith. Jawaharlal knew this. He knew his government was shackled by restraint, prevented from taking action, thwarted from meeting the needs of its citizens. It was for action that he longed, any action, so long as it was constructive. Gandhiji wanted the same thing; and it was the desire for action as much as anything else that kept him constantly on the go, attempting to reconcile, avert, and deter violence.

Jinnah also knew that action was needed, and perhaps that was why he insisted on the opposite. Every day that he stalled, every hour that the Interim Government was kept inactive, his position looked stronger and his bargaining power increased. Soon it might no longer be a question of accepting or rejecting the partition of India. It might only be a question of whether anyone could tolerate further indecision.

Of the three major forces in British India—the Indian National Congress, the Muslim League, and His Majesty's Government—only one was free to act. At the time he arrived Mountbatten was the only man in the open and able to move. He carried a clear mandate to effect the transfer of power by obtaining a unitary government for British India and the Indian states, if possible, within the Commonwealth; or to recommend to London what other steps were to be taken. He lost no time in getting under way.

When, at an introductory meeting and with Nehru's urging, he proposed to Jinnah that there be an appeal to all groups to cease violence and desist from fighting, Jinnah asked Lord Mountbatten whether, in reference to India, he did not agree that what the patient needed under the circumstances was immediate surgery. "Indeed, that may be so," Mountbatten countered, "but, in order to insure the survival of the patient, don't you think it would be best to give him the benefit of an anesthetic?"

On April 14, a Peace Appeal was issued, signed by Mohandas Karamchand Gandhi and Mohammed Ali Jinnah, calling for *the avoidance in speech and writing of all incitement to violence.* The appeal was read over the air. It was printed on the front pages of newspapers and flashed onto the screens of movie theaters. In backward and disturbed areas, leaflets were dropped from airplanes. A few days afterward, when Gandhi and Jinnah met for the first time in many years, Jinnah laid further stress upon the appeal by saying: "Mr. Gandhi and I both are of the opinion that we must do our best to see that the appeal is carried out." Temporarily, there was to be order, as Mountbatten had insisted, so that India could turn her attention to other matters.

Preparations were mapped for a strategic campaign. The English governors of the provinces were summoned to the viceregal palace, praised for their diligence, and instructed to hold on for another few weeks and be on guard against emergencies. The princes trekked to Delhi with pomp and fanfare but returned to their states in disarray, having been told that their rights would lapse within the immediately foreseeable future, that their territories would undoubtedly be merged in independent India, and they were to prepare for the advent of democracy. The army was reassigned to troubled areas.

Representatives of the press were given full and on-the-spot information on all developments but commanded not to fan the raging fires of speculation and retaliation. Administrative questions were dealt with quickly and in as much of a spirit of cooperation as possible in order to prevent details from getting in the way of larger issues. Leaders were consulted, enabled to confer with His Majesty's representatives at any hour of the day or night, and encouraged to carefully and sincerely measure the tempers of their communities.

Every second, every means was lent to the winning of a decision as to when and how England was to let go.

It was beautiful and timely that at this moment Lady Mountbatten and Indira Nehru, newly wed to Feroze Shah Gandhi, from Bombay, were able to meet and to assume their respective places on the Indian scene. Their constant presence lent both grace and intelligence to confused and ugly circumstances. Indira was every inch her mother's child, shy but warm, serene, and trustworthy. During the spring of 1947, her father needed her to serve as his hostess and counselor. Lady Mountbatten was her English counterpart, beautiful but humble, sensible, fearless, and steady.

The two women shared a loving concern for humanity and they were of immense help to the Viceroy and the Prime Minister of the Interim Government in the midst of strife. They launched relief drives on behalf of those who were homeless. They visited stricken neighborhoods and they encouraged women's groups to help with rehabilitation. To social welfare and related undertakings they offered direction and sympathy. During days of torture, their spirit was a balm.

Mountbatten had arrived on March 22. By the end of three weeks, he had completed his first round of conferences with Indian party leaders. Moreover, he had personally established himself in the confidence of the Indian people as no other Viceroy had ever done, and had struck up a lasting friendship with the foremost leader of the nationalists, Nehru. All the same, there was no hint from any quarter that he had been less than impartial or, for all his energy, too swift to be fair. Words of praise for him were lavish and genuine.

On the first of May, Mountbatten was ready to present the draft of a plan for the transfer of power from English to

Indian hands. Two of his aides flew to London with his papers. Considering the instructions the man had been given and his popularity, there was little doubt but that England, at least, was going to accept what he proposed.

Whether India as a whole would or even could accept Mountbatten's plan was another matter. "The Congress want to inherit everything," Jinnah complained. "They would accept anything to deprive me of my Pakistan," he said. On the other hand, Nehru's opinion was that partition was "by nature wrong."

It was not certain whether Great Britain was going to recommend dividing the country, but there was a widespread fear that it might. Gandhiji, who would countenance no redrawing of boundaries, stated that the Indian National Congress should "not concede Pakistan, even if it is demanded at the point of a sword." Rajendra Prasad concurred with the Mahatma. "I have been and am against partition," Maulana Azad maintained. "Never has my objection been as strong as it is today."

Presented with such divergent opinions, Mountbatten was worried. "If only I could have had the job eighteen months earlier," he confided, "while there was still time to influence the outcome." He reported to his government, "There has been catastrophic deterioration of the situation during the last few months."

Despite indications to the contrary, however, as spring flushed and summer advanced across the plains of India, during March, April, and May of 1947, a change could be detected in the utterances of the Congress Party leaders and a lessening of tension was apparent. Vallabhbhai Patel was the first to try and express the new consensus of the group. "Whether we like it or not, there *are* two nations in India," he admitted. "It looks to me as if we have no alternative but to accept this fact." Gandhiji went to the Viceroy's house for a long and frank conversation, after which he concluded: "The British government will not be responsible for partition if it comes. The Viceroy will have no hand in it. But if both Hindus and Muslims cannot agree on anything else, then His Majesty's Government is left no choice."

Mountbatten tested Jinnah's reaction to draft proposals involving the partition of some states, as well as the ceding of certain well-defined territories to a new nation. He thought that the leader of the Muslim League was receptive to such plans and that he would not ask for more.

About this time, Jawaharlal Nehru, whose work in the government was subject to open and hostile criticism from the opposition, asked to call on his friend Maulana Azad. He was temporarily downhearted and thought the visit might do him good. When the meeting was over, the Maulana wrote in his diary: "It is clear to me that in spite of his repugnance to the idea of partition, Jawaharlal is coming to the conclusion day by day that there is no alternative." Rajendra Prasad, acting as president of the Constituent Assembly, began to prepare its members for the reality of Pakistan. It looked as if India were going to be split, and the Congress Party would accept that fact.

At such moments, it is easy for a statesman to make a pronouncement that is embittered and which he may subsequently regret. In the memoirs of those nearest to a public figure, there may later be revealed certain outbursts of anger and vituperation that smirch an otherwise fair record. The taking of a new position sometimes alienates old friends. From every perspective and for a long time Jawaharlal Nehru had been sorely tried.

People who saw him from a distance wondered how much longer the Prime Minister of the Interim Government had it in him to hold fast and act with integrity; but they need have had no fears. When it came to announcing his position in public, Panditji handled himself in a consistent and openhanded way.

"I have but one demand. Let it be clear," he requested of the Viceroy, "that the independent Union of India inherits all that has been called British India. But the United India for which we have labored through all these years is not one of coercion and compulsion. It is a free and willing association of free people. If Pakistan and the Muslim League wish to secede, that is their choice."

Others might label what was about to happen as "partition," "the break-up of the country," and "the division of a nation." Not Jawaharlal. The aspiration that had lured Indians forward to the heights of independence had been indivisible. Therefore, to him the country was one. As in a family, he said, certain brothers might choose to move away and establish their homes elsewhere, but that did not dissolve the primary relationships. Certainly there could be friendly feelings between the boys and their parents. The door would remain open, and they could come home if they liked. He took the same calm and homely view of his India and neighboring Pakistan.

On the evening of June 3, 1947, radio channels throughout the world were cleared for a momentous announcement. Utilizing the services of All-India Radio, with broadcasts beamed to Europe, England, and America, four leaders announced their agreement on a plan for the transfer of power in India. Mountbatten spoke first. He said that it was his firm opinion that a unified India would be by far the best solution when it came to independence, but it had been impossible to obtain agreement on any suggestions that would preserve unity. Therefore, partition would occur. Boundaries would forthwith be drawn between those areas of British India that had a Muslim majority and those that did not.

Other speakers were Nehru, Jinnah, and Baldev Singh, a Sikh whose people were destined to lose heavily when partition took place. "The announcement envisages on the one hand, the possibility of certain areas seceding from India," Jawaharlal said, "but on the other, the promise of a big advance toward complete independence. It is with no joy in my heart that I can commend these proposals to you, although you should also be assured I have no doubt in my mind that this is the right course for us." He went on to express his deep appreciation to Mountbatten for his labors at such a critical juncture; and all three of the Indian speakers asked everyone to help make the fulfillment of the Viceroy's assignment less difficult by enabling him to effect the transfer of power in a peaceful and orderly manner.

Starting the very next day, it was to that end that leaders of every persuasion attuned themselves, all government departments aligned themselves, and armies were directed to carry out their orders with the last ounce of speed. Since independence and Pakistan were coming, they were to come as soon as possible. August 15 was established as the earliest possible date. Everyone and everything on the subcontinent was lent to the task.

Within the day-to-day context of affairs, the onset of empire in India had been slow and inauspicious. If twentieth-century newspapermen had tried to cover the event, in all probability they would have put out such headlines as DEATH OF AKBAR CRUCIAL TO INTERESTS OF EAST INDIA COMPANY, or HAWKINS WINS TRADING POST BUT LOSSES HEAVY. It was only after a very long time that the iron power of Elizabeth's ambition and Hawkins's enterprise were manifest. Not very often are people rewarded by being permitted to see the role they play in history. For example, could a man by the name of Hume, an Englishman who helped found the Indian National Congress, even have dimly guessed the outcome of his endeavor?

The transfer of English power to Indian hands took place under very different circumstances. The spotlight of nations was turned upon Delhi. Newsreel cameras ground and press wires hummed. By any standards, the advent of freedom after so long a trial was a gorgeous spectacle, but the reason for world focus had very little to do with sensationalism or with idle curiosity. Seldom do men and women witness the end of an epoch in history, and rarely, if ever, is it enacted with the splendor and precision that accompanied the renunciation of empire in India.

FORTY-THREE DAYS LEFT TO PREPARE FOR TRANSFER OF POWER read the big, handmade calendar that hung on the wall of the Viceroy's office. "Discuss *Indian Independence Act* with leaders," Mountbatten had scribbled on the notepad of his desk. In its final form, the Indian Independence Act, which he held in his hand and which was about to be read and commented upon before introduction to the House of Commons, covered scarcely fifteen typewritten pages. "2/7/47, discussion," was scratched on the list of appointments for Jawaharlal Nehru. He ceased making revisions on his copy of the Act and gathered his papers together. "Agenda: Independence Act," was Jinnah's reminder. Actually, he had very few changes to recommend.

After having been written and revised in Delhi, the Indian Independence Act was presented and passed through Parliament, in London, with lightning speed. Yet, the pace of events was not allowed to detract in any way from the pageantry and dignity of the moment. When the bill was read out in the House of Commons, no less a person than

Winston Churchill lent the full weight of his support, after long and bitter years of hard-headed resistance to the Indian nationalists; and, at his bidding, opposition members rallied to the side of the Labor Party, recommending that independence be total and partition fast.

In the House of Lords there were masterful speeches. Former Viceroys and Provincial Governors all had their say. "The Act is an event unique in history," Lord Samuel proclaimed, "a treaty of peace without a war." Lord Listowel, Secretary of State, met journalists afterward in the India Office. "The Bill is without precedent in the history of this country," he took pains to emphasize. "Never before has such a large proportion of the world population achieved complete independence through legislation alone."

The goodwill engendered by England's offer of liberty to India was remarkable, and in newspapers and at dinner tables around the world the British Raj was favorably compared to an aristocrat of ancient line, about whom Shakespeare had written: "Nothing in his life became him like the leaving of it." It was true that nothing England had ever done on the subcontinent or anywhere else, for that matter, could be classed with what she was about to do. "The Transfer of Power stands as one of the greatest acts done in history by anyone," said Vallabhbhai Patel in a communiqué issued as Minister of Information and Broadcasting for the Interim Government of India.

Great Britain had expected and desired to hand over control to India and Pakistan as a single nation; but, if the two chose to divide, there is no doubt but that she wished well to both of them. No attention she gave to the one was denied the other, and every assistance was made available to Pakistan especially, which had very few resources, to enable it to get under way. As soon as the Indian Independence Act had been safely shepherded through Parliament, the Interim Government was split into two Provisional Governments, which met daily and provided a workable framework of government for each of the new nations. In addition, so that independence could be speeded along, the Provisional Governments were supplemented by a Partition Council, which took action on matters of immediate and mutual concern.

ELEVEN DAYS LEFT TO PREPARE FOR TRANSFER OF POWER announced the viceregal calendar. "Scarcely more than a fortnight," Jawaharlal realized, glancing up from his files. He had enjoyed the dinner party that Indira had arranged for several friends the night before and served in the garden; but, actually, he was working so hard that he had almost lost track of time and measured his days by actions taken, affairs settled, and questions decided instead of by hours. The subject up for consideration at the moment was no less a one than Dominion Status.

"Somehow people seem to have some doubts about this word *Dominion Status*," Mountbatten said by way of opening the conference in his office. "Let me be clear about it. It is absolute independence in every possible way, with the sole exception that the Member States of the British Commonwealth of Nations are linked together voluntarily. In fact, they look to one another for support, mutual trust, and in due course affection."

The Viceroy had chosen to deliver that speech advisedly, remembering how often and how fully Indian nationalists, Jawaharlal Nehru among them, had rejected Dominion Status. Actually, he didn't need to worry, for the atmosphere in which he was negotiating was a congenial one. There was nothing in the kind of association that he described to which the Congress Party would object. Indeed, they could see much to be gained from the voluntary association of nations having a common colonial heritage. In the end, both India and Pakistan were willing to opt for membership in the Commonwealth.

At twelve, midnight, on August 14, Lord Louis Mountbatten stood alone in his study. For the first time in months, there was no urgent business to be done. He had been to Karachi earlier in the day. He and Lady Mountbatten had attended the inauguration of the new government of Pakistan and then flown back to India in good time to take part in the ceremonies connected with The Appointed Day.* His official duties would be resumed shortly with a visit from Nehru and Prasad; but, meanwhile, there was very little left for him to do. He stepped up to the big wall calendar that he had requested to have hung behind his desk. ONE DAY LEFT TO PREPARE . . . it read. He looked at his watch. The hour was nearing twelve. He took the calendar down from the wall and placed it in the wastebasket. Then he turned out the desk lamp, sat down and waited, reflecting with some contentment upon the events of the recent past.

In the Parliament building, great arc lights played full upon the scene. As the hands of the clock approached the hour of twelve, a magical hush came over the Constituent Assembly. A man of slight build approached the Speaker's Chair, which was flanked on either side by his comrades of many years' association; Vallabhbhai Patel, Rajendra Prasad, Maulana Abul Kalam Azad, Acharya Kripalani, Jairamdas Doulatram, Syed Mahmud, Govind Ballabh Pant, others whose names were less well known but who were loved and

---

* In the Indian Independence Act, August 15, 1947, was referred to as The Appointed Day, and before independence occurred the term was popularly used.

admired; Shri Rajagopalachari, Diwan Chaman Lall, Jai-prakash Narain, Sarvepalli Radhakrishnan—a veritable pan-oply of greatness and of friendship.

Only one was absent upon that occasion, but his pres-ence was deeply felt. Gandhiji had chosen to celebrate The Appointed Day in Calcutta with the Muslim Governor of Bengal. Almost certainly the province was to be divided when the boundaries were announced, and the decision was going to be hard for Bengalis to take. In all probability, there would be violence. So Gandhi had told his friends that he thought it was better if he were on the spot where he could try his best to avert bloodshed; but his spirit and his prayers would be in Delhi and with them at that moment.

The speaker had not planned to talk from notes. He placed an elbow on the lectern and leaned his chin upon his hand. The clock was at the hour. "Long years ago," Panditji began, "we made a tryst with destiny, and now the time comes when we shall redeem our pledge, not wholly or in full measure, but very substantially. At the stroke of the midnight hour, when the world sleeps, India will wake to life and freedom."

Could anything in Asoka's empire, Akbar's, Elizabeth's, or Victoria's have matched the wonder of that day? "Let me formally invite you," said Prasad to Mountbatten, no longer the Viceroy, "to do us the honor of becoming the first Gover-nor-General of Independent India." "I accept," His Lord-ship replied, bowing. "But let me, in my turn, ask to be re-garded as one of yourselves." At nine in the morning, the leaders of the young nation were driven in state to the Vice-roy's house and a twenty-one-gun salute resounded through the city. The doors of the rich and stately Durbar Hall were swung open and there amidst the livery of kings, the cabinet ministers of Independent India were sworn in.

It was a nationwide holiday. An order went out to unlock the gates of jails and free all political prisoners. There was rejoicing in every village and town. Jugglers, folk dancers, and storytellers paraded through the streets. The smell of rose petals and incense perfumed the air. Fireworks, illuminations, and parties were planned for the evening. Drumming and merrymaking would go on till dawn.

Toward noon on that day the sky turned gray above the capital; but, even so, the celebrations continued. The morning round had been lavish and stately. The time had come for the flag-raising ceremony at the Soldiers' Monument. Light rain began to fall, but, undaunted, a jubilant throng collected.

Jawaharlal Nehru, Prime Minister of the new Republic of India, arrived at the monument to find an audience that was much, much larger than he had anticipated. The fluttering pennants of the Bengal Lancers, who constituted the body guard of the former Viceroy, heralded the appearance of the Mountbattens in their handsome black and gold carriage; but it was quite impossible for the Governor-General to reach the platform. The crowds were too great. He stood at attention and signaled to the Prime Minister that he would take the salute from where he was.

The rain diminished slightly. Jawaharlal Nehru stepped up to the flagpole. The band played "God Save the King." Slowly, the Union Jack of Great Britain was drawn from the masthead where it had flown for so long. The strains of the Indian national anthem were taken up and Panditji raised the flag of Independent India against a broken sky. No longer would that flag be hidden. It would never be destroyed. As it had flown in the villages, so now it would fly over the nation, triumphant.

Every face was lifted. Jawaharlal too had his eyes fixed

upon the banner. He kept his hand steady; but never in all his life had he sensed such anticipation. It was the crowning moment of all his years. *"Jai Hind, Jai Hind,* Victory to India," the people cried. The flag reached full mast. *"Jawaharlal ki jai! Jawaharlal ki jai!"* the multitude thundered. *"Mountbatten ki jai! Jai! Jai! Jai!"*

India's bravest hope had been fulfilled. The clouds parted; and, as if to set a seal upon a mighty document, a shimmering rainbow arched the sky. Swaraj was born.

part 3 *1947–1964*

New India they called it. Suddenly, all over the world, one saw references to it: "New India builds . . ."; "New India's rivers"; ". . . a child of the New India." Much there was that was new; but much there was too that was old. The spirit was new. The conditions were old. The challenge lay in linking the two.

In the same way that Elizabeth I of England had inherited practices from Akbar the Great, New India in its turn inherited certain traits and a machinery of government that had outlasted not one but two empires. Akbar had tried to bring peace between Muslims and Hindus. England had assumed the safety of both communities as her trust. Now India and Pakistan were jointly charged with that responsibility. The Islamic Republic of Pakistan had been carved out of the subcontinent and it had a majority of Muslims as its citizens; but India was home to a sufficient number of believers of Islam to make it the third-largest concentration of Muslims in the world. After the furies of partition had spent themselves, she was left with approximately forty million believers in Islam, and providing security for them was the most urgent necessity that confronted her.

Akbar had ruled by making alliances with local princes, and Great Britain had found it feasible to continue many of his arrangements. When Lord Mountbatten had been appointed Viceroy, there had been over six hundred such agreements still in effect with maharajas. When the date for independence had been set, he had called the princes together and had urged them, in view of what was about to happen, to merge their territories with either India or Pakistan, depending upon their location, their economic needs, and the religious makeup of their populations. By the time power was actually transferred from British to Indian hands, all but three of the princes had signified their choices.

The question of what was to happen to the princes was a burning one. Throughout the centuries they had ruled with unquestioned splendor, confident of the protection of the British Crown. When independence came, they were hardly prepared for it. Only a handful had bothered to concern themselves with modern statecraft; and if they wanted to unite, there were enough of them so that they could be a very disruptive force in a young nation. They had money, guards, and influence at their command.

The business of weaving the former Princely States into the fabric of divided India was entrusted to a special States Ministry, master-minded by Panditji and headed by Vallabhbhai Patel. Patel worked with discretion and dispatch. Within a year of the date of independence he had reached individual agreements with the rulers, agreements that guaranteed them personal wealth and protection as long as they lived, but deprived them and their families of power and inheritance. In a very short time, assimilation of their holdings was well nigh complete; and, by and large, the former rulers were satisfied that things had turned out as well as could be expected for them.

With the passing of the maharajas, India lost a dimension of ceremony and display. Their elephants, their glittering swords, and fairy-tale palaces had helped to capture the interest of generations in a faraway and mysterious land; but the trappings of feudalism had outlived their usefulness. Princes had no more of a role than any other citizens in a democracy; and it was high time that their kingdoms were opened to the light of learning and progress.

The rapid and complete integration of the majority of the former Princely States was one of New India's proudest achievements and one that was accomplished with amazing calm at a time when the country was otherwise rent by strife and malice. For, apart from all the rest, there was also Kashmir. In that state the inheritance of Hindu-Muslim feeling, entrenched within a prince's kingdom, touched off a conflagration that threatened to envelop the subcontinent.

Kashmir lies in the northwest corner of India, hemmed in by the fastnesses of the Himalaya mountains, but neighbor to Russia, China, Afghanistan, and Pakistan. Of the ancient trade routes that pass over the mountains from Central Asia to India, the one through Kashmir is the easiest. From Kashmir flow three mighty rivers, which water the plains of northern India and Pakistan: the Indus, the Jhelum, and the Chenab. At the time of partition, Kashmir was a territory about as large as Minnesota.

A little over four million people lived in Kashmir in 1947. They were farmers and artisans, concentrated largely in the mild and fertile valleys. Classified by religion, they were about seventy-seven percent Muslims, and the rest Hindus, Sikhs, and Buddhists. Their capital was at Srinagar, acknowledged to be one of the most beautiful spots in the world.

In 1586 Kashmir had been conquered by Akbar. With the collapse of the Mogul empire, the territory had passed to the hands of the Afghans and then to Ranjit Singh, a fiery leader of the Punjab in the early years of the nineteenth century. After his time, the East India Company had been able to conclude treaties that consolidated the scattered holdings in the area and placed Kashmir securely under the rule of a maharaja, a Hindu of the Dogra clan. It was a maharaja of the same clan who was ruling the state in 1947.

Early in the 1930's, a well-educated young reformist Muslim by the name of Sheikh Mohammed Abdullah had gone to Kashmir and had set about to improve the situation he found there. Up until then the maharaja had been recognized as the legal owner of all property in the state and the peasants were actually his chattels. The army was recruited from members of his clan and no one excepting his relatives was permitted to own a gun. He was a Hindu and instituted laws that discriminated against Muslims. In fact, his administration showed little or no sympathy with the people's wants and needs.

First of all, Sheikh Mohammed Abdullah tried to establish a more representative government in Kashmir. He gained popular support rather quickly. However, fighting broke out between his supporters and the forces of the maharaja, and Abdullah was taken prisoner. Thanks to the intervention of His Majesty's Government, he was later released and a commission was appointed to recommend constitutional and social changes in Kashmir. Certain reforms were agreed upon, but they were meager and, essentially, the maharaja retained much of his power throughout the 1930's and 1940's.

With the build-up to independence, tension mounted in the state. Sheikh Mohammed Abdullah affiliated his people's movement with the Indian National Congress. A rival group turned to the Muslim League for support. The maharaja was infuriated and finally exercised his right to close off his boundaries and handle affairs in the way in which he alone saw fit.

In July, 1947, when Lord Mountbatten convened the Chamber of Princes, he recommended strongly that they *accede* to either India or Pakistan immediately. In the case of Kashmir, he went even farther than that. He personally visited the state to impress upon the maharaja the necessity of his coming to a decision before The Appointed Day. The maharaja had already been involved in conversations with Mohammed Ali Jinnah that might lead to Kashmir's acceding to Pakistan, but as Lord Mountbatten stated later, "Had he acceded to Pakistan before August 14, 1947, the future Government of India had allowed me to give His Highness an assurance that no objection whatever would be raised by them." In view of what happened afterward, it is tragic that His Highness refused even to confer with Lord Mountbatten upon the occasion of that visit.

On August 12 the maharaja of Kashmir announced his willingness to negotiate "Standstill Agreements" with both India and Pakistan. On August 15 such an agreement was signed with Pakistan. It authorized Pakistan to operate the postal services within Kashmir, and obligated it to transport food and other necessities to the valley. This met the most urgent needs of the state, so the Indian agreement, which had been talked about, never materialized.

Within a few weeks, however, it looked as if the leadership of Pakistan was using the privileges accorded by the Standstill Agreement in order to force the maharaja of Kashmir to accede. Supplies that Pakistan tried to transport failed to reach their destinations. Important railway services were canceled. Kashmir complained that it was being made the victim of what amounted to an economic blockade. Pakistan countered with the statement that when Muslim refugees passed through Kashmiri territory, they were mistreated. Kashmir said it objected to having refugees cross the border carrying weapons. The maharaja and Jinnah argued at length, each accusing the other.

On October 21, 1947, tribesmen numbering in the thousands marched across the line between Pakistan and Kashmir and moved toward the capital at Srinagar. They were armed and well equipped. Their progress was swift. Over the mountains and down the Jhelum Valley Road they came, capturing the town of Mandu, sacking the village of Baramula, seizing a place called Mahura and taking command of the electric power plant that provided electricity for Srinagar.

On October 24, the maharaja requested troops from India. India answered that she could not send soldiers to Kashmir unless Kashmir were Indian territory. The maharaja offered to accede. At an emergency meeting of the Indian Cabinet held on October 26, his offer of accession to India was considered and accepted. Troops were flown to Kashmir.

The Indian army arrived when tribesmen were within five miles of Srinagar, having cut a savage, desolate path to their destination. The maharaja had fled for his life, taking with him his relatives, his jewels, his carpets, and his cars. He ensconced himself at the winter palace in Jammu. The state was without a head.

Nearly fifty thousand people were homeless as a result of the invasion. Millions of rupees' worth of property was lost. Livestock had been destroyed. The tribesmen had swept onward almost without hindrance and, in fact, more Muslims than Hindus had been killed as a result.

Vexed and bleeding India! How could she take under her wing still another territory, and one at war? Refugees were pouring into the country daily from the west and from the east, millions of new citizens to be clothed, to be fed, and to be housed and educated. Others were leaving, and must somehow be granted safe passage across the borders. Meanwhile, the skies of northern India were red from the fires of destruction. The streets of Delhi were in panic.

Yet, at heart she still believed that Hindus and Muslims were of one brotherhood. "So long as I am Prime Minister," Panditji said, "India will never become a Hindu state." He had never accepted the fact that because a man was a Muslim, he had to go and live elsewhere; nor that a state, even with a majority of Muslims, could not be part of free India. But how far were he and India to be compelled to go in defense of this idea? How long would they be tested?

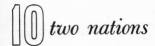

10 two nations

Dawn was beautiful in the valley. Mist clung to the lakes. Birds splashed by the water's edge and swooped upward in bright spirals toward the snows. A boatman glided his craft along the canal; but so deftly did he paddle that the surface of the stream was hardly ruffled. Temple bells rang for Hindus. Faithful Muslims, shrouded in embroidered shawls, knelt for prayer and inclined their heads toward Mecca. On his way to pasture the cowherd sang softly. In a pool at fabled Shalimar, scented lotus opened. Day broke across the wrinkled faces of the mountains and all the green gardens of Kashmir spread their splendor for the sun.

This was a scene every Indian schoolboy knew, for he head heard it described often in song and drama. The lovely valley of Kashmir amid the towering mountains was both the legendary birthplace of the Hindu god Krishna, and a paradise on earth, enhanced by the works of Mogul kings.

To Kashmir throughout the centuries travelers of all nations had journeyed to find rest, refreshment, and peace.

Jawaharlal Nehru, Prime Minister of independent India, knew Kashmir too. As a young man, he had trekked across its wild, high passes on foot, and had vowed that he would return to climb again every year. The demands of duty and office had prevented his fulfilling that vow, but the very thought of the valley and its majestic setting had been enough to give him strength sometimes when he had needed it in the midst of urgent business.

It was impossible for him to think of Kashmir without remembering Kamala, too. She had been a Kashmiri and had brought some of its loveliness with her to Anand Bhawan. It was in Kashmir that they had spent their honeymoon long years before, as had Indira and her husband. Yes, the Nehru family had had long associations, both personal and political, with the area, and the Prime Minister's memory of the place was of "a fair country and a peaceful people."

As his special plane now topped the peaks and raced toward the gorgeous valley, Panditji had his eyes glued to the window. In the seat ahead of him, Indira was keeping a sharp watch too; and when she saw the hills, and the people on the hills, she turned to her father and smiled. The Prime Minister's secretary, who had been working at some papers on the opposite side of the aisle, got up and came across. He leaned over an empty seat to have his own look at the sun-dazzled heights. This was Kashmir, the pilot announced. Without anyone's having spoken another word, a pleasant expectancy was conveyed from person to person in the cabin.

The plane touched down in Srinagar and the door opened. Along the edge of the airstrip Indian soldiers stood at attention. With a reassuring smile and a wave of his hand, the Prime Minister stepped out, followed by Indira. Resplendent in a black wool coat and fur cap, Sheikh Mohammed Abdullah, the young reformer to whom the government of Kashmir had been entrusted, strode forward. The two men met and clasped hands in greeting.

All Srinagar was out to welcome them. Standing side by side in an open jeep, Sheikh Mohammed and Jawaharlal toured the city. Along the narrow lanes and alleyways people were massed shoulder to shoulder, waving tiny Indian flags. Townsfolk peered over balconies and down from the flat tops of buildings in the marketplace. They tossed their caps and shouted as the leaders passed. Sheikh Mohammed Abdullah and the Prime Minister, each so vigorous and handsome in his own way, smiled and waved to them in return.

Fighting between the Indian army and the invading tribesmen was still in progress a short distance from Srinagar, and the Prime Minister's brief ride that morning could hardly have been called a triumphal tour. Remembering the opulence of the old days under the maharaja, some in the crowd must have been embarrassed at the meager display of welcome that had been prepared. But Panditji had come to Kashmir for other purposes than to ride in ceremony and he did not need flowered archways or sweet-smelling garlands to convince him of the people's affection. He saw it displayed on their earnest faces. There was no doubt but that the men, women, and tiny children who thronged about his car were glad to see him.

It was only when he got a chance to see the people at closer range that he could detect a shadow lurking behind the smiles. Then he saw that the faces of his hosts were not quite as trusting as they might have been, as happy or as confident. This hurt him, but he had expected it, considering what the population had just been through. Indira's sensitive eye soon caught the same message, and for a while it bothered her more than it did her father because she hadn't been as well prepared for it. It was a hard thing to explain and get used to right away.

With her sari drawn modestly around her head, the Prime Minister's daughter rode in the jeep that followed that of Jawaharlal Nehru and Sheikh Mohammed Abdullah. Her *namaskar* greetings were intended for the women and children primarily. She saw how worried they looked and she missed the effusive warmth with which she would have been received upon other occasions. She was touched to see how immensely relieved and strengthened the crowd was at sight of her father, how the old folk wept when they saw him and the young people pushed forward and tried to touch his feet *; but, all the same, they did not display the same vigor and enthusiasm they would have shown before independence.

Freedom had not brought them what they hoped it would, Indira realized with a sudden twinge of remorse, as she got down from the jeep and mingled with the crowd. She felt sympathy and a desire to comfort the gentle, frightened people that surrounded her. How could they have known what it would be like? she asked herself. They were so poor, so out of touch with the rest of the world for so long. Then, suddenly, they were engulfed in a conflict they had had no part in creating and were fighting for their very lives. Meanwhile, there was a gap of many, many years in knowledge and experience to be filled in. They could not help but feel bewildered, threatened, and withdrawn.

Land, taxes, water, food, schools, markets, and guns.

* It is a gesture of respect in India for a person to touch the ground and then with the same hand to touch the feet of an older person and one's own forehead. It is a way of saying: "I am blessed by being in contact with the dirt beneath your feet."

These were the things Sheikh Mohammed Abdullah, the Prime Minister, and their officers talked about behind closed doors for hours on that November day. Inside the conference room, the problems of Kashmir appeared to be manageable. The Prime Minister dealt with such questions daily; and, though decisions were never entirely in his own hands, when the same issues were raised in Srinagar as in Delhi, he could think of the ministers of the central government, whom he had left behind, predict what their opinions would be, and recommend action. Sitting in conference with Sheikh Mohammed and his men, he felt that the future of the state was assured, constructed as it was of strategies, agreements, budgets, and laws.

Yet, in the end, governments are constituted of people, however strong and necessary their policies are; and, in a democracy, those policies must be designed to meet the needs of people. Panditji knew that; and, as he listened to the long reports from the army, the officers of finance, and the agriculturalists, he found himself thinking of the farmers, the soldiers, the children, the shopkeepers, and the housewives he had seen and whom his informants represented.

The meeting was held around a table close to a latticed window. From time to time, birds flew in and out, oblivious of the formality of the occasion. The Prime Minister became aware of those tiny visitors as he had been aware of them during his long sessions in jail. Now, as then, they seemed to appear as messengers from another world.

Through the open lattice also came the muffled sounds of daily life. Panditji caught the cry of a peddler hawking his wares and he heard a mother crooning her baby to sleep. He found it harder and harder to concentrate upon what was being discussed in the room. As the day drew to a close, his head often turned in the direction of the window as if there were more to instruct him in the sight of homes and fields than in the documents that had been prepared for his signature.

That was November 11. On November 12 the sun rose again over the valley. The Prime Minister, Sheikh Mohammed Abdullah, and Indira were in a jeep, this time on their way out of Srinagar. In front of them was a military escort, and behind wound a long trail of army vehicles, crowded with guards, with officers, secretaries, and advisers whom the Prime Minister had brought with him from the capital. The procession was headed for the front and for the towns that had been invaded.

Panditji insisted that his party visit the most forward posts held by the Indian army. He wanted to see with his own eyes the conditions under which his men were fighting; and so, he spent a considerable amount of time scrambling over rocks and in and out of lookout posts, as well as rambling in the jeep and listening to the reports of field officers. He reviewed troops and gave official greetings to men on duty. Together, he and Indira watched the women's militia, for the most part made up of girls who had never appeared unveiled outside their homes until a few weeks ago. How proudly they went through their high-stepping drills for their Prime Minister!

The morning was difficult, but, despite its lessons, reassuring on the whole. The Prime Minister found that the spirits of the forces at the front were high. The officers were tireless. When he got back to Delhi, he would be able to say that the Indian line was confidently held. Moreover, wherever his party had gone—along treacherous mountain roads, through pastures and beside brooks, past farms, or tiny huts —as soon as they had caught sight of his vehicles, the peasants had shouted buoyantly, "Victory Victory to India! Victory to Hindus and Muslims together." They hadn't given up, not at all! On the contrary, they seemed to be completely one with events.

What was less assuring was the evidence he had found that the source of the trouble had not been local. Through the field glasses and telescopes located at widely scattered posts, the Prime Minister had observed steady lines of men and materials moving into position from the opposing side, their maneuvers well planned and orderly. In his own hands he had held guns that had belonged to the so-called tribes-men, not clumsy weapons but up-to-date rifles stamped with foreign trademarks. He had asked to be shown the list of prisoners and their identification cards. For the most part, the names were of boys whose homes were in the far north-west of old India, in the territory that had so lately become Pakistan. Evidence was pointing in that direction, but how hard it was, even now, for him to think of it as an enemy country.

It was nearly noon when the Prime Minister's party reached the town of Baramula on the way back to Srinagar. By contrast with the busy countryside and with Srinagar, the streets of the recently invaded town were silent. The approach lay through blackened rubble, and almost before the group knew it, their jeeps were well within the city limits. However, the Prime Minister soon sensed where he was and reacted immediately. Leaning forward in his seat, he tapped the driver on the shoulder. "Slowly! Slowly!" he commanded.

The jeep rolled over a temporary bridge, past a burned-out mosque, and around the ashes of a cluster of wooden shops. One remaining sign from the original build-ings stood miraculously intact, propped against a milestone. Otherwise, there was little to suggest that, just a few weeks before, this had been the bustling market center for fifteen thousand people. With a sudden look of dread, the Prime Minister ordered the driver to stop. "I had better get down now," he said.

The company alighted from the cars. As if they were explorers who had stumbled upon an ancient site, they picked their way carefully through the ruins, while the jeeps crawled along behind them. Painfully, the party tried to adjust to the desolate scene. Unconsciously, Indira reached for the loose end of her sari and drew it over her head. Panditji gazed, incredulous, at the destruction.

The little town of Baramula was one of several that had lain directly on the route of the invaders. It had been used as a strategic outpost as they advanced. Less than half the population survived. The place had been recaptured by Indian troops only a day or two before the visit of the Prime Minister.

There was a committee of survivors waiting to welcome the Prime Minister in what had been the center of town. They saw him approach on foot, turning aside often, bending down to speak to refugees who were camped in makeshift tents by the wayside. Through the haunted city the news had spread that Panditji had come. When they had heard it, wounded persons who had thought to hide their sorrows and their scars from sight of the party came out in spite of themselves. A stray child caught up with the Prime Minister and tagged along by his side, clinging to his hand. People began to collect.

The welcoming committee stood before a newly erected shrine. When he first set eyes upon it, the Prime Minister was tempted to smile, for the structure looked to him like an odd combination of all the shrines he had ever seen constructed anywhere in the world. It was built with a dome, like a mosque, but a picture of the Hindu god Krishna was hung upon it, while at the side fluttered a Buddhist prayer flag. Incense was burning and fresh garlands were strung across its face.

The Prime Minister greeted the townsfolk, then paused for a second and eyed their shrine. A man who had been appointed as host said quietly, "This is where he fell." When the Prime Minister gave no immediate sign of recognition, "Sherwani," the man explained. "You know Sherwani."

Yes, the Prime Minister did know Sherwani. Panditji remembered the first time he had met Sherwani when he had been a keen-eyed young worker in the Congress Party, an anxious and proud youth, eager for adventure. Perhaps the hills and forests encouraged the development of such characters, for Sherwani had become something of a Robin Hood in Kashmir. He had been wily and clever and had taken to turning up in unexpected places, quick to set right a wrong. The Kashmiris had loved Sherwani, the Prime Minister knew, as the downtrodden love their avengers. He had been almost a law unto himself, a wonderfully swashbuckling but persuasive character.

At the time of the invasion, a price had been set on Sherwani's head. He had avoided capture for a while because people had been anxious to protect him, but when he had been taken prisoner at last, the enemy planned to make use of him. They had brought him into the square at Baramula and had ordered him to profess allegiance to their side. He had refused to do so, and the tribesmen had killed him as a consequence; but his last words had been, *"Hindu-Mussalman ki jai!* Hindus and Muslims are brothers. They will win together."

Across the hills Sherwani's name was legend now, to be passed down through the generations as a hero. As a matter of fact, Panditji had wanted to be shown the spot where he

had fallen and to have the shrine pointed out to him; but
the importance of Sherwani's example had never revealed itself to him as clearly as it did when he stood among the few
survivors of the wretched city. *"Hindu-Mussalman ki jai!"*
The country must rise to that slogan and never let it die.

The Prime Minister reached out his hand and touched
the shrine. He took from his buttonhole the rose he had
slipped into it that morning. "What you have done is fitting," he said to the people. "In years to come all India will
worship at this place." He laid his rose before the picture,
mustered a smile, and raised one hand to his forehead in
farewell. With the other, he pushed his way through the
crowd. "Now we had better have a look at the mission," he
said to his secretary.

The mission had belonged to a foreign church and had
stood at the top of a hill on the outskirts of Baramula. There
had been a chapel, a school, and a dispensary tended by visiting nuns. The mission had housed one of the few hospitals
in Kashmir and for many, many years its doors had been
open night and day. But the gates were closed now; the loving sisters gone; and they would not return. The invasion
had brought the work of the mission to an end too. The
tribesmen had swept over the place like a scourge and what
they had left behind was blight and waste.

The Prime Minister heard the story of the attack on the
mission retold by his Kashmiri hosts. He saw the wreckage.
With his party, he walked through the ravaged rooms of the
hospital, the nursery, and the dispensary. The precious
equipment lay smashed, the bottles of medicine upturned,
the beds stolen or hacked to pieces. He stood amidst rubbish
in the remains of the former chapel, where broken statues
looked out through gaping walls into a lifeless compound.

He and his companions went to see what was left of the library and the school. Piles of torn and partially burned books lay about. The sight of these seemed to touch the Prime Minister especially, and he got down on his knees and fingered the crumbling pages. He was surrounded by the signs of plunder and vandalism—torn curtains, broken glass, ransacked cupboards—and worse still was the ominous silence that testified that whatever had been there which was live and warm and generous had been gutted and killed.

Old and deep run the traditions of Indian hospitality. Glad and grateful has the country been for mercy from whatever source it has come. At the height of the freedom struggle, Jawaharlal Nehru had said, "It is not the foreigner we fight. It is his policies." Afterward, despite the crimes committed by Hindus against Muslims, some of which had been enacted in Kashmir, the India of his dreams was still "a noble mansion in which all her children might dwell in safety." The Prime Minister knew full well that that structure would never be completed without many foreign hands helping in the process—in big ways, through governments, perhaps, but also in small and personal ways. The massacre of Baramula and the outrage suffered at its mission were like an ax striking at the taproot of his hope for the independent country.

The appearance of the mission compound exhausted the patience of one of the government secretaries. He clenched his fists and, half under his breath, muttered a threat to those who had wreaked such torment. His words were echoed by a young man from Delhi. Their sentiments had never been intended for the ears of the Prime Minister, but he heard them all the same. At the door of the library he turned and looked at the two men for a second with flashing eyes, as if he were about to reprimand them. Then he said to his group, "Let me be alone for a few minutes. I need to collect my thoughts."

Friends waited near the doorway, as quiet as the empty rooms around them. What was left of a broken chair was brought out for Indira. The rest of the party stood, each busy with his own thoughts, hardly daring to speak aloud, while Panditji walked by himself in the trampled garden.

At first the Prime Minister paced slowly back and forth on the garden paths, hands behind his back, head down. He went over to the tumbled-down wall and put his hand against the gatepost, as if to steady himself. He felt that the world as he knew it was slipping away. He had the sensation of flying, which he had so often had in dreams, but this time he hardly knew whether there was firm ground beneath him at all.

He looked down to the village in the valley, ruined. He had seen war damage before, more vast and terrifying, in China, in Spain, and even in England itself; but in those ruins he had always met a purpose that had spoken above the devastation, and out of the debris he had had a vision of a new world rising, more noble than the one that had passed. But where was the purpose in this? he asked. Where was the end, if brother were going to pursue brother, as was happening in Kashmir? He had seen violence, too, in his own India, when the British had set out to crush the freedom movement with such unremitting zeal. But in that too there had been purpose—an idea and a leader who kept before India ends more fine and just.

Jawaharlal Nehru walked along the weedy path. In a far corner of the garden, he saw a few flowers, still blooming. He bent down and gathered them.

Standing at the door of the library, the Prime Minister's

secretary glanced at his wristwatch; and, knowing that the flight to Delhi was scheduled to leave soon, he stepped out to call the Prime Minister. He saw him coming, bouquet in hand, but with a face so grave that he could not bring himself to speak.

Panditji approached the step, and putting one hand against the sagging doorjamb, he raised himself like an old man. His face was pale and drawn and he showed that he was wrestling with tragic thoughts. He barely took notice of the secretary, but placed the flowers in his hands. "Let's take them back to Gandhiji," he said. "They are the only clean things I can find for him in Baramula." After speaking these words, he remained with hands upraised, as if he had come to the end of what he could bring himself to do.

No one spoke. No one moved. The men looked away. Indira was sobbing. After a short while, her subdued cries seemed to reach the Prime Minister, for he looked at her. Then his glance moved from one face to another within the room. There he saw the shock and grief that his associates had suffered too.

Their sorrow called the Prime Minister forth from himself. He became alert. His shoulders straightened. He went to Indira and put his hand on her head lovingly. "Come," he said, "we are going back to Delhi. We have a very great deal to do." Leaving the group, he strode again to the door and was already in the jeep before the others had left their places.

Gradually, with enormous labors, the wheels of progress began to turn, and great India, like a lumbering bullock cart, was on its way as an independent nation. Panditji didn't do all that was done to set the state in motion, but he certainly did a lot. Most evenings the lights did not go out in the Prime Minister's residence until two or two-thirty, and he was up and on the go again at six-thirty. How he found time to do all the things he was expected to do, and then make time to do so much more, no one could ever quite figure out, but it looked as if the man were inexhaustible.

Official duties mattered; yet, it mattered just as much and sometimes more that people knew their Prime Minister was nearby, and that he cared. There is a famous story about him, told of the time when Hindu-Muslim riots were at white heat in Delhi, in late November, 1947. The Prime Minister insisted that he be taken through the areas where the riots were at their worst. With reluctance, police officials agreed to the journey and tried to keep him constantly under guard. But somehow Panditji escaped, just for a moment. When they again spotted him, he was scrambling across a roof to rescue two children—Muslims who were stranded all by themselves. How many times during those first months of Independence did he take his life into his own hands, just to make sure that someone else was safe!

He was pushed and overworked, called upon to supply answers for endless questions related to government, and to perform countless untried tasks. Nevertheless, he persisted relentlessly in the basic job of training, encouraging, and inspiring his citizens, whether they were highly placed or in common circumstances. One night a messenger came to his house with the news that a tremendous mob of refugees had arrived in Delhi from the Punjab. They had suffered terribly at the hands of persecutors along the way. They were from wealthy homes, people with ample lands and prestige who had been reduced to rags and were camping in an old fort. Hungry, excited, vengeful, they were ready to fight anyone who molested them. As soon as he heard the story, the Prime

Minister decided that he would talk to the refugees. "Tonight," he insisted. "After what they've been through, it
would be cruel to ask them to wait any longer."

So the Prime Minister went to the fort, driven in an
open jeep, taking a couple of friends and three or four policemen with him. When he got there, he stood on the hood
of the car with a flashlight and talked to the refugees; man
to man, father to father, son to son, as he put it. He said he
knew what they had suffered and he sympathized. Furthermore, he realized exactly how they felt; but the fact that
they had suffered did not give them the right to revenge
themselves on other helpless people. He insisted that they lay
down their arms; the pickaxes, the scythes, the stones, and
the mattocks they had seized. Alone and unflinching, with
supreme confidence and goodwill, he succeeded in getting
them to do as he bade. When the country was severed by
such distrust that neither neighbors nor families were at
peace, he taught them, by his own example, to be unafraid.

Yet, he was so fair! Were his eyes completely closed to
provocations? Didn't he ever break down and apportion
blame? Yes, of course he apportioned blame, at what he
deemed to be the proper time and in the councils of the
world where he believed there would be an effect, but never
personally and in a vindictive way. He wouldn't countenance hatred. Like Gandhiji, he distinguished between the
man and his actions, between what was fair and unfair, just
or unjust. To those two men, no other boundaries mattered.

Once, in the afternoon, a meeting at the Prime Minister's office was interrupted by a report that Hindus were
looting the shops of Muslims in New Delhi and that the police were merely standing by and doing nothing. Out onto
the thoroughfare sped Panditji and down into the heart of
the business district, where he found the report to be true.

Onto the sidewalk he leapt and into the shops he stormed, while the mob and the police stood back in surprise. He pulled the truncheons from the hands of the looters and ordered them to return to their jobs. The Prime Minister reprimanded the police stoutly. "If any man of you kills anyone of another community," he declared, "he will have to kill Jawaharlal first and over my body you will have to repeat the crime."

With such constant vigilance and his dramatic presence, he set a new standard for the behavior of a Prime Minister. So far as India was concerned, he refused to look back in anger. Rather, he looked ahead with hope. He believed in the country so strongly, and in her ability to overcome her own condition, that he was utterly heedless of himself when he acted on her behalf. Someone asked him if he died, what should be said of him; and he answered: "If people choose to think of me then, I should like them to say: 'He was a man who, with all his mind and heart, loved India and the Indian people.'" Battered and tormented, those people were imperiled. He was ready to give them all that he had.

Jawaharlal Nehru turned fifty-eight in the year of Independence, but his looks were youthful and boyish, and he matched them with his abounding energy. Equipped with a keen and practiced interest in all manner of things, ranging from science to ballet and government to mountain climbing, he was a delight to meet. Scholars, artists, and statesmen sought his company. It was his finest hour. To be with him was to be renewed.

"I used to drop in most evenings at Panditji's," his friend Badr-ud-din Tyabji said. "Often enough, he was too busy to spare me more than a fleeting smile or a few words, but his house and the personality which radiated from it, was wonderful tonic for persons like me, who were suffering from a sense of physical danger but were also mentally and emotionally sick at the turn which events had taken in the country which they loved."

One of the particularly nice accompaniments to Panditji's life at that time was the presence of his grandchildren. Indira had two sons, Rajiv and Sanjay, and they lived at the Prime Minister's residence. Jawaharlal was a gay, rambunctious companion for them. After having waited for him in the reception room, dignitaries and friends were sometimes surprised to see him appear with one of the youngsters astride his shoulders. When he chose, he could tell most wonderful stories while the little ones cuddled on his lap. He also kept a panda in the garden as a pet for himself and the boys.

November and December of 1947 ticked by. January, 1948, came and went. Then it was six months, a year, and more since Independence. The British had gone. The government had held. Children were born. Factories opened. Fields were plowed. Schools rose up. Partition, like the experience of prison, receded into the corners of men's minds. "We got over it," the Prime Minister explained in a conversation one day. "Getting over it rather strengthened us. We got over something as bad as ever it could be, we thought; we were not ever again going to have it as bad as that."

"Something as bad as ever it could be . . ." In the bloodbath of partition, seventeen million people were exchanged between India and Pakistan. Upward of two million perished. Production was completely disrupted. Kashmir was fought for but never fully won. India took its case to the United Nations, and Pakistan defended its side with fervor. So began a long series of investigations and negotiations that yielded nothing tangible in the long run, because basically the two countries were deadlocked over the idea of a democracy as opposed to a religious state, and neither could let go. Mohammed Ali Jinnah, the man most responsible for dividing the subcontinent in the first place, had died; but that did not roll back the curtain of history. His successors struggled feverishly to maintain a stable government and to feed their people. In its way, India faced the same challenge, although it had much more to work with; but Gandhiji, the beloved Bapu, was gone too, killed by an assassin's bullet.

In the fall of 1947, while Panditji appeared to be everywhere at all times, Gandhiji had been a rock, a silent, steadying force throughout the tumult. He took to stopping for a few hours or days at a time in trouble-ridden neighborhoods around Delhi. Indira stayed with him often and helped to organize workers to support him. His presence was like salve on an open wound. With his disciples he set up camp, as it were, but continued his ministry wherever he was. His prayer meetings were open to everyone. When circumstances looked bleak and insoluble, his old friends, the boys he had trained and who now held the reins of state, came in succession to his door, including at times Jawahar, troubled and distraught.

On January 30, 1948, Bapu's prayer meeting was held in the garden of Birla House. A fortnight before that, a bomb had exploded at one of the sessions. All the same, Gandhiji had refused police protection. That afternoon he walked through the garden gate dressed in simple khadi garments draped casually round his body. A young man stepped forth from the crowd as if to greet him. Gandhiji returned the greeting just before the boy fired three fatal shots. "*Hai Ram!* God lives!" Gandhiji cried. A few minutes later he was dead.

How gaunt Panditji looked when he went out to address the crowd, his face starkly silhouetted against the twilight sky. "The light has gone out of our lives," he said, "and there is darkness everywhere." He paused, reflecting. "The light has gone out, I said, and yet I was wrong. For that light was no ordinary light. The light that has illumined this country for these many, many years will illumine this country for many more years, and a thousand years later that light will still be seen. The world will see it and it will give solace to innumerable hearts. For that light represented something more than the immediate present. It represented the eternal truths. If we remember that, then it will be well with India."

There was so much for Jawaharlal to do by himself. At least it looked as if he were alone to the outsiders, to foreigners, to those who were used to associating India and the British, and to newspaper readers in other countries who could not pronounce or distinguish the unfamiliar names of his associates. For Vallabhbhai Patel was there. He differed with the Prime Minister at times, but for two full years Jawaharlal had the benefit of his experienced wisdom and determined command. Pandit Pant was there, serving faithfully as Chief Minister in Jawaharlal's home state. Rajendra Prasad lived in the tradition of Gandhi to the end, President of India from 1947–1963. Nan was there, gracious, experienced, and intelligent. She became in succession: Her Excellency, the Ambassador of India to the Union of Soviet Socialist Republics; Her Excellency, the Ambassador of India to the United States of America and to Mexico; Member of Parliament; leader of the Indian Delegation to the United Nations; Madame President of the United Nations General Assembly; High Commissioner to the Court of St. James; Ambassador to Ireland, and later, Ambassador to Spain. Indira was there, living in her father's house with her two small boys, a leading interpreter of her father's ideas, an officer in the Congress Party. Sarojini Naidu was there for a while, lightening everyone's burdens with her wholesome, incisive wit. Maulana Azad was there as Minister of Education, Baldev Singh too, Diwan Chaman Lall, Syed Mahmud —all friends of a lifetime, their loyalties and skills tested in the fires of the struggle for independence.*

Outsiders looked at the problems as well—at the poverty, the illiteracy, the stagnation of science, and the shame of partition. They questioned whether India was going to make it. The same question had occurred to Jawaharlal in prison, long years before. To those who questioned, he answered with a poem, which he had loved and quoted in *Toward Freedom*. It was his answer in 1930 and it was his answer in 1950.

> *We—move with new desires.*
> *For where we used to build and love*
> *Is no man's land, and only ghosts can live*
> *Between two fires.*

India was not burning. It was building.

---

* One who was not there was the fearless and lovable Badshah Khan. When partition took place, his territory went to Pakistan. His Congress Party friends would have been glad to have given him asylum in India, but he refused to leave those who had depended upon him. He stayed where he was, among the Pathans. After years of imprisonment in a Pakistani jail, the "Frontier Gandhi" died in 1956. It was a tragic end to a life that had been luminous with kindly effort.

▯▯ *building* *

Like a wind the Prime Minister swept across the clearing.
Like a storm he crested the rock-strewn hill. Behind him, as
behind a cloud, the midwinter sun was lowering. In his right
hand he carried a short walking stick, which he used from
time to time to accent his remarks. As at the approach of a
sudden shower, the men had come running from their jobs,
stumbling and pushing, hammers and ropes still in their
hands. Close-packed, they squatted in their work clothes,
amazed and awestruck by Panditji's appearance.

It was a lonely, scraggy hillside in the state of Bihar.
Away to the west, behind the workmen, lay a stretch of low
blue mountains. The valley below was a trough of excava-
tions, littered with embankments, furrowed by roads, dotted

* The incident reported here is a true one. The speech, however, is a
composite, with quotations chosen from several speeches which the Prime
Minister made on this theme at about this time.

with sandpiles, traced by ditches. At the side of the Prime Minister knelt a thin worker with a soiled cloth wound around his head as a turban. A heavy stone had been thrown down in front of him. All in all, it was an unlikely time and setting for a speech by a head of state.

At the hilltop, the Prime Minister towered above the crews. He looked exactly as he felt at that moment, like a *Sardar,* a foreman, addressing his workmen. Yet, he had wanted to stop, in defiance of time and his schedule, because there was something he felt that he must say. He chose his words carefully and delivered them with an emphasis that incised them deeply upon the minds of his audience.

It was to be a great day for India, to be hailed as a glorious beginning. When the sun set that night on the border of Bihar, in a remote corner of the vast country where oil lamps and slow-driven bullocks were taken for granted, before a cheering throng of ten thousand people, the Prime Minister was going to open the gates of the Bokaro Power Station, whose generators were ready to transmit light and energy over the wires to Calcutta, the steel mills of Jamshedpur, and the city of Patna. Given a proper network of installations, Bokaro had sufficient power to light every village in India. Within an area encompassing thousands of square miles, a revolution was about to take place in the lives of town and village people. Tomorrow they could partake of modern utilities and benefit.

Moreover, the Bokaro generating plant was but one segment of the plans for the development of the massive Damodar River Valley, plans that would bring flood control and irrigation as well as electricity to the peasants of Bihar and Bengal. It was the sons and grandsons of farmers who had assembled in a sheltered village on a summer's night in 1920 and had heard a promise made by a young aristocrat named

Jawaharlal Nehru who would see the fruition of his dream. They, who were but a few of India's millions, were now participants in projects devised for the welfare of all villagers. Designs that had first been discussed quietly during the days of The Raj, then delayed by the upheavals of partition, were being executed. The year was 1953, and India was reaping the fruits of nationhood.

The Prime Minister had been allotted just two days for Damodar. That was hardly enough, since he was as determined as ever to see everything. It meant there was a lot of territory to be covered. Many, many miles lay between the site of one dam and the next, and between the headworks and the irrigation canals. Panditji expected to have the complicated enterprise explained to him in detail. He needed to get a close look at charts and maps so that he could visualize the rivers and picture the farms as they were going to be when the work was completed.

If he had had only himself to consider, Panditji would certainly have chosen to spend far longer in such an exciting place and with the engineers, but the varied tasks of India called him on. If Damodar were worthy of his attention, so, too, were Hirakud, Bhakra-Nangal, and the Maithon dams, spanning wider rivers and steeper gorges. There was a new Chemical Institute to visit in Poona, one of ten, and a National Museum opening in Madras. Since India was so diverse, and he as Prime Minister stood at the hub of its development, like the villagers who would witness the coming of the lights, he had to be ready to absorb a lifetime of change in a few hours.

That day, however, the Prime Minister had felt more than equal to his task. He had delighted the young administrators with his friendly, genuine interest. He had questioned the draftsmen and the supervisors astutely. The engineers had been surprised by the range of the man's mechanical knowledge. Characteristically, he had been eager. He had been radiant. Invigorated by the sight of such a fascinating plan, ready to follow it all the way from the drawing board to the fields and the village huts, he had set a pace on the hillsides that was little short of a run.

On the dry embankment at the site of the Konar dam, a subsidiary designed to store the water that would cool the generators of Bokaro, the Prime Minister had come upon a single workman carrying stones. With able strength and rhythm, this man took on his head a boulder weighing several hundred pounds, mounted with it to the top of the hill, and dropped it there so that it could be fitted into place on the face of the dam. Other stone carriers mounted behind him. The first man descended to pick up another piece of rock and deliver it to its destination, then another, and another.

In his way, the stone carrier was typical of the people and the methods involved in raising the new structures of India, so typical that it was surprising that Panditji noticed him or singled him out of the crowd. In fact, after having watched the operation for a moment or two, the Prime Minister had started to go on. But then an idea had occurred to him and he had turned back.

"Tell me," he asked the lean, strong-muscled man who had first caught his eye, "tell me why it is that you carry stones like that one you just dropped?"

The workman was startled by the Prime Minister's unexpected inquiry. He thought perhaps he had displeased Mr. Nehru in some way. He dropped onto his knees, and in a subservient tone reminiscent of the years of empire, he answered, "My foreman tells me to, Sahib. I do my work. He pays me wages at the end of the week."

The Prime Minister looked shocked. Curious as to the cause of the incident, other stone carriers came up in their turn and stood in a little circle around their fellow workman and the Prime Minister. Panditji turned to one and then to another and repeated his question:"And you, what are you doing?"

With very little variation, the laborers gave essentially the same information that the first had given. Defensively at first, and then with somewhat more confidence, they explained the reasons for their work in simple, obvious terms. Either that or they shook their heads and said honestly, "We don't know."

The Prime Minister dealt with the stone carriers in a kindly way; but his eyes were troubled. He became pensive and considered just what he was going to do next. He looked around at his hosts, the engineers, quizzically. One of them started to speak. "You must understand, sir," he began.

Panditji raised his hand for silence. He was not going to have anyone tell him that he had happened to stop an ignorant man who could not be expected to furnish any more than the statements he had given. The Prime Minister took a firm grip on his walking stick and with a wide gesture he circled the hillside. "Send for them," he said, indicating the people who were scattered like sand over the face of the dam. "Call them up," he demanded. "I wish to speak to them. I have something they had better hear."

Looking directly down into their work-worn faces, the Prime Minister started to speak even before the laborers were all assembled. "It is not often that I get to leave my office in Delhi and come out to visit you," he said, "so, before I go, there are a few things I would like to say."

The Prime Minister paused for a second or two while others came and squatted at his feet. So fresh was he from meetings with his Cabinet Ministers, so used to repeating the formulas of economists and conversing in the jargon of politicians, that he had to think for a minute how he was going to put what was on his mind.

"In that office in Delhi, where I spend my days, there is a map," he explained. "It is a huge map. It takes up one whole wall of my office and spreads from one side to the other," he said, marking out the area of his map with his stick in the air. "It is a map of India; and it shows the hills, the plains, the coasts, the railways, towns, and villages. So, even while I am shut up in my office, you could say that I am face to face with India all the time. But I often put a question to myself. 'Is this really India, this map on the wall?' I say. 'Is this our *Bharat Mata,* Mother India?' And the answer keeps coming back to me, 'No, this is not India; for India is people, the sons and daughters of Bharat Mata. They are India.' "

The Prime Minister paused and surveyed his audience. He used his stick to point out persons in the crowd. "It is you, and you, and you too," he said, singling out a scantily clothed old man with a hoe in his hand, a woman with an iron tray full of mortar, and a little boy who was carrying a goatskin of water slung across his back. "It is all of us," he emphasized, pointing first at himself and then at the engineers. "We are India."

"And you most of all," he proclaimed, addressing the stone carriers, "for she can only be as strong as the men who are ready to carry her burdens."

"Upon that map I also see great rivers," he continued. "They come tumbling out of the mountains of the north and for centuries they have watered and refreshed our land on their way to the sea. It is the rivers which make India what it is, a fertile land, instead of a desert. We could not live without them.

"But the rivers are not always kindly rivers. Sometimes the rivers are like unruly children," he commented, allowing himself to slip into the picturesque habits of speech that are characteristic of countryfolk. "And like unruly children anywhere, these rivers are not very well behaved. They destroy things, not because they are bad, but simply because they have not yet learned their proper places."

"Now it is you," he explained, pointing again at his audience. "It is you who must take on the job of controlling the rivers, and making them behave themselves. If they are left to plunder our lands as they have done in times past, our fields will be ravaged and our grain stores empty. Then, if that happens, what becomes of our India, our future and our dream?

"Long years ago," the Prime Minister reminded his listeners, "in this country of ours, we dared to dream of freedom, of a nation loosed from the bonds of colonialism. Mahatma Gandhi was father to that dream, and he helped us to fulfill it in large measure. But the old dream does not fit us any longer. We have won our independence. We must dare to dream a new dream not only of freedom but freedom which includes plenty for everyone, for the outcast and the peasant, the Muslim as well as the Hindu. And, in the fulfillment of that new dream, you people play a major part, because, ultimately, whether or not it comes true depends on you."

Panditji was quiet for a few seconds, letting his words sink in upon the minds of the assembly. A thrill of pride had stirred the ragged workmen at his feet. He could see it on their faces and in the way they were sitting, muscles poised, ears strained for his words. He went on, but in a less strident tone, speaking more as a friend than an instructor.

"Also, on my desk in Delhi," he said, "are plans, many, many plans, bound together in one big book which is called 'The First Five-Year Plan for the Development of India.' In that book there are plans for helping farmers to raise more food. There are plans for building hospitals. There are plans for starting factories. There is a particularly wonderful plan called *community development,* which has been designed to help you make your villages better places in which to live and raise your families.

"They hold something for all of us," Panditji reflected happily, "the five-year plans. But they, too, describe only the barest outlines of what India can do, once she is on the road to meeting her own needs."

The Prime Minister had been addressing his audience with eyes lowered almost as if musing to himself. Now, however, he set back his shoulders and looked again at the crowd. His voice resumed its usual cadence and he spoke earnestly. "Yet, without you," he reiterated, "without you men and women of India, the plans would only remain where they are, on paper. The fulfillment of the plans depends upon how you and I and all of us together approach our daily tasks."

The Prime Minister no longer tried to restrain himself or consider whether his choice of language was appropriate for this particular gathering. The strength of his feeling poured forth in ripe and impressive phrases. "India's real strength lies in the capacity of her people for disciplined work. Only hard work can bring us wealth and rid us of our poverty. Each one of us, therefore, man or woman, young or old, must work and toil. Rest is not for us. We did not win our freedom so that we might rest afterwards, but in order to work harder to hold onto and strengthen that freedom.

"Whatever you are asked to do," the Prime Minister said emphatically, "remember there is a great difference between the voluntary labor of a free man working for wages on an object of his own choice and the drudgery of a slave for a master. We labor as free men and women. It is freedom which accords us the dignity for which we and our ancestors longed. Let us not lay it aside, knowingly or unwittingly.

"Our labors, yours and mine, as free men and women are laying the foundations of a great future," the Prime Minister concluded. "Our labor of love for the cause of India will endure. For the fact is that we are building, brick by brick, the great dwelling place of free India.

"There is joy in such work," he affirmed, tossing his head and grinning. "There is joy. Because, even when we have departed, our work will be there for future generations to see.

"Therefore," Panditji insisted, again aiming his remarks at the workman he had first interrogated, "if anyone dares to stop you at a busy time of day and asks you what you are doing in an out-of-the-way place like this, while you measure and lift and unload your stones, you tell them that you are laying the foundations of the future, for you are."

There was hardly a stir on the hillside. The breeze had calmed down and blew more gently. The Prime Minister said farewell to the man at his feet. He put out his hand and pulled him up and indicated that he should go back to his job. He waved to the others, gesturing them to their labors, as well. Then, as if to set an example, Panditji started off too, precisely in the direction in which he had been headed before he had caught sight of the stone carriers. He took up his conversation with the engineers exactly where he had left it; and he evidenced the same dynamic interest in all that was about to happen as he had shown before.

In the fall of 1949 Panditji took a journey he had anticipated for years. Boarding a plane at Palam Airport, New Delhi, he and Indira flew to Washington, D. C. Nan, who was serving as India's Ambassador, was there to greet them. So, too, was President Truman.

The next three weeks were packed with activity, even when judged by the standards of one of the world's busiest men. Upon arrival, the Prime Minister of India addressed a joint session of the House of Representatives and the Senate. He visited the Washington Monument, Mount Vernon, the Jefferson and Lincoln memorials, and he spoke at the United Nations. He lectured on major university campuses clear across the country from New York to San Francisco. He climbed to the tops of skyscrapers and rode upon freeways. His quick step and ready smile invited friends and conversations at every crossroads. While he was at Columbia University, the honorary degree of Doctor of Laws was conferred upon him by Dwight D. Eisenhower. Albert Einstein opened his home to the illustrious statesman. Eleanor Roosevelt received him. It was all so wonderful, so fast, and exciting that at the end of his stay, when someone asked, "Well, how do you like America?" Panditji quipped, "It's very nice, indeed, but I've decided that no one should ever come to America for the *first* time."

He had dreamed of coming long ago when he had been a student; but, as he explained, that had not been meant to be. There were other things that had had to be done first; and yet, Jawaharlal Nehru had continued to think that there were several good reasons for taking a trip to America. Because of the revolutionary heritage common to both countries, he always thought of India and the United States as partners. He spoke of Washington, Jefferson, Lincoln, and Thoreau as "the torchbearers of freedom," and he explained in 1949 that he had come hoping to catch hold of something of the fire that had burned within their hearts. He wished to acknowledge a long-standing debt to them, he said, and to others of their countrymen—President Franklin D. Roosevelt in particular, who had understood India's yearning for freedom and had helped to convince England that it was sincere and just. Moreover, he longed to present his country, which was largely unfamiliar to Americans—the India of villages and humble, willing people—in a friendly light; and he needed to secure America's cooperation in plans for development.

But he did not come empty-handed, or as a beggar might have come, with hands outstretched. He came as an equal, and bearing an important message. The United States and the Soviet Union were locked in a cold war, which had followed quickly after World War II. Only the most essential information was passed between the two great powers at the time. Every move on the part of one was regarded with suspicion by the other. Like giants, they seemed to bestride the earth, holding peace and goodwill captive between them. Yet, for all their displays of power, it looked as if the Soviet and America were actually afraid—afraid of attack, afraid of the use of the very weapons they had striven to manufacture, afraid of infiltration, afraid even of ideas that were new, strange, or distasteful. In such a circumstance, Panditji's message was: "Don't be afraid. Fear is something which you yourselves have created. When you are afraid, you blind yourselves to the possibilities of action. Nothing which can happen to you from the outside can ever be as bad as inner weakness. Don't doubt yourselves."

Two gifts had been garnered from the years of trial in India: independence and courage, the very kind of courage the world of the 1940's and the early 1950's needed, courage to face systems bigger than oneself, and better organized, to face them with moral conviction and the belief that they were amenable to change. Gandhiji had come forth in 1920 with the command "Do not be afraid!" Following his lead, the country had tested and withstood a mighty empire. It needed no further convincing of the power of that injunction.

Yet, if it had wanted proof, daily and on a worldwide front, India was receiving up-to-the minute evidence of its influence. Using their illustrious neighbor as an example, Ceylon and Burma had gone on to achieve their independence in 1948, and Indonesia won hers in 1949. On the very brink of partition, the first Asian Relations Conference in history had been convened in Delhi and by popular insistence was followed up with regional meetings on specific topics, which led to the planning of the momentous Afro-Asian Conference of 1955. In the Korean crisis of 1950, India offered to mediate and did so successfully. Her emissaries were highly praised. Dr. Radhakrishnan had rendered magnificent service as Ambassador to the Soviet Union at a critical time. Madame Vijaya Lakshmi Pandit was destined to be the first woman elected as President of the General Assembly of the United Nations.

Because of its refusal to ally itself with any of the strategic powers, the country was being offered free access to the best technical and scientific assistance available anywhere in the world, and was able to use it without political sanction. The notion of an "area of peace," which India advocated, as distinct from *East* or *West,* was assuming major importance in the thinking of foreign statesmen. Regardless of how smaller (or much larger) Asian states might choose to conduct themselves in the international arena, India's deeds and words were treated with respect and accorded a large measure of trust.

Independent India had burst upon the world scene with meteoric speed. Within a few months of having achieved its nationhood, it had become intimately involved with the United Nations. It was articulate and active in the British Commonwealth of Nations. It had qualified fully as a participant in international social and cultural activities, and was in the forefront of negotiations with heads of state. Its voice had been persuasively raised on behalf of humanity, justice, and peace. Its leadership qualities were manifest and the authority of Jawaharlal Nehru, its Prime Minister, was frequently felt in ruling quarters. He was everywhere—witnessing, conferencing, encouraging, and reconciling.

The remarkable emergence of India could not help but attract notice and comment in world capitals and on behalf of citizens. It was noted by many as progress; by some, it is true, as interference; but by more than a minority as an affirmation of the essential truths that underlie human endeavor and which could profitably guide relations among countries. By and large, India's nonaligned position was heralded as providing an alternative to the split-up of nations into two armed and hostile camps. Its offers of mediation were well received.

Because relatively little was known of the country, however, people tended to take India's actions and Mr. Nehru's analyses of world affairs at face value. Probably very few recognized the effect that emergence or independence itself had had upon the Indian point of view. All the same, to Indians, to Asians in particular, to former colonial peoples, and certainly to Britain, the roots of the policies that India advocated were apparent, deep, predictable, and tried.

First and foremost, India stood for full equality among the races of the world. How far it was willing to go in upholding that principle was shown by its position in relation to South Africa as late in Panditji's life as 1961, when the Union of South Africa was expelled from the British Commonwealth of Nations because of its discriminatory policies. The Prime Minister himself attended the conference that made the decision to do that. "We were sorry to do it," he said, explaining the action to members of the Indian Parliament, "but there was no other way. It was in South Africa that Mahatma Gandhi made his first stand, and it was on the same issue. To have given in would have been a negation of our long-held principle that humanity is one, regardless of status, race, or religion."

India thought of itself as an Asian nation, and, therefore, the inheritor of a long and unique tradition. Gautama Buddha, "The Enlightened One," had been born on Indian soil in the sixth century B.C. Great cities and universities had flowered on the Indian plains from earliest times. Long before the discovery of America, learned emissaries had passed to and fro across the boundaries between India and other countries. And, curiously enough, the very empire Indians had struggled to overthrow in the twentieth century A.D. had served to insulate India and other parts of Asia sufficiently from European contact to perpetuate habits of thought and conduct and a point of view that were distinctly in contrast to those of the west.

India was also anticolonial. It had been her opposition to colonialism that had caused modern India to rise and assert herself. When that effort had been crowned with success, she was ready to take up the same cause on behalf of other subject peoples. Not only did she intervene sympathetically on their behalf, but she helped to interpret the insecurity, the wounded sense of pride, and the lack of self-esteem that colonialism engendered in its subjects. As a result, the world as a whole was wiser in its dealings with young Asian and African nationalists.

On all counts, India spoke with a voice hitherto un-heard in the councils of nations and she naturally gave utter-ance to the strivings and longings of subject and formerly colonial peoples. Therefore, she quickly attracted a retinue of countries that were unallied and outside the East-West complex—Indonesia, Burma, Ceylon, Egypt, Ghana, and Yu-goslavia, to name but a few. This group became welded into something called "A Third Force," which was able to move adroitly and to a large extent without arousing suspicions of its dealings with the Great Powers, even though it incorpo-rated a substantial segment of the world's populations. India had assumed the lead in representing nations too weak to stand alone but, once united, too strong to be ignored.

It would have been presumptuous to have thought that satyagraha, which had produced such splendid results on a national scale, could have been applied in a world context amidst unpredictable circumstances and given the existence of modern weapons. Nevertheless, India was anxious to push the method as far as it would go. Speaking in the halls of Congress in Washington, D.C., Panditji said:

> *How far can the principle of nonviolence be applied in wider spheres of action? I do not know for situations differ and the means to prevent evil have to be shaped and set according to the nature of the evil. Yet I have no doubt that the basic approach which lay behind that technique of action which we used was the right approach in human*

*affairs and the only approach that ultimately solves a prob-
lem satisfactorily.*

Free and vigorously confident of having discovered a
force of astounding dimensions, India was eager for other
nations to test nonviolence. Her anxiety brought grumblings
of criticism from some quarters and elicited the charge that
the newly independent country thought itself morally superior to the rest of the world. But whether people wanted to
listen or not, India felt that she could hardly keep silence.
All indications were that the ability to destroy had outrun
the capacity for maintaining peace among nations. Every attempt had to be made to devise a sane and reasoned solution.

Speaking as Minister of External Affairs, a post he held
simultaneously with that of Prime Minister, Jawaharlal
Nehru was the most famous interpreter of Indian sentiments; but the people backed his government to the limit.
When the time came to test the popularity of its policies at
the polls in 1957, 365 Congress Party candidates were elected
to Parliament out of a possible total of 489. Moreover, citizens had offered to give a full measure of their time and effort to trying to fill the gap that existed in their knowledge
of other countries. They had traveled. They had gone to
night schools and attended seminars. If misdemeanors and
injustices were perpetrated, as they thought they had been in
connection with British action on the Suez Canal in 1956,
Indians had responded immediately. Basically, the tenets of
foreign policy that Panditji adhered to were understood by
them to be the right ones and embodied the very notions to
which they wanted to give voice. They enjoyed the acclaim
and prestige that came their way in return.

Therefore, when the Prime Minister went on missions

to the trouble spots of the world, in the fullest sense he traveled as an emissary of the Indian people. All the same, no one could deny that he was a rare and eloquent human being, a man endowed with versatility, breadth, and power of intellect. Unremittingly and on a hitherto unprecedented scale, he sought to effect personal relations between the atomic powers and the neutral states, between communist and noncommunist countries, between industrially advanced societies and the underdeveloped parts of the world. The climate of opinion and affairs of nations changed as a consequence.

The trip Mr. Nehru took to the United States in 1949 was the first of three to that country which he enjoyed over the next thirteen years. He also journeyed to China, the Soviet Union, Southeast Asia, Japan, almost every country of Europe, to Great Britain and North Africa as well. In the decade of the fifties, if there were unrest, it was likely that the Prime Minister of India would appear without delay. With a smile on his face, high courage, a ready wit, his hand extended, often pictured with a child by his side, he toured the continents, calm of purpose and steady of resolve. He became the most talked about, the most photographed, the most frequently consulted and proclaimed man of the generation.

12 *honor, praise, and glory*

The setting was Rashtrapati Bhawan, the stately home of the President of India. It was a summer evening. Inside, incense glowed; and through the windows came the soothing sound of water rippling over the cascades of the Mogul Gardens. The sleek black limousines of diplomats swept through the heavy gates and up the graveled drive. Footmen wearing crested turbans opened doors and escorted handsomely dressed ladies and gentlemen to the reception rooms where Cabinet Ministers and officials of the government mingled happily with foreign guests. The murmur of voices drifted pleasantly through halls festooned with garlands. Emissaries had donned full-dress regalia. Indian women were glamorous in tissue-thin saris embroidered with gold and silver threads. This was a beautiful and distinguished occasion.

President Rajendra Prasad, ordinarily so quiet and reserved, was enlivened and good humored. He had earned the

reputation of being a man of notably simple tastes. His un-
pretentious figure had never seemed to have adapted itself
completely to the grandeur of his surroundings; yet at his
party he was obviously enjoying the role of head of state and
host. His eyes were sparkling. His manner was genial.

By the side of Rajendra Prasad stood the wise and witty
Dr. Radhakrishnan, Vice-President of New India. The two
men were in the midst of their most seasoned friends and acquaintances. The warmth and affection they felt for one another were evident, and the esteem they accorded their foreign visitors was no less sincere. There was something especially cordial about the atmosphere of Rashtrapati Bhawan
that evening. Envoys sensed it the moment they entered. The
rooms were richly festive; the hospitality free and unrestrained.

Rajendra Prasad received his guests at the end of a long
hall where he could keep his eye on both the door and the
reception rooms. Rather frequently he interrupted a pleasant conversation with a foreign dignitary, excused himself
quietly, and took a quick look at his wristwatch. Those who
were standing closest to him saw him run his eyes over the
assembly, taking note of who was present and who had yet to
arrive. But if his glance happened to meet that of a colleague, a sidelong wink might be exchanged between them.
A smile twitched persistently at the corners of the President's
mouth; and from time to time he fingered his heavy mous-
tache deliberately, as if trying to draw a curtain over a secret
delight that it might not yet be time to disclose.

The dinner hour approached, and a swift tropical twilight enveloped the great house. The last violent colors cast
up by the setting sun streaked the sky above the capital as
yet another car drew up the hill, passed the mounted sen-
tries, and raced through the iron gates of Rashtrapati Bha-

wan. An aged but handsome figure alighted. He was dressed in white silk, spun and woven by hand. A Congress Party cap was set upon his head. In his buttonhole he had tucked a fresh red rose. The servants saluted and stood at attention.

Jawaharlal Nehru, Prime Minister and Minister for External Affairs for India, mounted the steps of the President's house slowly, wrapped in thought. A fragment of the day's heavy work still weighed upon his mind. He looked preoccupied; but as soon as he entered the gala hall, his presence was noted.

Conversation became subdued. The diplomats, all of whom Mr. Nehru had met and most of whom he knew by name, paused and bowed. The Indian ladies joined their palms in greeting and foreign women graciously inclined their heads. With much the same courtesy they would have shown a ruling monarch, the guests stepped to one side and let Panditji pass. His Indian associates beamed. For a second the Prime Minister looked a bit surprised and shy; but then, smiling broadly, he walked smartly up the path that had been cleared for him, to greet his President.

The evening's function was indeed out of the ordinary, for it was of a kind usually reserved for the highest-ranking dignitaries who came from abroad to visit India. The time-honored portraits of the former viceregal banquet hall gazed down upon tables adorned with flowers and twinkling lights. Glimmering silver plate was laid on the spotless cloths. Platters were heaped with steaming rice and pungent sauces. Mouth-watering sweetmeats were passed by liveried bearers. The air was laden with the smell of blossoms and spice. At the head table, Rajendra Prasad presided; but this time at his right, as guest of honor, was one of India's own sons, Jawaharlal Nehru.

The date was July 16, 1955. Panditji had come home

and the country was rejoicing. For three full days Indian newspapers had been filled with accounts of his journey and its attainments. The Prime Minister had been greeted with a tumultuous ovation and a civic reception at the airport in Bombay. His cabinet had met in special session to welcome him. He had reported to a breathless crowd of thousands in Delhi that afternoon.

The people of India made no attempt to conceal their adulation. They paraded for their Panditji and displayed his picture. They erected arches of flowers along his route and sang his praises. When his plane had touched down in the capital, eager, cheering crowds had broken through all barriers and had defied the police and ground crews to let them see him, to get next to him, to touch him. The country was proud, immensely proud, of its Prime Minister and his accomplishments, and relieved at his homecoming. The reasons for their pride were not hard to ascertain. Jawaharlal Nehru was unequaled in his time. They loved him. He had gone far and done much.

Years before, when India had faced her darkest hour and the country had been prey to suspicion and fright, Mohandas Gandhi had picked up his staff and walked from village to village to make peace. His words had been simple and his actions direct. He had appealed to the warring factions to have tolerance for one another, regardless of their beliefs or the propaganda they had imbibed. His brave pilgrimage had given quiet testimony to what he preached and his house had become a sanctuary where parties to both sides of a conflict could meet. In his presence, a breach had often been healed. That had been in 1946 and 1947, when India had been sundered by discord and the outside world had waited anxiously for news of its welfare. Out of the ashes of hatred the Mahatma had helped two nations to rise.

In the early part of the 1950's the world itself faced darkness. For the first time in history, men had the ultimate power to destroy life on their planet forever; and they were consciously divided into two separate and hostile camps. The United Nations, which was the established spokesman for humanity, was young and foundering. The threat of imminent conflict between the major powers and the shadow of universal destruction gripped men's minds and bred suspicion. Worse than that, it planted despair where could have been hope, encouraged hatred instead of love, and diverted the resources urgently needed for development to the manufacture of weapons.

It was then that Jawaharlal Nehru set out, leaving for the moment the hard-won tasks of Indian development: the redrawing of the state boundaries, the teaching of a common language, the integration of tribal peoples, the defense of Kashmir, the abolition of the landlord system, the revision of age-old laws, and the routing of the last remnants of imperial domination. With absolute faith that experience in solving their own problems would fit his countrymen for things to come, he turned his attention to the one job no one else was willing to do. He decided to travel to both East and West, to carry a message of goodwill to Russia and to the United States of America, to China, to Egypt, to Yugoslavia, to Japan, France, Germany and Austria, to Czechoslovakia, Italy, Indonesia, Canada, and England. He was ready to approach the United Nations itself.

Wherever he went, he conferred with heads of states, but he also insisted upon mixing with the common people as well. He talked about the forces that were pulling nations apart and asked leaders to reflect upon matters with open minds and restrain themselves from taking sides. He openly discredited the idea that prestige would come simply from amassing arms, money, or know-how. He discarded the notion that force alone should determine the outcome of national conflicts and substituted the concept of personal mediation in world affairs. "Friendship and cooperation between countries is not only essential but natural," he said. "I stand here to offer both in the pursuit of justice, liberty, and peace."

In all modesty, the Prime Minister called attention to other nations and to other statesmen who were also trying to break the impasse between East and West. He spoke with honor of the kindly efforts of persons such as Mrs. Roosevelt and Adlai Stevenson from the United States, Albert Schweitzer in Lambaréné, Dag Hammarskjöld of Sweden, Premier U Nu of Burma. He reminded the wealthy nations of the poverty of most of Asia and Africa. He said: "Man does not live by politics alone. I can tell you it is not Jawaharlal Nehru who speaks to you, but all the striving peoples of the world who want a chance to enjoy freedom from hunger and live in peace."

He spent two weeks in the Soviet Union on the eve of high-level conferences between that nation and the United States. Amid surroundings of deep resentment and mistrust, he entreated Russia to forgo undue interference in the affairs of other nations. He suggested that it look upon the pacts and agreements it was about to negotiate in a constructive way. "Let your coming together with another country be because you like one another and wish to cooperate," he counseled, "and not because you dislike others and wish to do them injury."

At this juncture in his life, Nehru couldn't take time to rehearse his speeches or to submit them to anyone in advance. He simply had to speak exactly what came to his mind, and encourage some kind of give and take between himself and the audience, for he did not want his addresses to be regarded as fixed pronouncements. They were merely stepping-stones toward understanding. How he wished that he could do something more than talk; yet in what other way, he asked, could he reach people, so many people, quickly and effectively?

He believed in person-to-person contact, was honestly touched by sight of the cheerful, trusting faces of workers who were waiting for him at the gates of a Russian factory, and he trusted implicitly that sincerity was conveyed when he accepted their greetings and could tell them: "In spite of the differences in our methods, there is not an unfriendly feeling between Indians and the people of the Soviet Union." He really hadn't the slightest doubt but that Russians in all walks of life could open their minds to the truth that: "Out of war or the threat of war or continuous preparation for war no goodwill can emerge." Life as men knew it on the face of the earth depended upon peoples' uprooting violence and cultivating the conditions of peace. He was convinced they wanted to do it, and would do it, if they were approached in the right way.

As Panditji made his slow expedition across Russia, the Middle East, and Europe, citizens watched and policy makers gave heed. The places he stayed became islands where honest feelings were discussed in an atmosphere of trust. Not everyone was going to heed his counsel, of course; but, as he took his way steadily through villages and towns and capitals, across deserts and over mountains, in and out of schools, mines, and industrial plants, his majestic poise and fearless figure was inspiring. His message was always the same: "The world is full of dangers, fears, and suspicions, but the way to meet danger is not to run away from it and the way to overcome fear and suspicion is not to submit to them."

The sight of such a man, the example of the nation behind him, had a powerful effect upon a frenzied world. The Prime Minister managed to establish lines of communication between decision makers. He fostered hope among the common people. In view of his words, sophisticated and somewhat callous materialists paused to reconsider the ends for which they were striving. America and Russia began to think of one another as nations of human beings rather than mere systems, and their policies relaxed somewhat. Small, young nations realized that they mattered in the world context. Blocs of opinion began to dissolve. Policy makers thought twice before they took actions that would be exposed to the light of humane criticism.

The Prime Minister's journey was accompanied by enormous acclaim from many and diverse quarters. After his visit to the Soviet Union, West German students thronged the airport where his plane came in for an unscheduled stop in the middle of the night. He was offered the honorary citizenship of Belgrade in communist Yugoslavia. At Vatican City he was met at the gates by cardinals and escorted in solemn procession to the throne room of the Pope. His Holiness hailed him with the greeting "We welcome heartily a great statesman and an eminent Prime Minister." As Panditji's aircraft swept in to Cairo, a mighty shout went up from the crowds: "Long live the messenger of peace!" When he left London after a call at No. 10 Downing Street, Sir Winston Churchill, long an opponent of Indian freedom, a renowned orator who had once described Jawaharlal Nehru as "a man of straw of whom in a few years no trace will remain," sent him a personal message of gratitude for his undertaking, and wished him Godspeed on so important a journey.

Now he had come home, back to the unanswered questions and the unfulfilled aspirations of India. The job of building a united, self-sufficient nation on his own soil was far from complete. The perpetual demands for creating, rapidly and efficiently, the structure of modern society pressed upon him. He didn't have much longer. If there were one monument he wished to leave behind, it was 400 million people capable of governing themselves. But this required leadership, food, tools, education, experience, money, and opportunity. There must be some rest, too, he thought—some reward for a population that had worked so hard.

The Prime Minister tried to be realistic. No single journey of any man, however unafraid and persuasive, was going to serve to halt the careening arms race upon which the mighty powers were focused. For peace to be installed in the world, there would have to be many, many people who shared his views and were articulate. There would have to be an outcry of the world's population which could not be stilled. Leaders of the Great Powers had to expect to deal in open and forthright honesty with one another. Latin America, more of Africa, and the whole of the Middle East would have to be brought within the orbit of wholesome influence. The United Nations would have to be supported, strengthened, and expanded.

The magnitude of the enterprise he had conceived caused Jawaharlal Nehru to think back to the conditions that had prevailed in India during the 1920's. Convincement was a slow process, and he wondered whether the world had time enough for convincement in the 1950's. As he had at certain stages in the freedom struggle, he again felt somewhat apprehensive. The men who had supported him and had helped him to become what he was were no longer young. Soon a new crowd would be taking over. How much did he speak for them? How much was he talking for himself when he went abroad, or could he say he represented a country fundamentally committed to the ways of peace?

At the close of the state banquet at Rashtrapati Bhawan, Rajendra Prasad rose to make an announcement. For the benefit of distinguished and foreign visitors he explained: "We have assembled this evening to express our joy at the safe return of our Prime Minister, Jawaharlal Nehru, from a strenuous tour in different countries of Europe and North Africa." With genuine satisfaction, the President then reviewed the notable itinerary and made a special point of saying: "India has followed with avidity and eagerness the news of the splendid welcome which has been extended by the governments and peoples of the various countries which our Prime Minister has visited."

The President's speech was not long or involved. He had never thought his powers of expression measured up to those of associates like Jawaharlal or Dr. Radhakrishnan, and he had always found it much easier to put across the message of his lifetime in deeds rather than words. All the same, he had things he wanted to say and he was determined not to let his modesty deter him.

"We are an ancient country," he remarked, "but a very young republic, and it is a matter of gratification to us to know how our activities and policies are being appreciated and how they raise our honor and prestige.

"We hold and believe," the President affirmed, "that peace is necessary for the welfare and prosperity of all peoples of the world, and more so in this age of great scientific achievements and weapons which have left before humanity the choice between the renunciation of war and total destruction."

At the outset of the President's talk, Jawaharlal had sat

with sober and immobile features, but as his friend warmed to the presentation, the Prime Minister's stance softened, his face relaxed. The President answered directly the questions Panditji had been asking himself. He could not have chosen better words. "In upholding and supporting the cause of peace," Rajendra Prasad continued, "we are voicing in our own humble way the yearnings of millions and millions of men and women all over the world, and no wonder our Prime Minister, who has been the chief interpreter of this policy of ours in this age, has been the recipient of such ovation."

Rajendra Prasad looked down at the silver-haired man at his side. He drew a small box from the pocket of his achkan. He paused, as if considering just how he would phrase what he had to say next. Perhaps, too, he remembered the simple meeting places where he had faced Jawaharlal Nehru in the past and the impact of the conversations that had passed between them in times of contest and danger. He bowed his head and spoke with characteristic humility.

"I have been wondering," the President said, "how the people of this country can express their gratitude to you in a concrete form so that you and all may see how an entire nation is behind you in your great endeavor."

Panditji cocked his head curiously. The President bade him rise. He stood and Rajendra Prasad reached out an arm to rest it lovingly upon his shoulder.

"Your lifelong services to our nation are written in letters of gold upon every page of our recent history," the President of India proclaimed, looking straight into the eyes of his Prime Minister, "and this latest phase in your great career, this heroic effort in the cause of peace for mankind has served to embellish the gold, or, as our ancient proverb says, 'added more charm and beauty to it by giving it a sweet scent.' "

The President withdrew his hand from Jawaharlal's shoulder and fingered the tiny box he held in his hand. He cleared his throat and smiled benignly. The moment he had anticipated so pleasantly had at last arrived. "I have felt," he said, "that I can do no better than confer upon you the award of Bharat Ratna, which is the highest award of honor which the Indian Government can bestow."

The President took from its case a handsome medal, which is very seldom struck, and attached it to the coat of his Prime Minister. He turned swiftly back to the assembly and raised his glass. "I would request you all," he said to his guests, "to join me in wishing our Prime Minister many happy years of health and vigor so that he may serve still more his country and the world at large."

The assembly rose and drank. They sat, leaving Panditji standing alone at the head of the table. The moment was deeply significant. Jawaharlal had often been the giver of awards and encouragement to his people, but relatively seldom the recipient. In a voice shaken with emotion, he thanked the President for his kind words. With reference to the honor that had been accorded him, he said he did not know to whom, or how, to render gratitude.

"In this work, there are no leaders and no followers," he stated with humility. "The time when threats were effective in world affairs is long past. No question of saving face or prestige should come in the way of a human and civilized approach to the problems of our age. Our task is the preservation of peace, and, indeed, of our civilization. To this task let us bend our energies. We can find fellowship and strength in the presence of one another."

Envoys were on their feet and clapping. Government functionaries nodded their heads and waved. Had the nation as a whole been able to add anything more, it would have been the quiet applause traditionally reserved only for its greatest performers. *"Sadhu, sadhu,* Holy, holy," they would have whispered.

The border between India and China is 2,500 miles long and runs across some of the highest and most nearly impenetrable country of the world. Until the twentieth century, the two countries could boast of having enjoyed two thousand years of friendship, made possible in part by the existence of that same border. Mule trains crossed back and forth over well-chosen and traditional routes. Mountaineers occasionally obtained permission to pass in order to gain access to a specific peak. The border countries of Tibet, Nepal, Sikkim, and Bhutan were relatively small and of little concern to the world at large; and otherwise, nobody bothered himself very much about the existence or location of the boundaries, least of all the scattered tribal folk whose villages may have lain astride the lines, but whose contacts with their governments or the outside world were extremely limited.

Modern transportation, communication, and methods of warfare have made isolation impossible. Airplanes easily span great distances, and leap the highest peaks of the world. Radios transmit news instantaneously back and forth between spots that it might take months to reach on foot or horseback, and warfare is waged in hitherto remote and seemingly inaccessible places.

When India assumed responsibility for its own affairs in 1947, Tibet, the Himalayan peaks, and the tribal villages were still out of the way and cut off from the mainstream of endeavor. The illusion of their remoteness and the persistence of their exotic customs appealed to certain adventurers and romantic individuals, although everyone knew that the way of life in such places was bound to change. China took over Tibet in October, 1950. The United States sent its first foreign aid mission to Nepal in 1952. Mt. Everest was scaled in June, 1953.

If there was one among its neighbors in the community of nations with whom India desired to have friendship most of all, and especially during the years of new nationhood, it was China—and the reasons for this were not necessarily strategic. First of all, the background of stable, friendly relations maintained for two thousand years had had an effect. It was a matter of pride to both nations that there had been no war between them and, as a consequence, Indians naturally thought of the Chinese in a close and amicable way. And there were other justifications for not stirring up mistrust. Both countries needed time to establish themselves politically. Economic development within their own borders presented an urgent and powerful challenge.

India, by accident of history, was linked to the West and found it easy to converse with and relate to Western nations, while China had remained completely Eastern. The Western nations had almost all rejected the communist government which was in power in Peking. Given her deep-seated desire for reconciliation, India saw herself as a go-between, a window for China upon the West. All the same, it would be wrong to conclude that India courted the friendship of China for purposes of prestige and influence alone. It is probably more correct to say that, as in the case of most other peoples, Indians were attracted to the Chinese because they liked them, because they felt a common bond with them, and because they trusted them.

In 1939, Jawaharlal Nehru had visited Nationalist China as the guest of Generalissimo and Madame Chiang

Kai-shek. Upon that occasion, he had been struck by the depth and power of the revolution that was transforming the country. As he saw it, China was being driven forward by the necessity to break with a feudal past, the attraction of modern industrial means, and the desire for political expression. It was these factors, he said, rather than the appeal of any one well-defined and immutable system which instilled such ardor in Chinese youth. Therefore, it is not surprising that when communism became an accomplished fact in China, India should have recognized it almost immediately. Indians saw that their friends on the other side of the mountains were on the move, motivated by some of the same impulses that had inspired their own freedom movement. The Chinese, it is true, were taking a somewhat different path in pursuit of their goals; but, underneath it all, the country was having its growing pains and hardships the same as India. Certainly the two nations could understand and sympathize with one another.

Having recognized the existence of a communist government in China and having exchanged diplomatic representatives, India took a further step in regard to her neighbor. She consistently advocated that China be seated in the United Nations. To certain other nations, that point of view seemed naïve and overly solicitous; but, to the majority of Indian statesmen, communism in China was a fact of life. They knew the country was strong. They foresaw the implications of its having adopted a rigid ideology. Considering these factors alone and laying aside for the moment India's long-standing championship of the underdog, they advocated that China be brought within the orbit of international discussion and sanction without delay.

Again, it was the Prime Minister who gave most vivid and articulate interpretation to the relationship that existed between his country and China, but he was not the only one in action by any means. Here, as elsewhere, a people's feeling found ready means for expression. Indian dancers gave performances in China. Merchants negotiated trade contracts. Professors, ministers, importers, and workers traveled north and came back amazed with the hospitality that had been extended to them, electrified by what they had seen happening in Shanghai, in Chungking, and in Peking.

India was ahead, just ahead of China, they said, in terms of material well-being; but what energy, what vitality the people were applying to their tasks! How vast the country was, how thrilling its overall plans for development. How well conceived were the undertakings, how well executed the labors. If India really believed in the effectiveness of democracy, then it was up to her to prove that she could go as fast and do as much as China. Her young people especially, the students and technicians, were mightily impressed and enthusiastic about China.

When China occupied Tibet in 1950, its proximity to India was felt and there was need for a statement of policy that would reaffirm China's friendly intentions. At that time, a Sino-Indian agreement was reached which took care of such matters as trade and defense and was intended to allay doubts and fears that might have arisen on the part of the Indians. The preamble to the agreement included the famous Panch Sheel, five principles, which were proposed by China in the first place and which spelled out the position of the two countries so far as one another were concerned.

The Panch Sheel stated that India and China had resolved to enter into the agreement with the understanding that it was based upon mutual respect for one another's rights to its own territory, with the assurance that neither one would advance against the other, with the promise that

294 · PART 3   1947-1964

neither would interfere in the domestic affairs of its neighbor, with the pledge that both were to deal with each other on the basis of equality and with the statement that they looked forward to peaceful coexistence. The Panch Sheel were warmly endorsed by India and were signed independently by at least a dozen other nations of Asia within a few months.

Of the five points agreed upon, the most heralded in India was the one that insured nonaggression. For her part, the country had no plans whatsoever for pushing her boundaries farther to the north. It was difficult to conceive that China would try to cross the Himalayas, although, as India had stated repeatedly, if it came to a defense of her borders, she had every intention of fighting.

Understandably, what the country wanted most of all was to be left in peace. She did not want to be forced to divert her time and energies to the purposes of war. She did not wish to have to deflect her resources from the building of machinery and apply them to the manufacture of guns. She did not choose to divert her attention from the major questions of worldwide disarmament and become party to a strategy of defense. If she were to continue to occupy a position of leadership among small and developing nations, it was imperative that she not be overridden by someone stronger and better equipped than herself. She did not like to contemplate the eventuality of submission any more than she liked to consider taking up arms at all. She would fight if she had to, if she were compelled to defend her own territory, but she hoped that she would never have to face that circumstance.

What Panditji thought and what he did in regard to China was so inextricably woven into his life as a whole as to be indistinguishable from the fabric of his personality and philosophy. Who was the man whose pictures appeared on the front pages of newspapers at this time, arm in arm with Chou En-lai? It was the same man, older, to be sure, and in many ways wiser, but the same high-principled individual who had said, "It is not the foreigner we fight, but his policies!" and who had warned his countrymen twenty-five years earlier that: "As soon as one begins to think of the other side as a mass or a crowd, the human link seems to go. We forget that crowds also consist of individuals, of men and women and children who love and hate and suffer."

Who was it who was off on a trip to Peking and speaking of the brotherhood that existed between his countrymen and the people of China? It was the man who had said in a broadcast to the nation in September, 1946: "We are of Asia and the peoples of Asia are nearer and closer to us than others."

And what manner of person was this who sat down and tried to negotiate with the government of Communist China? Did he really place his faith in a slip of paper called Panch Sheel? In answer to that exact question, put to him by international news reporters in 1959, the Prime Minister of India replied:

> *If they are good principles, they remain good whatever individuals or a country may do. People seem to think that the so-called Panch Sheel is some temporary arrangement to meet a temporary set of circumstances. It is not. It is a basic approach to international affairs and to life generally. . . . If we believe in Panch Sheel, we follow it, even if no country in the wide world follows it. Of course, it cannot be easily followed in a one-sided way, but that is a different matter. Our attitude will be to follow it, if we believe in it, and we do.*

13 *bent to the storm*

Panditji fidgeted. Outwardly he tried to appear calm, but inwardly he was disturbed. He paced back and forth on the hot tarmac before the hangar. He spoke nervously with friends who were assembled at the airfield. Even the little girl who was with him, so prim and pretty in her white dress, with a high, stiff bow atop her black curls, could not distract his attention. The Prime Minister squeezed the child's hand almost too tightly as she marched alongside him. From minute to minute he consulted his watch and his eyes scanned the white-hot heavens.

Out of the north came the impatient roar of planes. Eight Vampire jets of the Indian Air Force hurtled into view, nested carefully around a heavy-framed Viscount. The aircraft dipped low over the field, causing a windstorm of sharp, dry dust. The Vampires peeled off, permitting the Viscount to land. Its engines screeched to a halt and soldiers opened the door. Two men emerged, dressed in soft gray. From the spectators in front of the terminal building came a restrained murmur of greeting. The Prime Minister and the little girl, who clutched a bouquet of flowers, went forth to meet the arrivals.

Across a narrow strip of asphalt, the two men faced each other, then shook hands. Jawaharlal Nehru, Prime Minister of India, and Chou En-lai, Premier of Communist China, had met several times before. The Prime Minister had toured China in 1954. Chou En-lai had visited India in 1954, and again in 1956 and 1957, when he had been received with a thunderous, prolonged welcome. Both men had been prominent figures in the Asian and African Statesmen's Conference at Bandung. Musicians, playwrights, scholars, and scientists had traveled back and forth between the two countries steadily during the past few years, enjoying cordial receptions. The picture of these two officials embracing one another good-heartedly as they had said farewell at this same airport in January, 1957, had been spread across the newspapers of the world.

This time, too, the cameras of the world's newsmen were poised upon the scene at Palam Airport. But as the Prime Minister stepped forward, his eyes were lowered and his smile stiff. The little girl presented her flowers, as she had been instructed to do, but looked questioningly at the visiting Premier. He put out his hand, accepted the bouquet, and glanced uneasily at the quiet crowd. Cameras clicked. Panditji led the way to the microphones.

Standing before the loudspeakers, speaking in a clear and even tone, the Prime Minister did a thing that was, for him, quite out of the ordinary. He who had always insisted upon speaking extemporaneously read a speech that had been written out in advance and printed in Hindi. His words were repeated in Chinese by a government official who stood at his side. When the first sentence of the Prime Minister's prepared talk was translated, the Chinese Premier looked up quickly, startled and surprised. However, he managed to compose himself almost immediately and evidenced no further sign of shock.

The Prime Minister had chosen his words consciously and with great care. He recalled the warmth of the welcome that had been accorded the Premier on previous visits and he described the bond of friendship that had been generated by past discussions. "But unfortunately," he said, and a keen sense of personal disappointment crept into his voice, "other events have taken place since then which have put a great strain on this bond of friendship and given a shock to our people. Thus our relations have been imperiled for the present and for the future and the very basis on which they stood has been shaken."

Taken on the surface, these were not harsh words, nor were they fighting words. They had not been spoken in bitterness or anger. They might also have been voiced by any Indian who had sufficient learning and status to express them, so well did they indicate the mood of the country at the time. But for the man who uttered them, they were sad words. He hated to believe that any person or any nation was ill-intentioned. He much preferred to operate in an atmosphere of trust, to work with confidence that a right and well-chosen method would bring forth a good and beneficial result. But China, acting through the man who stood before him, had deceived him; and the Prime Minister was deeply hurt.

Friendship with all countries, regardless of their internal politics, had been a cornerstone of Indian policy from the outset of independence. Long, long before the Transfer

of Power, when the Congress Party had been beset by punitive decrees and hope of ultimate liberty was slight, Jawaharlal Nehru had written from behind prison walls: "I do not
know what India will be like or what she will do when she is
free. But I know that those of her people who stand for national independence today stand for the widest internationalism." Later, when a new government had stood upon the
threshold of freedom, the Prime Minister had spoken honestly of the intangible tie that bound his people to their
neighbors in Asia. By all counts, the political system in
China must be accepted and tolerated and warm associations
were to be encouraged with the Chinese people.

India was not a communist country. It had chosen to establish a democracy when it became free, albeit a democracy
in which the government had power to do a large part of the
planning and to manage industrial development. However,
during the years that had followed immediately after the
onset of freedom, India's leaders had seen the world divided
between two armed camps, as it were. The desire of these
men for peace had been far stronger than any loyalty they
had felt for either side; and, so, they had kept up relations
with both communist and noncommunist countries and most
especially they had encouraged support of nations which,
like their own, were trying to establish a nonaligned and independent position.

India had been busy, desperately busy. Steel mills were
rising above the plains. The machines of giant factories were
beginning to turn. Brand-new laboratories were being
opened. Roads and power lines were pushing their ways
across the deserts. Jungle forests had been felled and homes
made for refugees. The number of persons in school had increased. By day and night one heard youngsters and old people chanting lessons. Books were being printed and sold, lots

of books on many subjects, and theaters had been opened. The aspect, the techniques, the interests, and the outlook of the country were changing.

Then, suddenly, news broke that China had completed a hundred-mile road across the Aksai Chin plateau of northern India. The Aksai Chin was a remote strip of territory which lay close to the northernmost boundary, but it was strategic for Chinese purposes since it linked Sinkiang Province and Tibet. The Aksai Chin was wild and virtually uninhabited land, and certainly of little use to the people of the subcontinent. But why had China taken the liberty of building the road, Indians asked, and when had the construction taken place? Why had China not honored the fact that Indian troops were deployed on the borders of Kashmir rather than along the Chinese boundaries? Besides, if China had wanted to have a small area of land, why had it not asked for it outright, and arranged for it honorably? The situation raised many questions that were disturbing in their implications.

The Aksai Chin incident provoked the government of India to make investigations and to reveal to the people that over a period of five years there had been intermittent skirmishes between Indians and Chinese at widely separated points along the border. These had taken place in the east as well as on the western fringes of the boundary. Certain inroads had been made by the Chinese, which had aggravated hostile and separatist tribal people. Resentment had been stirred up.

Mr. Nehru, who had had previous knowledge of the incidents, had hoped that perhaps they could be kept under control until an appropriate time when the whole border question might be opened for review and settlement. Now, unfortunately, circumstances demanded that the situation be handled in an atmosphere of impatience and fear. The Indian people were alerted. The army was on guard. Peace was endangered.

So Premier Chou En-lai was invited to come to Delhi and was met at the airport by the Prime Minister on a blisteringly hot day in 1960. Ostensibly, the Chinese Premier had come to confer with the Vice President, Dr. Radhakrishnan, whose knowledge of Chinese and communist affairs was extensive, to talk with other ministers and governors of the border states, and at length with the Prime Minister.

A library of documents had been set aside for use of the Chinese Premier at Rashtrapati Bhawan. Timeworn maps had been retraced and copies of imperial agreements amassed. Every attempt was made on behalf of the Indian government to make available to the government of China means for offering a plausible and studied solution to the border problem. Mr. Nehru freed himself for ten full hours of conferencing. Indian officials tentatively raised the possibility of India's exchanging the Aksai Chin for Chinese withdrawal from the northeast frontier.

The talks stretched out over three days. An ominous silence pervaded the capital. Rumors of a breakdown in the negotiations were circulated. The people of India became fretful. They complained. Panditji warned: "We have to be particularly careful at a moment of difficulty such as this, that we function and we say whatever we have to say with dignity and wisdom but that does not mean moderating any policy."

Chou En-lai had few comments. In comparison with the fundamental question of preserving friendly relations between the two countries, he referred to the border encroachments as "a limited and temporary situation." Nevertheless, when the maps were presented, he claimed on behalf of his government 51,000 square miles of territory which India had regarded as her own; 12,000 of those miles were already occupied by Chinese troops. He conceded no blame and left without compromise. The most hopeful word published after his visit was that the discussions were incomplete and must be continued.

India was grim, sobered by the loss of its territory and wounded by the disdain of its friendship. Animosity toward Chou En-lai had reached such a point in Delhi that the security police had had to cordon off all roads used by the visiting dignitaries, and the forces regarded the safety of the Premier as the most difficult assignment with which they had ever been asked to cope. The Prime Minister faced his people. "Much has been done which we think should be undone," he admitted, "but even so, we realize that we have raised the banner of peace before other countries and we and the world can ill afford for us to let this slip from our hands. We face a great and powerful nation which is aggressive. It might be so whether or not it was a communist nation, of course. But the situation has worsened in the sense that we can no longer be sure that more may not happen."

Chou En-lai did not return. The boundary dispute dragged on. Questions over the issue recurred in the Indian Parliament. Unrest increased. The disappointment suffered by the Indian people gave way first to coldness and then to hostility toward their northern neighbor. Border incidents continued. They sparked enmity. More land was usurped by the Chinese. It looked as if India would be forced to retaliate.

On October 11, 1962, China struck with unprecedented force. On October 12, Indian newspapers carried the blazing headline INDIAN CASUALTIES MOUNT AS FIGHTING FLARES UP ON NORTHEAST FRONTIER. Winter was coming on. The Chinese had maneuvered into an advanced stronghold. They were fighting down from a ridge at a height of over 12,000 feet. Their forces were backed by heavy equipment. Fresh troops were moving up behind them. Nehru gave orders to the Indian army to clear every point south of the traditional border. Guns, tanks, cavalry, and footsoldiers went into action.

On October 16 it was reported that Chinese fighters were well advanced along the eastern section of India's northern boundary. At this juncture, it was discovered that Indian defenses were woefully inadequate to the challenge. A hasty attempt was made to reassign soldiers from along the Pakistan border. In no uncertain terms, the Prime Minister demanded that the Chinese government withdraw its thrust.

The headlines of October 21 read: CHINESE OPEN FIERCE OFFENSIVE. Heavy defense was necessitated, both on the Aksai Chin plateau and in the Northeast Frontier of India, areas separated by a distance of nearly 1,000 miles. Struggling against wretched weather conditions, experienced mountain combat troops were rushing to get into position. Recruitment of raw forces was under way.

Two key posts were lost. In the world's press, Indian resistance to the Chinese was described as "nothing less than heroic." A nationwide state of emergency was declared. To help meet the rocketing costs of defense, people volunteered their private fortunes to the government. Following the example of Indira Gandhi, women sold their jewelry * and contributed the money to the armed forces.

On the evening of October 22, the Prime Minister broadcast to a serious but determined nation. Nothing, with the exception of the freedom struggle, had ever produced

---

* In a country such as India, until very recently, people were unused to banks. They kept their savings at home and often invested them in gold jewelry, which was convenient to carry and relatively easy to safeguard.

such unity among his countrymen. They were terrified, but they had no intentions of yielding to Chinese force. They had not won their independence only to surrender it again.

The Indian people were angry with China and critical of certain of their own government departments, notably the Department of Defense, which had left them ill prepared for this contingency. They knew that their military efforts had to be overhauled and stepped up and they were already on the move toward doing something about that. But there could not be the slightest letdown in their customary labors on behalf of development and no hint of withdrawal from a position that offered constant promise of negotiation, mediation, and peace.

The Prime Minister's words were measured and his pace steady. His voice sounded strained, but there was no fatigue in his courage. "I am speaking to you after a long interval," he said to the nation. "I feel, however, that I must speak to you about the grave situation which has arisen on our frontiers. We are men and women of peace in this country, conditioned to the ways of peace. We are unused to the necessities of war but the time has come for us to realize fully the menace that threatens the freedom of our people and our independence."

His calm was admirable; his fortitude sustaining. "We have to meet a powerful and unscrupulous opponent," he stated in all honesty. "We have, therefore, to build up our strength and power to face this situation adequately and with confidence. The conflict may continue for long. We must prepare ourselves mentally and otherwise. We must have faith in ourselves and I am certain that faith and our labors will triumph. *No other result is conceivable.*"

He was supremely willing, and vigorous far in excess of his years. "We shall have to carry a heavy burden, all of us," he warned, "whatever our vocations may be. The price of freedom now has to be paid in full measure. Perhaps we were growing too soft and taking things for granted. But freedom can never be taken for granted. It requires always awareness, strength, and austerity."

He hadn't given up! "We have followed a policy of non-alignment and sought the friendship of all nations," he reflected. "I believe in that policy fully and we shall continue to follow it," he declared.

The nation needed him, and they needed his faith in their abilities. The future was dark and menacing, but if Panditji were with them, they could manage. "I wish you well," he concluded, "and whatever may befall I want you to hold your heads high and have faith and full confidence in the future."

Mobilization for the Chinese invasion had to be well-nigh total. As a consequence, young India learned a vital and timely lesson, which was that upon every pair of shoulders rested some responsibility for vigilance, bravery, and action. The people had had Panditji with them for so long, he was so capable, and they had come to depend upon him so completely, that they had almost forgotten that he would not be with them forever. Moreover, they had known, but had hardly comprehended, that although he could do the work of perhaps twenty men, he still could not encompass everything. He had told them, but now experience reinforced his view, that ultimately a nation's image and a nation's strength is that of her people marching together.

For reasons never fully explained, the Chinese arrested their invasion and did not proceed, as they might have done, despite wintry snows, to the plains of India. They withdrew to the positions they had occupied before the attack of 1962. Diplomatic relations could be maintained between the two countries. Nehru offered to renew discussions of the border question. All the same, however, India continued to modernize its combat forces. A Defense Council was established to coordinate military activities within the government.

Meanwhile, the country went on with its daily tasks—the planning, the sowing, the harvesting; on with the training, the building, the growing, the changing. But the load was lightened a bit for the Prime Minister. Work was spread among more and younger hands after 1962. Indira had served as President of the Congress Party and was recognized in her own right as having a capacity for politics. She began to be more active. A man named Y. B. Chavan replaced the discredited Krishna Menon as Minister of Defense at the very height of the Chinese invasion. Dr. Radhakrishnan followed Rajendra Prasad as President, and a Muslim became Vice-President. Lal Bahadur Shastri, a relative newcomer of prominence, became Panditji's assistant.

In 1961, an American journalist who was a long-standing friend of the Prime Minister, had paid a call and had had a chance to interview Jawaharlal Nehru.

"What will you do," he had asked, "when you are freed from government responsibilities?"

Panditji had looked puzzled. "You mean, what would I do if I retired?" he had replied.

"Yes," the journalist had said.

For the first time in their long acquaintance, the journalist had seen pain on Panditji's face and had found him at a loss for words. The Prime Minister had been slow in answering. "Well, I suppose there are some things I could do," he had said without any particular enthusiasm. "But I really haven't thought much about it."

Why should he have thought about it? he asked. He was

almost never sick. But basically, he supposed, and correctly, he hadn't thought about what he would do afterward because he loved his job and it dismayed him to think he would ever have to leave it—leave the labors, leave the challenge, leave the people.

Panditji's remarkable strength and agility were famous. Some friends commented that he looked somewhat tired after his latest American tour in the autumn of 1961, but before long he was quite rested. He had a kidney infection during the spring of 1962 and he remained in bed for a week or so; but, again, he made a good recovery. Soon after New Year's in 1964, while he was on an official visit to the state of Orissa, he suffered a slight stroke, but that too was minor. By spring he was keeping the same whirlwind schedule that he had maintained ever since the year previous to the Transfer of Power—appearing in Parliament once or twice a week to answer questions, attending to the duties of office, entertaining the President of Sudan, working on a television series to be broadcast in the United States, arranging for a fresh series of talks on Kashmir, flying to the mountains for a weekend, anticipating a trip to London for a conference of the Prime Ministers of the Commonwealth, hoping to see his friend Mountbatten while he was there.

On the morning of May 26, 1964, the Prime Minister woke early and complained of having a pain in his left side. However, he made light of whatever it was and said he did not want to bother a doctor by having him come to the house at that hour. He lay down when the pain increased, but shortly afterward he became unconscious. He never reawakened. He was dead, of a heart attack, at about two o'clock that afternoon.

The world mourned his passing, but not as the people of India did. The country was numb, struck by a loss too great for tears. Their sense of sorrow and loneliness could

hardly be assuaged. The vast concourse of people who attended his last journey to the banks of the Jumna was as
large as any that had ever attended him when he had been
alive.

A few days later Nan read out his will. He asked that
his body be burned, but without ritual. A few of his remains
he wanted to have scattered in the Ganges River. He had
written:

> *The Ganges reminds me of the snow-covered peaks and
> deep valleys of the Himalayas, which I loved so much, and
> of the rich and vast plains below, where my life and work
> have been cast. Smiling and dancing in the summer morn
> ing sunlight, and dark and gloomy and full of mystery as
> evening shadows fall; a narrow, slow, and graceful stream in
> winter, and a vast roaring thing during monsoon, broad
> bosomed almost as the sea, and with something of the sea's
> power to destroy, the Ganges has been to me a symbol and
> a memory of the past of India, running into the present,
> and flowing on to the great ocean of the future.*

But he requested that the rest of his ashes be taken
aloft, high in an aircraft, and then "scattered over the fields
where the peasants of India toil." He wanted them "to mingle with the dust of the soil of India and so to become an indistinguishable part of her."

Even in his dying there was grace and he found a way to
express his sense of wonder and adventure, along with his
generous love for the Indian people. Once, too, someone had
asked him to speak of Gandhiji. In a pensive mood he had
answered: "I suppose that in years to come the world will
scarcely believe that such a one as that did walk the earth. A
few there are who seem not to have been moulded of the
common clay, but set apart for some high purpose." He
might, with all humility, have been speaking of himself.

index